SETTLE IT!

...and be Blessed

MONTSERRAT

Orlando, Florida

SETTLE IT!

. . . and be Blessed

When you're in the fight of your life

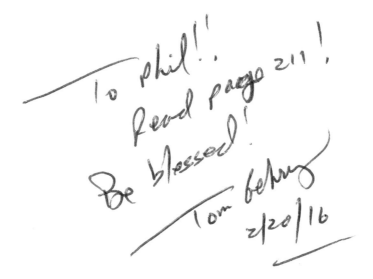

To phil!!.
Read page 211!
Be blessed!
Tom Gehring
2/20/16

Tom Gehring

CONTENTS

Introduction

After thirty years of fighting, I put my sword down. Thirty hard-core years of litigation, trials, arbitrations, mediations, wars, battles, fights, and brawls. I could fight no longer.

I was thankful, and still am, that early on in my career as a trial lawyer I made Jesus Christ my Senior Partner. I know a good partner when I work with one. He was, is, and will always be, the best. Still, have no doubt, even with Jesus as my partner, it was incredibly *hard work*. Just ask my non-existent family. Just ask my cat.

After I put my sword down, my Senior Partner told me to write this book. He's my Senior Partner, I do what he tells me to. It always works out.

He said he wanted to pour out his blessings on his sons and daughters and that to do so they must do all they can to settle all the burdens and trials that have come their way and would continue to come their way. In our last days, there should be nothing separating us from a close relationship with God.

He also said: "*Surely I am coming quickly.*"

And I know what he meant, for today, and for eternity.

I pray this book helps you.

PART
I

Settle It!

. . . and do it quickly

Settle It
. . . and do it quickly

Peace, make every effort

"You know Tom, everybody has something they need to settle in their life. *Everybody!* Some sort of trial, a dispute with someone, a problem in their family, or sometimes worse—a problem with themselves."

Harry Goldberg had invited me to lunch at a little restaurant in Santa Monica. "How long ago was that trial you helped me with? It seems like a lifetime ago."

"That was about twenty-five years ago, Harry. Long time ago," I said as I remembered back.

"I've often thought about how that trial changed my life," Harry said. "How old were you then?"

"Mercy! I was about . . . thirty-one years old."

"I was probably," he sat back and thought, "sixty-one or so. All I remember was that, I was in the fight of my life. Everything was on the line. You know, that trial put my whole life in perspective. Ever since then, in every situation, I have," Harry pursed his lips together and I thought I saw a little tear well up, "made every effort possible to make peace when a dispute rose up, or when I had a fight in the family, or when I needed to get something right with myself. I remembered to *make every effort*.[1] You know Tom, as I get closer to the end of my life, I have realized what a great lesson that was."

The menus were lying unread on the table. The waiter walked up to his old familiar customer: "Do you want to order now, Harry?"

"No, not yet, I'm waiting for some friends."

"Friends?" I asked.

---

[1] Romans 14:19. "Let us make every effort to do what leads to peace and to mutual edification."

Harry carried on. "I remember early in the case when you asked me to read and meditate on the Beatitudes. You really wanted badly to settle the case."

"Perhaps, I was scared to death of who I was up against," I said.

"You called them 'Jesus' Eight-Step Program.' I told you 'I'm Jewish, Jews don't believe in Jesus.' So, we compromised and I agreed to read the Psalms. I did pretty good reading the Psalms. They seemed to bring some peace. Then I read Psalm 95. 'Today, if you hear his voice, do not harden your hearts.'[2] I was in the fight of my life. My heart was so hardened." Harry shook his head. "So hardened. So much had led up to that place in my life, and I realized that I was the most tired man on the planet. Tired! Disconnected. No amount of sleep would have given me the *rest* I needed. Where had it all gotten me? Psalm 95 helped me to change, because I decided to hear his voice. His voice was always there. I actually listened to God. And there, right there in the middle of that trial I started to know true rest.[3] Strange huh? I found out that rest did not mean sleep. You can only get true rest from one source." Harry pointed up. "And if you want that rest, you have to listen. And do what he tells you to. Surrender."

"Friends? You have friends coming?" I asked again. I smiled; perhaps I wanted to lighten things up.

"One last thing, Tom. You'll get a serious kick out of this. About six months ago I got my wife to do your 8-to-3 rule, to try to get her to quit smoking. *All these years.* She tried everything, patches, medications, meditations, willpower, you name it. Finally, I said, 'your problem is you're trying to do it on your own strength. You need God to help.' I explained your 8-to-3 rule. But, of course, she remembered it, because it saved our daughter's marriage a few years ago. So, she decided if it could save a marriage, it could save her. So, she did it!! For seven days. And—she quit! Amazing, all these years. . . . She said it was simple, one morning at 3:00 a.m. while praying, she said the Lord told her she had to quit now, and that he wanted to add some more years for her to be with me and the kids, here on earth. So, she quit. Imagine that? That was six months ago. She hasn't had a cigarette since. No matter how young or how old you are, there is always something to settle in your life, right Tom?"

"Right, Harry," I said.

Harry laughed and sipped his ice water. "You know, Tom, we've been through a lot together. And one thing you've always said was to settle matters quickly. Not *hastily*, but quickly. There's a difference. And if you will do that, God will bless you."

---

2 Psalm 95:8-11. "Today, if you hear his voice, do not harden your hearts as you did at Meribah, as you did that day at Massah in the desert, where your fathers tested and tried me, though they had seen what I did. For forty years I was angry with that generation; I said, 'They are a people whose hearts go astray, and they have not known my ways.' So I declared on oath in my anger, 'They shall never enter my rest.'"

3 Id. See also Hebrews 4:11. "Let us, therefore, make every effort to enter that rest . . . ."

"And *to bless* means to confer abundant and effective life upon you and endue you with power for success, prosperity, and longevity,"[4] I said. Perhaps I was pontificating a little.

"Yes," said Harry. "And only God can do that, and has done that for me."

"Yes," I said back to Harry. "Better is one day in his courts than a thousand elsewhere,"[5] quoting one of Harry's favorite Psalms. I was feeling exhausted from a long week in court.

Harry smiled at me. "I love that Psalm. I sure want to know *exactly* what it means? But, I'm running out of time." He smiled again and shifted in his chair. I noticed that he was looking over my shoulder. "So much has been on my mind lately that I wanted to have this lunch with you today. So that's why I called you."

And so we talked on for a while.

Then, Janie Blythe walked up to our table. "Is this a bad time?" She was full of smiles and sass as she arrived. When I saw her, I jumped. Janie Blythe, what was she doing here? I had fought a case for her some years back. Then I saw Mike Harrison walk up. Mike Harrison!! What was he doing here?

I had *really* fought a battle for him years ago. Then Sarah Bleu. Then Dr. Ezra Ezekiel. Then Giovanni Moretti, with his two brothers.

And then I saw some more old friends walk up. Lots of them.

As they slowly took their seats, they were greeting each other, hugging, talking, kisses on the cheek. The waiters apparently knew of the plan; extra chairs and tables emerged.

Harry looked at me.

"Tom, it's time. You need to write some of this down. You helped a lot of people."

"Harry, I haven't helped anyone. All glory to God, not me."

Harry looked around: "Well, bottom line: I called a meeting."

For twenty-five years now, when Harry called a meeting, I went.

I'm not a theologian

I journal a lot, a whole lot. It started years ago, when I was in panic mode on some of my early cases, or when a friend came to me with a major personal problem. I would kneel down, pray, and ask God to tell me what to do. He always did. I took copious notes. These cases and problems were real. People had really serious problems. And I needed help, if I was going to help them. I did exactly what God told me to do. As time went on, I told my clients how we were going to attack their problems, and they joined me in my strategy, which was really God's strategy.

And things worked out.

---

4 Cf. R. Laird Harris, Gleason L. Archer, Jr., Bruce K. Waltke, *Theological Wordbook of the Old Testament* (Chicago, IL: Moody Publishers, 1980), p.132.

5 Psalm 84:10,12. "Better is one day in your courts than a thousand elsewhere; I would rather be a doorkeeper in the house of my God than dwell in the tents of the wicked. . . . O Lord Almighty, blessed is the man who trusts in you."

After that lunch with Harry and my old clients and friends, I went home and pulled together some of my old journal entries. The first thing I wanted to confirm was: Why God seemed to really bless people if they did everything they could to settle a dispute with someone, or settle a problem or matter in their own life. Mercy, the first thing made clear was that—I'm not a theologian.

I'm just a trial lawyer that has fought enough to know that I would do anything and everything I could to convince you to settle all the "its" in your life, and do it quickly. In addition to a dispute you may have with someone, or a legal action going on in your life, there are many other issues and challenges in your life that you should settle, and settle quickly.

God wants to bless you.

Let him.

A major blessing that started a long time ago

There was a reason that God blessed Abram after he settled a dispute with Lot.

> "The Lord said to Abram after Lot had parted from him, 'Lift up your eyes from where you are and look north and south, east and west. All the land you see I will give to you and your offspring forever. I will make your offspring like the dust of the earth, so that if anyone could count the dust, then your offspring could be counted. Go, walk through the length and breadth of the land, for I am giving it to you.'"[6]

There had been quarreling between Abram's and Lot's herdsmen. So Abram said: "Let's not have quarreling between you and me, or between your herdsmen and mine, for we are brothers. Is not the whole land before you? Let's part company. If you go to the left, I'll go to the right; if you go to the right, I'll go to the left."[7]

So, here's Abram giving Lot the first choice as to the land he can have, even though Abram, as uncle to his nephew Lot, could have taken first choice on seniority alone. So Lot chooses what he certainly thought was the better land.

> "Lot looked up and saw that the whole plain of the Jordan was well watered, like the garden of the Lord, like the land of Egypt, toward Zoar. (This was before the Lord destroyed Sodom and Gomorrah.) So Lot chose for himself the whole plain of the Jordan and set out toward the east. The two men parted company: Abram lived in the land of Canaan, while Lot lived among the cities of the plain and pitched his tents near Sodom. Now the men of Sodom were wicked and were sinning greatly against the Lord."[8]

---

6 Genesis 13:14-17.
7 Genesis 13:8-9.
8 Genesis 13:10-13.

Abram placed full confidence in the Lord; he gave Lot the first choice as to the land, and immediately thereafter, he was blessed by the Lord. And as for Lot, who "chose for himself," he chose the land next to two of the worst cities in the world, Sodom and Gomorrah, and placed himself and his family in a terrible position. For his faithfulness, God promised Abram that he and his offspring would be blessed *forever* and would receive all the land, even what Lot had chosen.

If you had been litigating and counseling as long as I have, you would have seen this phenomenon play out over and over again. The phenomenon is simple, if there is an opportunity to bless the other person first for the sake of resolution, then do it. Work closely with God, indeed, place full confidence in him, to resolve the conflicts in your life and he will bless you, and you will be a blessing to others. No need to try and understand it, it's just the way God is. "Trust in the Lord with all your heart and lean not on your own understanding; in all your ways acknowledge him, and he will make your paths straight."[9]

Settle matters quickly

Things that God wants you to do in life, he usually wants you to do quickly, especially urgent things like settling the lawsuit in your life, or settling a dispute with your spouse, or a brother or friend, or settling a major personal issue like an addiction. There is a reason that David ran *quickly* to the battle line to meet Goliath and take him down.[10] And not just take him down, but kill him, and use Goliath's own sword to chop off his head and end the giant's defiance. Similarly, Jesus said, "Settle matters quickly with your adversary who is taking you to court."[11] If you had spent thirty years in court as I have, *you know that you know that you know*, that God wants you to settle matters quickly with your adversary, or a family member, or your neighbor, or even with yourself if there is sin or conflict in your heart.

"Therefore, if you are offering your gift at the altar and there remember that your brother has something against you, leave your gift there in front of the altar. First go and be reconciled to your brother, then come and offer your gift.

Settle matters quickly with your adversary who is taking you to court. Do it while you are still with him on the way, or he may hand you over to the judge, and the judge may hand you over to the officer, and you may be thrown into prison. I tell you the truth, you will not get out until you have paid the last penny."[12]

---

9 Proverbs 3:5-6.

10 1 Samuel 17:48.

11 Matthew 5:25.

12 Matthew 5:23-26. See also Luke 12:57-59. "Why don't you judge for yourselves what is right? As you are going with your adversary to the magistrate, try hard to be reconciled to him on the way, or he may drag you off to the judge, and the judge turn you over to the officer, and the officer throw you into prison. I tell you, you will not get out until you have paid the last penny."

These are Jesus' words. Jesus, the ultimate mediator, says, settle matters *quickly.* As a lawyer, a courtroom warrior, I know, that if you don't do everything you can to settle the matter quickly, you will pay dearly with your money, your precious time, the mental anguish, pain, and resulting ramifications if you insist on delaying the resolution or pursuing the battle. And yet, you will still suffer even more than that, because you will miss blessings in your life and your relationship with God will suffer.

This book is about settling it . . . or winning it. To do what's right, or righteous, you must stay close to God. There's no other *way.* "Dear Children, do not let anyone lead you astray. He who does what is right is righteous, just as he is righteous."[13] In the challenges, battles, issues and problems I talk about in this book, there really is very little room for a mistake. Act justly, love mercy, and walk humbly with your God, especially in times of conflict, especially when you're in the fight of your life.[14]

And, don't forget, make Jesus the Senior Partner of your life. He is the ultimate mediator. "For there is one God and one mediator between God and men, the man Christ Jesus, who gave himself as a ransom for all men—the testimony given in its proper time."[15]

When you're in the fight of your life, remember the very last words of Jesus in Revelation. I've remembered them as I've walked up the steps of a courthouse, ready to give an opening statement, ready to do battle. I've remembered them when I had one last chance to settle a case, or one last chance to reach out and be a blessing to someone. I've remembered them when I was personally in bad shape and needed help. Jesus' last words apply to the situation you are in right now. They are not for some distant unknown time. They are for now also. Jesus said, "I am the Root and the Offspring of David, and the bright Morning Star."[16]

This is the very same David that ran *quickly* toward the battle line.

Jesus' last words in the Bible were: "*Surely I am coming quickly.*"[17]

If you need him, and ask him, he will come quickly.[18]

This is *still* . . . a revelation.

T+

---

13 1 John 3:7.
14 Micah 6:8. "He has showed you, O man, what is good. And what does the Lord require of you? To act justly and to love mercy and to walk humbly with your God."
15 1 Timothy 2:5.
16 Revelation 22:16.
17 Revelation 22:20 (NKJV).
18 Psalm 40:13. "Be pleased, O Lord, to save me; O Lord, come quickly to help me." Psalm 40:17. "You are my help and my deliverer; You are my God, do not delay."

The Take Away 1
Settle matters quickly in your life.

1. Settle matters quickly in your life, whether it be a lawsuit, a dispute with your spouse, your child, a neighbor, a friend, and just as important, yourself. Make every effort to do what leads to peace.

2. Things that God wants you to do in life, he usually wants you to do quickly, especially urgent things like settling the lawsuit, or settling a dispute with your spouse, a brother or friend, or settling a major personal issue like an addiction. There is a reason David ran quickly to the battle line to meet Goliath and take him down.

3. When you settle matters quickly in your life, God will bless you. He will confer abundant and effective life upon you and endue you with power for success, prosperity, and longevity.

4. God calls you to settle matters quickly in your life. You will need His help to do that. So, ask Him, and He, indeed, will come *quickly*, to help you.

You Be the Peacemaker

The Eight-Step Program

You don't qualify to win it,
 unless you've done everything to settle it

I wanted all my clients to be peacemakers. If they came to me they were usually in a mess, a big mess. Therefore, I wanted them to be peacemakers. And most of the time I knew that peacemaking would not come easy to them. The world doesn't train people for that. Their natural selves didn't tell them to do that. They were in the "right," and they should win. Their gut reaction was to fight it and win it. I would tell them that: *You don't qualify to win it, unless you've done everything to settle it.*

That didn't make sense to them. They had heard I won my trials, so they came to me. They wanted to win. I told them I didn't win because I'm some grand manipulator of the facts and law. I told them I won because I always did everything I could to settle it. Indeed, I had discovered a great correlation between making every effort possible to settle it, and increasing your chances of winning it. Indeed, my process of making every effort to settle it was a big part of why I expected to win it. *God wants to bless you by settling it, and he wants to protect you by winning it.* Strive for the blessing to get the protection. Believe me, an old trial lawyer, you really want that *blessing* if you settle it, but you really need that *protection* to win it.

If you settle it, great, God will bless you. If you have done everything you can in a godly way to settle it, but you can't, then you go on.
 Then you need to win it.

The real reason you win it is because God wants to protect you, not because he wants you to "win" it. Mediators talk about how the best settlements are when both sides leave disappointed. That is often true. You may be disappointed, but you're still blessed. An earthly disappointment is temporary and worth it—for a godly blessing. And a godly blessing is more valuable and important than an earthly "win."

Are you hot or are you cold?

Are you hot or are you cold? If you're hot, good. If you're cold, good. But if you are neither, that's "bad."

I like rehab centers. The reason is simple, they are a place where it is much easier to find those people that are hot, and those that are cold. Over and over again in rehab centers, I've seen God do something miraculous to people filled with cold despair, hopelessness and hatred, by turning it into healing, hopefulness and love, or do something with hot passion by turning it into a zeal for life and helping others, and in both cases changing lives. But, God can't do anything with those that are neither hot nor cold. In Revelation, God says: "I know your deeds, that you are neither cold nor hot. I wish you were either one or the other! So, because you are lukewarm—neither hot nor cold—I am about to spit you out of my mouth."[1]

This is *still* . . . a revelation.

I've been blessed to counsel and work for rehab centers while carrying on with my trial work. I've also been blessed to speak at rehab centers. Indeed, speaking at a rehab center can be gratifying because of the responsiveness of the audience. The reason for the responsiveness is simple, to paraphrase Socrates and Cicero: "The best flavoring for drink, is thirst." On the other hand, courthouses are often vast bastions of the lukewarm people. That's why I like the experience of the bookends of working both in courthouses and in rehab centers. Courthouses are often the homes of the lukewarms, and rehabs are often the homes to the hot and cold ones. It's easier to find God in the rehab centers. No one seems to find God in the courthouses. There is at least one good reason why the courthouses are filled with the "lukewarms," and why God doesn't want you there. If you are engaged in preparation for a trial, or at trial, or in the courthouse for just about any reason, you are wasting time, you are *not* going about your purpose for life, you are burning up precious time and resources on something that, in even the best of circumstances, will not bring you a good return. Clearly, God wants you to *settle matters quickly with your adversary;* on the other hand, the devil wants you to waste as much time as possible *with your adversary*. If you had to pick one type of building where people clearly are wasting the most time and resources in their life for the least return—pick the courthouse. Next time you're there, observe, and you will agree.

---

1 Revelation 3:15-16.

If you're a lukewarm, you can't be a peacemaker. In a courthouse setting, a lot of times it's easier to fight than to do the hard work of settling. Lukewarms won't do the godly introspection necessary to resolve a matter. I think there is at least one profound reason why God doesn't like the "lukewarms," and would just as soon spit them out of his mouth. The reason can be summed up in one word: laziness. Lukewarms are lazy. And, if you are one of the more comfortable ones in life, you are probably the laziest. And a lazy person can never do the Eight-Step Program. Only *children of light* can do the Eight-Step Program. "Those who believe that self-interest should be brought under the discipline of a higher law" can be called "children of light," as Reinhold Niebuhr said.[2]

The Eight-Step Program; It's really a Battle Plan

Picture yourself outside the courthouse, 111 North Hill Street, downtown Los Angeles, State of California. You've been there since 7:00 a.m. to beat the traffic, and to sit with me in a little coffee shop while I sip coffee with cream, no sugar, getting ready for the opening statement. At 8:00 a.m. you enter the courthouse with me. You're basically out of control at that moment. You are now in my hands, and the hands of a judge and/or jury. That's it. In the most prosaic way, you can be stoic enough to think that a trial is nothing more than a complicated way of reaching a decision.[3] But, it will be an earthly decision. There are many people in prisons, divorced, broken, hospitalized, among many other things, because of *earthly* decisions—and their failure to seek God's decision.

It's now 9:00 a.m. You're sitting in the hallway outside Department 56. The trial is about to start. In your case, the first part of the trial, the jury selection process, is about to start. You see forty potential jurors sitting in the hallway. They stare at you. The parties and counsel stare at each other. You feel a churning in your stomach that you've never felt. The churning is an indefinable kind of grinding feeling. You have to suck air on occasion, having forgotten to breathe. This is real. You feel your life is on the line. One way or the other, it usually is. But, the judge is busy, so he orders all counsel and the parties to a settlement conference, usually with one of his buddies, a judge down the hall. You've got one last shot at settling the case.

I'm the lawyer, I'm blessed, I represent a peacemaker.

But, it wasn't always that way.

If you've been my client, we would have already made many formal and informal settlement offers and overtures. You will have seen how I integrate our settlement efforts into my successful efforts to win the trial. For the most part, the judge and jury were going to see every effort we made to resolve the matter. I wasn't going to keep it a secret, or privileged. It was out in the open.

---

2 Reinhold Niebuhr, *The Children of Light and the Children of Darkness* (New York: Charles Scribner's Son, 1944), p. 9. See, Luke 16:8.
3 See Chapter 13, fn 6.

Everybody would know. No hiding. Settling and winning were not separate issues to me. If the offers weren't accepted, it was their loss. Once the deadline to accept the offer had passed, or the trial had started, the offers were off the table. Then the protection would kick in. It was too late, for them.

Several years ago, on a sunny Monday morning in the middle of summer, my client, Doug Cooke, and I were in this situation. I'd been there many times before during my career. For some clients, this is usually their first time, and, they hope the last. But—it *wasn't* Doug's first time. Doug's first time was a long time ago. Doug was a different person a long time ago. This time would be much different.

Doug and I were ready when the judge ordered both sides and all counsel, to a settlement conference. A typical settlement conference in the Los Angeles Superior Courts is usually anything but typical. Every judge does it somewhat differently; every judge has his or her own style. Still, the settlement judge will know that if we don't settle the case we will go straight to trial, there will be no turning back. In most cases that provides for a certain amount of leverage because the lawyers and the parties to the case will always have at least some hidden trepidation about the stress and outcome of the case. The settlement judge will act as a neutral third party who will hear both sides of the case, possibly read some of the pleadings, analyze the facts, the law, and potential damages and try to get the parties to settle. He will often caucus with one side at a time to hear each party's story, best and worst arguments, and legal and factual position on the case. The settlement judge will poke holes in each party's case, and try to convince the parties to settle. He will try to elicit offers from each side, and then go back and forth between the two sides trying to convince the parties to settle. The process tends to take up the amount of time allotted for the process. In other words, it can take an hour, or it can take all day. As a practical matter, a settlement conference, especially a last-minute one, is usually different from a mediation in that the judge is usually more aggressive in his settlement style and attempts to settle the case, there is less time to work with, and the pressure of the upcoming trial increases the stakes of the failure to settle.

In Doug Cooke's case, we had actually drafted the settlement agreement two years before, when we first proposed the settlement between the parties. Our position hadn't changed. The other side was never willing to settle, and weren't willing to negotiate. Weren't willing to even talk about settlement. That happens sometimes. Sometimes all the time. The opposition sometimes sees the overtures to settle as signs of weakness, not realizing that they are sowing the seeds of their own defeat. In this case, we had fought for two solid years. They were shooting for big bucks, my client's trademark, and lots of damages for various *alleged* infringements. I had worked the case up legally and spiritually. The Lord was there.

You want to make sure "The Lord Is There" when you are in court, or in the middle of whatever dispute you have. In the book of Ezekiel, when the evil princes of Edom looked down from their lofty mountaintop at the land of the Israelites, Israel and Judah, they thought it would be easy pickings. In their arrogance, the princes said, "These two nations and countries will be ours and we will take possession of them." But there was one huge, impenetrable problem: "The Lord was there."[4] Edom's confidence was their undoing, and Edom would be left "desolate."[5] As Charles Spurgeon once said about this story, which is the story of *our* lives, "We are constantly opposed, and yet perpetually preserved!" As long as God is there. God doesn't want you to "win" because he wants you to win, he wants you to win because he wants to protect and preserve you.

If you want to quit alcohol, go to AA and work through the Twelve-Step Program. If you put your heart into it, you will quit alcohol. If you want to be a peacemaker, if you want to resolve the fight of your life, and you put your heart into it, go through Jesus' Eight-Step Program—the Beatitudes.[6] Jesus put this program together a few thousand years ago. Certainly, the Beatitudes have incredible depth and insight on many levels, but if you are in the fight of your life, they are Jesus' Eight-Step Program to turn you into a peacemaker.

Kneel down.

Remember, *you* be the peacemaker. If you're a peacemaker, you're a child of God. If you're not, you're something else. And you don't want to be something else. You could be one of the *children of darkness.*[7] That's not good.

We'll get to that.

"I'm not a peacemaker, I'm a moneymaker, and I will never be called a child of God"

Doug Cooke and I go way back. In the fall of 1984, I put Doug in a rehab center for the fifth time. He had a "little" problem with alcohol and cocaine, and sometimes—whatever else was available. He would, time and again, work with a recovery counselor and immerse himself in a Twelve-Step Program. Doug's business was in clothing and all the products that came out of the Santa Barbara surfing culture. His company was successful, and Doug was wealthy. On this fifth occasion, however, within a few days of putting him into the rehab center, he got sued by a large vendor. His company could, sometimes, function without him, but it certainly suffered, and I thought this latest lawsuit looked really serious. Doug owed a lot of money. But, all he wanted to talk about and do—was fight. He mentioned over and over again that there was this certain "guy" that owned

---

4 Ezekiel 35:10.

5 Ezekiel 35:15.

6 Matthew 5:1-10 (KJV).

7 As Niebuhr said: "The children of darkness are evil because they know no law beyond the self. They are wise, though evil, because they understand the power of self-interest." Niebuhr, *The Children of Light and the Children of Darkness*, p. 10. See John 8:12-17 where Jesus talks about the children of the Devil. "You belong to your father, the devil, and you want to carry out your father's desire."

the company, but he didn't mention his name. Doug said he could beat him. And, he told me I had been successful before against other vendors, so I'd simply win again, or somehow get it resolved.

But, this time—I refused.

One night I went to visit Doug at the rehab center for the last time. I was done, I was under pressure from my law partners to produce billable hours, and I was burned out on being his lawyer and friend.

I remember the look on Doug's face. It was stone cold. I remember him saying to me: "I understand. I'm done with myself too. I'm done. I can't kick this, I always plateau out, and eventually relapse."

Where was the fight? Where was the euphoria from a few days ago? Something had dissipated over the past few days.

"Tom, I'm done. I can't go on. I can't kick this. Wish I could, but I can't. Done, finished."

I remember sitting there listening. And . . . trying to talk myself into not caring. But, it was difficult.

Looking back on that evening makes me think of a verse I learned a long time after that night: "He has made everything beautiful in its time. He has also set eternity in the hearts of men; yet they cannot fathom what God has done from beginning to end."[8]

These were the "beginnings" for me. I had so much to learn, and nowhere to go to learn it. Somewhere deep down inside me, from somewhere I wasn't aware of, I told Doug that it was time for him to do Jesus' Eight-Step Program. I had no idea where that idea came from.

I told him we'd do it together.

I remember Doug looking at me and saying: "Fine, I'm done anyway. What do I have to lose?"

So, we did it together. Two beginners. No clue, no help.

In the fall of 1984, a drug addict and a lawyer methodically did Jesus' Eight-Step Program. We had no idea what we were doing. I wasn't a Christian, he wasn't sober. No one was guiding us, yet we felt guided. I remember the feeling and rhythm of those months in the sense that nothing was structured, but Doug and I would "meditate" on one verse for about a week, and then go to the next verse. We thought we "knew" how to meditate, we were up on the latest trends, so that's what we did. Eventually we agreed that we'd actually try to pray. We figured that wasn't a big deal, we'd just talk to God like we talked to each other. My law firm senior partner, Murray Katz, had assigned me to a really big case involving a few radio stations, I was over my head, and Doug eventually got out of rehab and went back to work. We stuck to the Program. We just felt in our hearts we were supposed to.

---

8 Ecclesiastes 3:11.

We also had Doug's case to deal with, but in those days in particular, litigation was expected to drag on forever. And Doug felt he was making money off the money he wasn't paying the other guy. He seemed okay, and I didn't have a clue.

Then the week came when we began to meditate and pray the Seventh Step. That week, Doug got sober permanently, and I changed permanently. "Blessed *are* the peacemakers: for they shall be called the children of God." I didn't know then what I know now, what I'm sure of now, what I've tested now for twenty-six years: The Beatitudes are in perfect order and seven is the number for perfection in the Bible. It was a Monday night in late October 1984. Doug and I were having coffee at a coffee shop in Santa Monica. We were discussing Jesus' Eight-Step Program.

"Tom, I'm a thief," Doug finally said. He hung his head and told me what going through the first six steps had done for him. During the week before, while meditating and praying on the Sixth Step his heart broke and he cried for hours. "Blessed *are* the pure in heart: for they shall see God."

Doug drowned himself in another sip of coffee. "Tom, you just can't meditate on this stuff and not change. I'd be lying to you if I didn't tell you that I tried to keep up the facade for all these weeks, but I can't. There is nothing pure in heart about me, I'm not merciful, I don't thirst for righteousness, I'm not meek, I don't mourn, and I'm certainly not poor in spirit. There's nothing *poor, or pure,* about me!"

I think I was getting the point. In the moment of silence, I took a sip of my own coffee, hovering over my cup for sanctuary.

Doug looked up. "There were no thunderbolts, no clashes of thunder. I just realized something. It just sunk in."

"Yes," I said.

"I'm not a peacemaker, I'm a moneymaker, and I will *never* be called a child of God."

If ever there was a moment when I felt I saw someone change in a flash . . .

"Tom, I owe that vendor the money. Every penny of it. I was wrong, I am wrong, and I'm going to fix it. I'm going to apologize and try and work out a way to pay his company back. I'm done; I'll never do that again."

I told him I understood and that I would help him.

Start day.

As we left the coffee shop, Doug looked at me and said: "Sandy Collins."

"What?" I said.

"Sandy Collins. . . ." Doug looked down and shook his head. "He's the 'vendor.' I know him well. Married to Lindy, and they have two daughters. He's a good man. I . . . owe him the money."

The Beatitudes

Now we know we have to go up to the "mountain" to get these eight steps from Jesus, just as Moses went up on Mount Sinai to get the Ten Commandments.

For me, kneeling down was my way to go up to the mountainside; I needed the blessing. "And it shall come to pass in the last days, *that* the mountain of the Lord's house shall be established in the top of the mountains, and shall be exalted above the hills; and all nations shall flow unto it."[9]

> "AND SEEING the multitudes, he went up into a mountain: and when
>   he was set, his disciples came unto him:
> And he opened his mouth, and taught them,
> saying,
> Blessed *are* the poor in spirit: for theirs is the kingdom of heaven.
> Blessed *are* they who mourn: for they shall be comforted.
> Blessed *are* the meek: for they shall inherit the earth.
> Blessed *are* they which do hunger and thirst after righteousness: for
>   they shall be filled.
> Blessed *are* the merciful: for they shall obtain mercy.
> Blessed *are* the pure in heart: for they shall see God.
> Blessed *are* the peacemakers: for they shall be called the children of
>   God.
> Blessed *are* they which are persecuted for righteousness' sake: for
>   theirs is the kingdom of heaven."[10]

Jesus would have made a great lawyer. In my case, he was a great Senior Partner. His words (or directives) are concise, *in perfect order*, and to the point. And, very powerful. The Beatitudes are not a scrambled set of principles that Jesus just threw out there for general guidance. No, there is perfect order, and there is a reason for the order from one through eight. When in the battle of your life, study the Beatitudes in order, meditate on them, and ask God what he wants to tell you in each step so that he turns you into a peacemaker. I can assure you that God will come through for you. Please believe this, have faith, and work through Jesus' Eight-Step Program.

As to the other side, your opponent, your adversary, well, let God work on him, or her, or it, or the situation. You know, the battle belongs to the Lord.[11] After thirty years of fieldwork with the Lord, I can assure you that if you do your part, he will do his part. He loves having a partner that wants to work with him. Consider it fieldwork.

Get your fieldwork started.

You be the peacemaker

Step Seven: "Blessed *are* the peacemakers: for they shall be called the children of God." I love well-placed punctuation such as a colon. A lawyer should respect

---

9   Isaiah 2:2 (KJV).

10   Matthew 5:1-10 (KJV).

11   2 Chronicles 20:15. "This is what the Lord says to you: 'Do not be afraid or discouraged because of this vast army. For the battle in not yours, but God's.'" See also, Exodus 14:14: "The Lord will fight for you; you need only be still." See also, 1 Samuel 17:47.

perfect punctuation. For each "blessed," Jesus provides an illustration. When Jesus illustrates—take notice. He's telling you what the reward will be, in this life, and for eternity. A lawyer also respects the word "shall." When a judge says he *shall* do something, there's no "maybe" about it. He is expressing more than a strong intention. He believes he has a duty to do something, or, more broadly, is required to do something.[12]

You become a peacemaker when the first six Beatitudes characterize your life. The best I can do is assure you that if you work through the first six steps, God will make you a peacemaker, you will be blessed, and you will know that you know that you know, that you are a child of God. And, when you do your part as a peacemaker, God will do his part.

The Beatitudes are also known as *makarisms*, that is, "blessings." Early Christian scholars saw that for each "blessing," there was another side to the story, a curse or reproach, if you had led someone astray or hurt them. Scholars believe there was a reason that Matthew placed the reproaches in Chapter 23, because that marks the conclusion of Jesus' public ministry in that Jesus only teaches his disciples after that, not the public. The reproach to Step Seven, "Blessed *are* the peacemakers: for they shall be called the children of God," (Matthew 5:9), can be found in Matthew 23:15.

And it's serious.

"Woe unto you, scribes and Pharisees, hypocrites! for ye compass sea and land to make one proselyte, and when he is made, ye make him twofold more the child of hell than yourselves."[13] In the courthouses, in the rehab centers, in life, you can find the peacemakers, and you can see why they are called the children of God. You can also see those that are *not* peacemakers, and you can see why they are the children of hell.

Either way, they are easy to spot.

Especially, in the long run.

And, by now, I've had a long run.

"The creation waits in eager expectation for the sons of God to be revealed."[14]

You will not waver

Twenty-three years ago, on a Monday night in a little coffee shop in Santa Monica, everything started to change. Within two weeks of that night, with no planning, no coordination, and no knowledge of what the other guy was doing, we both felt called to walk to an altar and surrender our lives to a Savior. And that was it. We never wavered after that.

But, more on that later.

---

12 See, Black's Law Dictionary, Seventh Edition, Bryan A. Garner, Editor in Chief.
13 Matthew 23:15 (KJV).
14 Romans 8:19.

Twenty-three years later, in 2007, on a Monday morning, Doug Cooke and I walked down the hall to take part in a settlement conference.

Doug's company had continued to prosper over the years. Several years ago, a competitor accused Doug and his company of unfair competition and trademark infringement. Doug and his company hadn't done anything wrong, and he went out of his way to show how any confusions in the marketplace could be resolved. He and I made several very reasonable and generous offers. We even drafted up the settlement agreement and sent it to his opponents and their lawyers. But, we never received any favorable response. Instead, they sued Doug. That was a year ago. Now, we were about to go to trial. Doug had done everything he could to settle it.

Now, we expected to win it.

Judge Crowley was our settlement judge. He started the settlement conference by having both lawyers summarize their cases, the facts and supporting law, and an analysis of the damages. That took about forty minutes. Again, the process is always different, but the goal is always the same: to settle the case. After the lawyers summarized their clients case, the judge went through several hours of going back and forth between the two sides, meeting with each side alone with their lawyers present. The settlement judge's back and forth process included some arm twisting, a lot of critiquing of each sides' case, and some fresh perspective from a settlement judge that had also been a trial judge for twenty-five years. But, something was different, the other side was much more peaceful this time around, whereas our previous attempts at settlement and one previous mediation had been hostilely received. This day had a good feel to it.

Doug and I were now in our fifties. So, on the breaks, while the judge was meeting with the other side, we reminisced about the old days, and in particular, the fall of 1984 and our first efforts with Jesus' Eight-Step Program. What we talked about the most was—the Eighth Step.

Step eight: Blessed *are* they which are persecuted for righteousness' sake: for theirs is the kingdom of heaven. As Isaiah said: "And the work of righteousness shall be peace; and the effect of righteousness quietness and assurance forever."[15] This is the bedrock step. This is good news, because you don't need to worry. If, you are persecuted for righteousness' sake—you will not waver. You cannot be moved. After going through Jesus' Eight-Step program, you indeed will be blessed. St. Thomas Aquinas in *Summa Theological* said:

> "The eighth beatitude is a confirmation and declaration of all those that precede. Because from the very fact that a man is confirmed in poverty of spirit, meekness, and the rest, it follows that no persecution will induce him to renounce them. Hence the eighth beatitude corresponds, in a way, to all the preceding seven."

---

15 Isaiah 32:17 (KJV).

If you make it through the first seven steps, and those steps characterize your life, you will be steadfast. *You will not waver.* You will be called a child of God, you will know what that feels like—and you will not turn back. Ever. You will be for God, forever. And, of course, he will be for you. Indeed, God will be your front guard and your rear guard. "For you shall not go out with haste, nor go by flight; for the Lord will go before you, and the God of Israel *will be* your rear guard."[16]

Settle matters quickly, not hastily, Part 1

By 2007, Doug had been a peacemaker for about twenty-three years. When the dispute first arose about two years before, he went into peacemaking mode. He made proposals to the other side, went out of his way to look for a solution, and *set his mind* to settle the dispute. And yet, the lawsuit came a year after that. And Doug went back to work again to resolve the matter. What's important here is that Doug settled the matter quickly in his heart and by his actions, and he directed me to draft up a generous settlement agreement.
And then he let God take over.

As time goes on, and discernment settles in, I know in my heart the difference between doing something "quickly," and doing something "hastily." "Quickly," is a good thing. "Hastily," is a bad thing. In my lawyer world, hastily usually means fearfully and superficially. As I said, when God wants you to do something, he usually wants you to do it quickly, but not hastily.[17] Indeed, even an angel of the Lord, when freeing Peter from prison, struck Peter in the side and woke him up, saying: "Get up quickly."[18]

And on that day, after two years of attacks by the other side, Judge Crowley, toward the end of the mediation asked both sides to commit to a "mediator's recommendation," that is, he asked both sides to agree in advance to whatever his terms would be to settle the case. Doug quickly agreed. And, so did the other side.
Judge Crowley made his recommendation.
Doug at first was surprised, but then decided he shouldn't be surprised.
The judge's recommendation was exactly what Doug had proposed two years earlier. And, we already had the settlement agreement drafted. The case settled.

Doug was a peacemaker in action. During the settlement conference, something became clear. Doug's opponent, had changed. He was different. Eventually, he was ready to make peace. "When a man's ways are pleasing to the Lord, he makes even his enemies live at peace with him."[19]

---

16 Isaiah 52:12 (NKJV).
17 Proverbs 19:2. "It is not good to have zeal without knowledge, nor to be hasty and miss the way." Proverbs 25:8 (NIV). "What you have seen with your eyes do not bring hastily to court, for what will you do in the end if your neighbor puts you to shame?"
18 Acts 12:7 (NASB). "Behold, an angel of the Lord suddenly appeared and a light shone in the cell; and he struck Peter's side and woke him up, saying 'Get up quickly.' And his chains fell off his hands."
19 Proverbs 16:7.

Turn the battle over to the Lord

I've spent thirty years at the crossroads of human conflict. Let me tell you a secret about the Beatitudes, Jesus' Eight-Step Program. I know the Beatitudes have amazing depth, and so much applicability in other areas of your life. But, when you are in the fight of your life, here's the secret:

The Eight-Step Program, it's really a battle plan.

It's a plan to turn the battle over to the Lord.

T+

The Take Away 2
"You" be the peacemaker.

1. "You" be the *peacemaker*, and you will be called a child of God. This is not something you can be lukewarm about. God doesn't like the lukewarms, and would just as soon spit them out of his mouth. Lukewarms wait for the other person to be the peacemaker.

2. God doesn't want you to "win" the lawsuit or battle in your life because he wants you to win, he wants you to win because he wants to protect and preserve you. *You don't qualify to win it, unless you've done everything to settle it.*

3. Jesus has an **Eight-Step Program**. The Eight-Step Program is really a *Battle Plan*, a Plan to turn the battle over to the Lord. Indeed, the battle belongs to the Lord.

   This is Jesus' Eight-Step Program, the Beatitudes:

   Blessed *are* the poor in spirit: for theirs is the kingdom of heaven.
   Blessed *are* they who mourn: for they shall be comforted.
   Blessed *are* the meek: for they shall inherit the earth.
   Blessed *are* they which do hunger and thirst after righteousness: for they shall be filled.
   Blessed *are* the merciful: for they shall obtain mercy.
   Blessed *are* the pure in heart: for they shall see God.
   Blessed *are* the peacemakers: for they shall be called the children of God.
   Blessed *are* they which are persecuted for righteousness' sake: for theirs is the kingdom of heaven.

4. **Settle matters *quickly* in your life, not hastily.** Quickly done is godly done. Hastily done is humanly done, it is done fearfully and superficially. *It is not good to have zeal without knowledge, nor to be hasty and miss the way.*

   Remember, when a man's ways are pleasing to the Lord, he makes even his enemies live at peace with him.

My First Tool

Speak to your problem

Going up to the mountain
Inquire of the Lord

The last words ascribed to Jesus in the Bible were, "*Surely I am coming quickly.*"[1] And, as I said, if you need him, he will come quickly. But, *it helps if you ask.* Indeed, it helps if you *inquire of the Lord*.[2] Early on in my walk, I didn't know I needed to ask. But, I did ask out of desperation. God always does things consistent with his word. Here again, Jesus laid it out: "So I say to you: Ask and it will be given to you; seek and you will find; knock and the door will be opened to you. For everyone who asks receives; he who seeks finds; and to him who knocks, the door will be opened."[3] I remember the first time I asked. I needed help, and I needed it quickly. Don't let the naysayers, the lukewarms, question God's timing. Ask for help, and ask God to respond *quickly*. Let the lukewarms wait around. Indeed, they don't even know to ask. When David ran quickly to the battle line, he wasn't lukewarm about his assignment, and neither should you be.

And neither will God be.

I remember so many times over the years going "up to the mountain." Many of those times were to get help in resolving, solving, or settling a big case. Eventually, the full value of Isaiah set in:

---

1 Revelation 22:20 (NKJV).
2 See, Joshua 9:14, to understand the consequences when the "men of Israel . . . did not *inquire of the Lord.*" Or see 1 Samuel 30:8, ". . . and David *inquired of the Lord*, 'Shall I pursue this raiding party? Will I overtake them?' 'Pursue them,' he answered. 'You will certainly overtake them and succeed in the rescue.'" And see, 1 Samuel 23:2.
3 Luke 11:9-10.

"Many peoples will come and say,
  'Come, let us go up to the mountain of the Lord,
    to the house of the God of Jacob.
He will teach us his ways,
    so that we may walk in his paths.'
The law will go out from Zion,
    the work of the Lord from Jerusalem.
He will judge between the nations
    and will *settle disputes for many peoples.*
They will beat their swords into plowshares
    and their spears into pruning hooks.
Nation will not take up sword against nation,
    nor will they train for war anymore.
Come, O house of Jacob,
    let us walk in the light of the Lord."[4]

I remember the early days of my career when I would "go up to the mountain." But I also remember the weight on my shoulders when I had to go down off the mountain. As the years went on, I remember not only the weight on my shoulders, but it was as if my feet were heavier. Like I had to trudge down that mountain, feeling like a failure if I didn't settle the case, settle the matter, or resolve the situation. Whenever I was in a trial, I felt I was in a valley. The *valley of decision.*[5] But I felt protected, and as I beat my plowshare back into a sword, and my pruning hook back into a spear, the angst and disappointment I felt, would change. I knew I'd be okay, *if God was there.*[6] And, I knew I'd be okay if I had done everything I could to settle it.

But if I didn't settle it, I was going to win it. "Beat your plowshares into swords, and your pruning hooks into spears: let the weak say, I *am* strong."[7]

Coming off the mountain

When you're in the fight of your life, choose your tools carefully, and know how to use them. You will need those tools. I promise you. I use my set of God-given tools for all occasions. But I especially use them—in court. Believe me, when you are on the firing line, you will need tools. I feel so sorry for those who don't have a good set of God-given tools. You will need tools, but you have to ask him for them. If you are in the fight of your life, just kneel down, and ask God for help, and ask him for a set of tools. He will give them to you. *Customized.* Customized just for you.

In May 1985, I had just started a jury trial in the courthouse in downtown Los Angeles, fourth floor, department 36. It was a long first day, picking the jury, then

---

4 Isaiah 2:3-5. See also, Micah 4:2-3.
5 Joel 3:14.
6 Ezekiel 35:10.
7 Joel 3:10 (KJV).

making opening statements. By the end of the day, I was exhausted. But worse, I was scared to death. I was up against five, count 'em *five*, of the best trial lawyers in the country, two from right here in Los Angeles. The two local lawyers were the types that waved to all the judges if they saw them in the hall: "Hi John"; "Hey Judge, good to see you"; "Clarence, you're looking good, will you be there Saturday night? —Great!" The judges would yell back to them: "Counselor, good to see you, congratulations on the ruling"; "BJ, good to see you too"; "Of course I'll be there, wouldn't miss it!" They'd been around a long time. Me? Nobody knew *me*. I felt like a baby lawyer compared to *that team*. They made me feel like a baby *everything*.

I was also a baby Christian.

It had been six months since I had answered an altar call all by myself in a little West Los Angeles church I had stopped in on a Wednesday night on the way home from my Century City office at a big law firm. I still think of the angel who sent me there. Anyway, six months later, I was still feeling brand new in my rather disorganized new Christian life. I ended up going to St. Monica's Catholic church in Santa Monica because I was raised Catholic so I went where I thought I was supposed to go. I was quickly *discovered* by a pretty girl named Tobi who asked me if I would play piano for the church.

I said, "yes."

Why did the senior partner, Murray Katz, put me on this huge case? Was he crazy? I was outmatched, and by the end of the first day after opening statements, I felt it even more. At the last minute, Murray saw fit to add two lawyers to my team, *just to help out a little*. It seemed way too late for that, but I would take all the help I could get as my faith floundered. One guy was fifteen years older than me and much more experienced, and the other one was my age. The older lawyer, Chuck, unbeknownst to me had a little drug problem that he would feed on the breaks, but other than that he was pretty smart. Stan, the lawyer my age, was very helpful, but more scared than me and not willing to do anything in the trial that required opening his mouth. My motley little crew was pretty pathetic. But a couple of the female jurors were kind of cute, so I felt like my opening statement went fairly well. I was grasping.

At 4:30 in the late afternoon in that hot little courtroom (courtrooms are always hot during trial), we all left the courtroom. Stan headed home with a stack of papers to work on for the case, watch the Dodgers on TV and drink a beer, and Chuck went to do some cocaine and go home to his wife. This was the mid-80s; think *LA Law*. They were my back-up lawyers, this case was my problem, not theirs.

My client was Harry Goldberg, and he owned two radio stations, unless of course, I lost the trial, and then he would own—*no* stations. The plaintiffs were bound and determined to take the radio stations from Harry at a bargain basement price based on a set of deal memos that I was arguing were not binding.

Harry had gotten in over his head financially and without a good lawyer, had gone back and forth with the plaintiffs (before they were the plaintiffs) with a bunch of written and signed deal memos. Harry was in poor financial condition. After that first day in trial, Harry and I walked down the courthouse hall into the attorney conference room. I could see he was concerned. That was about when I realized why I was the lead trial lawyer on the case. I was all Harry could afford. I was the "B" team. And Murray threw in a couple "C" team lawyers at the start of the trial to bolster me up a little bit—against the best team of plaintiffs' lawyers in the inner galaxy. They even dressed so well it scared me. Everything matched. Navy blue. They looked like the Blue Angels when they walked down the hall in unison. When they sat at counsel's table they sat in unison. They even went to the bathroom together, although one was a female and she would peel off at just the right moment to veer into the ladies room as if it was all choreographed.

I was in my khaki-colored suit I picked up cheap in the garment district (I had five of them, same color). Only a few coffee stains on two of them. I had on my standard issue white button-down shirt. Striped tie. All on sale.

I just didn't know yet, but my outfit was going to pay off.

Excuse me, Mr. Goldberg, there's a handgun in your briefcase

Once we were in the attorney conference room, Harry slipped open his old tan leather briefcase and took out his notes from the day. I gulped a cup of coffee; my khaki suit would get another stain. We went over his notes, his thoughts, his concerns about the day. And then he reminded me that if we lost the trial he would lose everything, his life's work, his passion, his love, the reason he got up in the morning, the way he supported his family, the way he employed his family, and his only contribution to a lost and foreboding world, but not necessarily in that order. He talked about his collection of antique radios; maybe I could somehow use them in the trial. He loved his radio stations. Then Harry opened up his briefcase to slip his notes back in. That's when I saw it. A handgun in his briefcase.

"Excuse me, Mr. Goldberg, there's a handgun in your briefcase," I said, with a jolt.

"Yes, and it's loaded," he said, pursing his lips tightly and speaking firmly.

"Why do you have a loaded handgun in your briefcase?" I muttered.

"Because if I lose this case, I'm going to shoot everyone of those bastards, (he paused to look me in the eye) before they even leave the courtroom."

"The plaintiffs"!? I tried to calm my shock.

"Yes. And their lawyers." His thumbs were poised on the locking clasps of his briefcase. I still remember the double clicking sound when he locked both clasps with simultaneous proficiency.

Then he looked me in the eye: "See you in court in the morning."

He didn't wait for a comment from me, or even a goodbye. I watched his lonely large figure walk all the way down the courthouse hall and out the door.

I remember thinking: "Hmmm—he means it."

Need I tell you?

They didn't have metal detectors in the courthouse in those days.

My first tool

All I remember was panic that night when I went home. I just had to call Murray Katz and tell him that Harry had a loaded gun in his briefcase, and if I lost the case he was going to blow away the plaintiffs and their lawyers. I did the math, and decided he probably wouldn't have enough bullets left over to shoot me. I wondered if he brought refills. I didn't know what to do. I figured I couldn't call Murray, I certainly didn't have his number, I was a lowly associate. I was too stressed to prepare for court the next day. I didn't have a dog. My heart was pounding. I literally remember saying to myself, "well, I guess it's about time, I give this ol' Christianity thing a whirl." It was either that or a stiff drink. Up to then, for the last six months my walk had been easy. I was going to church at St. Monica's, playing piano in the little church band, meeting new friends, hugging people, the usual mush-mush stuff. Even after six months, I still wasn't comfortable with all the hugging these Christians did. What's that about? Still, the Catholics assured me that even lawyers could go to heaven, so, all things considered, I was doing pretty good.

So I knelt down. That alone was a big step for me. I was a big-shot rising star lawyer (in my own mind), to kneel down just didn't make sense to me. I had done some kneeling in the Catholic Mass service, but everyone knelt at specified times, kind of automatically. I figured those kneel-downs didn't count. I was just doing what everyone did. But the kneel-down that night counted. I *chose* to kneel down. I was desperate. I was in a panic. I had no hope. This trial was *not* just another test I could gin-up on and pass with flying colors. I needed help, and I needed it quickly. So, I asked the Lord for help, and told him I needed it quickly. I said it out loud; I wasn't sure why at that moment.

My spiritual dimension was, shall I say, lacking, before I knelt down that night. After I knelt down, well, that's a different story. The Lord told me immediately to *speak* to my problem, and to cast it into the sea. That's exactly what I heard in my heart, so I did it. I stood up, just like I was in court and I started speaking to my problem. I spoke it out loud, loud enough for my neighbor to hear. Loud enough at times for the neighborhood to hear. I said: *I speak to the Plaintiffs, and in particular to Knoll Radio Company (the main Plaintiff), and to Billy Joe Hollister (the other plaintiff and owner of Knoll), and to Brendan Jones, Bruce Jenson, Philip Rawlings, and Ann Davis (the Plaintiffs' lawyers)—and I cast them into the sea in Jesus' name. I speak to the Plaintiffs, and in particular to Knoll Radio Company (the main Plaintiff), and to Billy Joe Hollister (the Owner), and to Brendan Jones, Bruce*

Jenson, Philip Rawlings, and Ann Davis (the Plaintiffs lawyers)—and I cast them into the sea in Jesus' name. I say it again, I speak to the Plaintiffs, and in particular to Knoll Radio Company (the main Plaintiff), and to Billy Joe Hollister (the Owner), and to Brendan Jones, Bruce Jenson, Philip Rawlings, and Ann Davis (the Plaintiffs' lawyers)—and I cast them into the sea in Jesus' name.—Cast them into the sea in Jesus name. Cast them into the sea in Jesus' name. Cast them into the sea in Jesus' name. I take authority over them in Jesus' name. I have faith in you Lord. And throughout this trial, I will put all my faith in you Lord. This is your trial, and I put my full trust in you. Period. Amen!

Then, I went to sleep. I had a dream. In my dream my Counselor said: *"Tell the just man ALL is well."*[8]

And I slept perfectly until the alarm went off at 4:30 a.m.

T+

---

8 See, Isaiah 3:10. And years later I came across this verse in *Story of a Soul*, The Autobiography of St. Thérèse of Lisieux, Manuscript C (Washington D.C.: ICS Publications, 1996), p. 207.

The Take Away 3
Speak to your problem.

1. To have victory over the problem in your life, your first tool is to *speak* to your problem, and cast it into the sea in Jesus' name—cast it into the sea in Jesus' name. Have no doubt in your heart, but believe that what you say will happen, and it will be done for you. Believe that you have received the victory, and it will be yours.

2. When you are in the fight of your life, you must *inquire of the Lord.* Jesus' last recorded words in the Bible are, *Surely I am coming quickly.* Ask God for help, and ask Him to respond—*quickly!* He will.

3. David *inquired of the Lord*, "Shall I pursue this raiding party? Will I overtake them?" "Pursue them," the Lord answered. "You will certainly overtake them and succeed in the rescue."

Inquire of the Lord to make sure the Lord is with you. He will be. Have faith.

4. If you can't settle it, then win it. Beat your plowshares into swords, and your pruning hooks into spears: let the weak say, I *am* strong.

You *say* (speak it out loud) to yourself, *I am strong.*

Show Me Your Tools

ddarssa

My dependency problem; the Lord doesn't like self-sufficiency

For the next twenty-four years, I would occasionally be back in department 36, the site of the Knoll Radio Company vs. Harry Goldberg case. As the years went by, my tools became a little more refined. They had to, I led a life of serious warfare. I was never blessed with a nice, simple, easy-going peaceful little life. Every day seemed like open warfare to me. No quiet weekends. I had no personal life. I felt God was using me to defend my friends and clients from people or companies who had attacked them. He brought a lot of cases to me. If they attacked my clients, most of the time they also attacked me. As it is sometimes said, being a trial lawyer is like standing between the dog and the fire hydrant. You're going to get hit, you're just not sure how hard *or what with*. It won't be fun. It is not enjoyable. There is no way to understand the life of a trial lawyer unless you lived the life. The only trial lawyers I knew that were happy, were lawyers I didn't know. I borrowed that line from Dennis Prager, who said: "The only people I know that are happy are people I don't know." That statement was in Prager's book *Happiness Is A Serious Problem*. I agree with Prager. The problem is that when you really get to know those supposedly "happy" people, you find that they really aren't so happy. If you've been a trial lawyer for thirty years, you end up thinking that no one is happy, especially the lawyers. And, statistically speaking, 25 percent of all lawyers have dependency problems. Drugs, alcohol, or other dependency issues.

I also had a dependency problem: I depended on the Lord. It was serious. I *really* depended on the Lord. Of all the Christian lawyers, I know, like my close friends, Dan, Dave, Sam, etc., because they had a serious dependency problem like me, they were fine. No problems. We chose who and what to be dependent on. We were, and are, steadfast. We ain't wavering. It won't happen.

I can assure you after thirty years of fighting that any form of self-sufficiency is a fraud on your "self." Even my friends that have gone through AA know that. Please ask God for help. In my case, I learned to become downright pushy about it. When you are in the fight of your life you absolutely simply have to stop the typical lukewarm mushy half-baked approach to things. By the time twenty years had rolled by after the Harry Goldberg trial—I was a much more focused fighter. I always had the *desire*, I would make a *decision*, I would *ask* God for it, I would *receive* it, I would *see* it, I would *speak* it, and I would *act* on it. And I would not waver. Period. *ddarssa.* Back in 1985, I was just getting started. The battles I had in courtrooms were just part of the story. What I saw in rehab centers, and sometimes in day-to-day life, was just as serious.

The whole book of Isaiah is a manual on how to deal with the battles of your life. As a trial lawyer and warrior studying this book, literally reading it like a law school textbook, you see that a life that fails to hit the mark of a good relationship with God is going to get you off track. It is going to force you to self-sufficiency, and that will lead you to ruin. You simply can't win a trial, and you can't win an important battle in life without getting right and staying right with God.

"Woe to the obstinate children,"
    declares the Lord,
"*to those who carry out plans that are not mine,*
    forming an alliance, but not by my spirit,
    heaping sin upon sin;
who go down to Egypt
    without consulting me;
who look for help to Pharaoh's protection,
    to Egypt's shade for refuge.
But Pharaoh's protection will be to your shame,
    Egypt's shade will bring you disgrace.
Though they have officials in Zoan
    and their envoys have arrived in Hanes,
everyone will be put to shame
    because of a people useless to them,
who bring neither help nor advantage,
    but only shame and disgrace."[1]

There was a time when Israel, and in particular, the city of Jerusalem, also called the Valley of Vision, was going to be attacked by their enemies from Elam and Kir, states that were under Assyrian rule. And here you have the Israelites looking to every means of protection possible, assessing and assembling their weaponry, assessing potential breaches in their defenses, storing up water, counting their buildings and tearing down houses to fortify the walls, and even forming alliances with their pagan neighbors. But they did not look to God.

---

1 Isaiah 30:1-5.

"And you looked in that day
    to the weapons in the Palace of the Forest;
you saw that the City of David
    had many breaches in its defenses;
you stored up water
    in the Lower Pool.
You counted the buildings in Jerusalem
    and tore down houses to strengthen the wall.
You built a reservoir between the two walls
    for the water of the Old Pool,
but you did not look to the One who made it,
    or have regard for the One who planned it long ago.[2]

Textbooks in law school are good. The book of Isaiah should be included. And one of the case studies should be Chapter 22. It *is* a case study. The Lord called the Israelites to *call* on Him, to weep and wail and put on sackcloth. But the Israelites were focused on self-sufficiency. They were so focused, they had given up hope. In a long legal career you get to see those that have given up hope. Look what the Israelites did:

"There is joy and revelry,
    slaughtering of cattle and killing of sheep,
    eating of meat and drinking of wine!
'Let us eat and drink,' you say,
    'for tomorrow we die!'"[3]

The Lord is there

It is worth repeating, you want the Lord there with you in the fight of your life. Spurgeon would have been a good lawyer. Again, he said: "*We are constantly opposed, and yet perpetually preserved!*" As the Lord said: "This is the one I esteem: he who is humble and contrite in spirit, and trembles at my word."[4]

I got to the point that I really didn't have a choice. The Holy Spirit would slam me if I got off the path and tried to be self-sufficient. I said to the Lord a long time ago, "choose me." He did. They were tough battles, right up to the end of my thirty-year stint. I absolutely had to depend on Jesus, and the Holy Spirit was ruthless with me to stay on the path. Just plain ruthless. Besides, I had to be up at 4:30 a.m. the next morning, and I couldn't have any distractions.

None.

---

2 Isaiah 22:8-11.
3 Isaiah 22:13.
4 Isaiah 66:2.

Back to the battle

The trial is a crucible for the people of faith. It grinds out all the impurities of passivity and indecision.

The Lord's repertoire of tools for battle is endless. He has his own set of tools for you. Seek them out. Be wary of those tools assigned to others. Look for those assigned to you. A slingshot for one warrior may be a bow and arrow for the other.

And back in May 1985, on a Tuesday, the alarm went off at 4:30 a.m., and as soon as my feet swung off the bed and hit the floor, I launched into the use of my first tool. And mercy, I went at it. Maybe a *little softer*, but loud enough for it to resonate where it counted. I said: *I speak to the plaintiffs, and in particular to Knoll Radio Company (the main plaintiff), and to Billy Joe Hollister (the other plaintiff and owner of Knoll), and to Brendan Jones, Bruce Jenson, Philip Rawlings, and Ann Davis (the plaintiffs' lawyers)—and I cast them into the sea in Jesus' name. I speak to the plaintiffs, and in particular to Knoll Radio Company, and to Billy Joe Hollister, and to Brendan Jones, Bruce Jenson, Philip Rawlings, and Ann Davis—and I cast them into the sea in Jesus' name. I say it again, I speak to the plaintiffs, and in particular to Knoll Radio Company, and to Billy Joe Hollister, and to Brendan Jones, Bruce Jenson, Philip Rawlings, and Ann Davis—and I cast them into the sea in Jesus' name. —Cast them into the sea in Jesus name. Cast them into the sea in Jesus' name. Cast them into the sea in Jesus' name. I take authority over them in Jesus' name. I have faith in you Lord. And throughout this trial, I will put all my faith in you Lord. This is your trial, and I put my full trust into you. Period. Amen!*

I put on my khaki suit, a white button-down shirt, a striped tie, fresh for the day. To the jury, I would look exactly like I did yesterday. I packed up my briefcase and headed down to court. I was at the little coffee shop outside the courthouse by 7:00 a.m.

Harry was already there waiting for me. His firm look, and pursed lips said: *Don't ask me to discard the gun.*

My look back, and perceptible nod said: *You won't need the gun. We're going to win.*

But, I did say: "Harry! *ALL* is well."

Harry studied me: "You look different."

I looked exactly the same. I nodded: "I spoke to my Counselor last night, I received instruction."

"Good," Harry said. He assumed I spoke with Murray Katz, or one of the other senior partners.

I *did* speak to a Senior Partner—my Senior Partner.

Later, Harry noticed a different step in my walk as we approached the doors of the courthouse: "What was your counselor's advice?"

"To speak to my problem," I said.

Harry glanced at me—but the Blue Angels, in formation, were gliding into the courthouse right then. Their greetings to an audience of friends drew our attention, but we just kept walking.

These days were the beginning of my dependency problem. Day number two of trial was about to begin.

I had no business being in a trial of this magnitude. I had already had some trials, but nothing like this. Still, by then, I basically had a style. But the style really jelled in this case: on day two. Day two was a whole different story from day one. There they were, the Blue Angels, four in a row, sitting there at counsel's table, stacks of files everywhere, boxes strewn behind them on the floor. Pads of paper, pens, documents on the table in front of them. What a mess, even for the Blue Angels.

Then there was me. By myself, with Harry sitting next to me. I had one yellow pad in front of me. Nothing written on it yet. And one sharpened pencil next to it. That was it. Even Harry wondered if he hadn't made a horrible mistake settling for me, the "B" team. My two back-up lawyers sat in the first row of the audience. I was going to take on the other side all by myself. I made that decision at 4:30 a.m. They didn't want to open their mouths anyway. As for the plaintiffs, because they were the plaintiffs, protocol said that they sat the closest to the jury. So the jury saw the Blue Angels sitting in a row directly in front of them. They had to look down the line of the Blue Angels, past all their files, boxes, pads, pens and documents, to see me, and Harry, with nothing in front of us on the table except my blank yellow pad, and my sharpened number 2 pencil next to it.

And, then, they called their first witness, Billy Joe Hollister, the plaintiff and the owner of Knoll Radio Company, *born and bred in Texas*, "and proud of it." Ol' BJ strode to the witness box like one of his sailboats had just caught the perfect wind to take him to the lead. Oh, the smugness—Billy Joe Hollister—Bill to his second-tier friends, and "BJ" to his first-tier friends and his pretty wife sitting in the front row. My thought at the time: *I'm sorry, this is a business case, you don't need the little wifeypoo sitting there in the front row cooing for her husband.* But there she was, straight from central casting.

I thought about bringing my cat to court.

Billy Joe Hollister spent the morning on the stand dutifully answering the spoon-fed questions his lawyer lifted to him on a cloud. From my standpoint, I saw a man that had betrayed his homespun roots of hard work, family, community, faith and contribution—and replaced them with skullduggery, favoritism, manipulation, leverage, and opportunism. But, from a worldly standpoint, "BJ" had a good morning, he was doing well, and his cooing wife, and the other Blue Angels were happy and impressed all morning long, right up until lunch. Three and a half hours of a beautifully laid out direct exam of their star witness. As we left the courtroom for lunch, "BJ" caught my eye and nodded at me: "I look forward to doing business with you later, Skip."

What was that—some kind of boating reference? I wished it was the Old West, I would have spit at him. Okay, maybe not, but still . . . . Anyway, I knew what the "business" was that he wanted to do with me later. He figured he would eat me alive during my cross-examination of him.

Let him read the menu all he wants, I'm not on it.

So, we went to lunch, from 12:00 noon to 1:30 p.m. Harry paced, and I prepared. Harry was nervous; he was sure he had lost. He wanted to throw in the towel; aren't lawyers supposed to object more, why wasn't I bouncing up like crazy and making a scene? Don't I know that BJ is destroying him? Harry's lips were pursed, and his eyes glaring. I went to the men's room. And I spoke again. I said: *I speak to the plaintiffs, and in particular to Knoll Radio Company, and to Billy Joe Hollister, and to Brendan Jones, Bruce Jenson, Philip Rawlings, and Ann Davis, and I cast them into the sea in Jesus' name. I speak to the plaintiffs, and in particular to Knoll Radio Company, and to Billy Joe Hollister, and to Brendan Jones, Bruce Jenson, Philip Rawlings, and Ann Davis—and I cast them into the sea in Jesus' name. I say it again, I speak to the plaintiffs, and in particular to Knoll Radio Company, and to Billy Joe Hollister, and to Brendan Jones, Bruce Jenson, Philip Rawlings, and Ann Davis—and I cast them into the sea in Jesus' name.—Cast them into the sea in Jesus name. Cast them into the sea in Jesus' name. Cast them into the sea in Jesus' name. I take authority over them in Jesus' name. I have faith in you Lord. And throughout this trial, I will put all my faith in you Lord. This is your trial, and I put my full trust into you. Period. Amen!*

The other lawyers in the bathroom thought I was crazy.

I was a *little* crazy. So much of what happened that day I didn't understand until later in my Christian walk. Billy Joe Hollister took the stand again after lunch, and his first-chair lawyer, Brendan Jones, spent about another half hour with him until 2:00 p.m. and then I suddenly heard Jones say to the judge: "No further questions, your Honor."

Judge Roth looked down at me: "Your witness, counsel."

There is something about the slow opening of a file cabinet that shakes up a smug witness like BJ. Behind me, I had brought in my two trial metal file cabinets: 52 inches high, 18 ½ inches wide, four-drawer, legal size. Kind of old style, a little weathered, but clean as a whistle. I had found them used; I liked them used. And they were loaded, believe me. I stood up, swung around slowly, grabbed the handle of the first file cabinet, top drawer, and slowly opened the drawer. In a quiet courtroom, you can hear every click of the old drawer as it slowly opens. The click in the witness's mind is even louder. I like the *old* file cabinets. Then, all too slowly, I reached in and grabbed a thick file with rubber bands around it and lifted it out, and slowly walked to the podium where I made sure the file hit the top landing of the podium with an appropriate *—thud.*

The "thud" in one note, is designed to convey the following: *BJ, you assumed wrong, I wasn't just sitting there taking no notes, I was so prepared, I didn't need notes. The file cabinets in this courtroom belong to me. They're loaded. The pencil sharpener fastened at the top of one of the cabinets is mine. The one time I sharpened my pencil was during the moment that your lawyer, Brendan Jones, was asking you the most critical question, and the jury didn't even pay attention, because that was the moment I decided to sharpen my pencil. The thermos sitting on top of the file cabinet next to the pencil sharpener is also mine. The one time I poured myself a little hot tea, was the very moment that Brendan Jones was asking you the second most critical question, and the jury didn't even pay attention, because that was the moment I decided to casually pour myself a little hot tea and take an unconcerned sip.*

Billy Joe Hollister, sitting there in the witness seat, to the left of the judge, twitched in his seat for the first time. In a quiet courtroom, a twitch can be loud. The leather chair, the rollers on the bottom hitting the hardwood floor, the lack of oil in its joints, you can't get away with even a twitch. Even the judge looked over at ol' BJ. *Did he really twitch?*

And, at the very moment of BJ's first twitch, my two C-team players, entered the courtroom in lock-step fashion as they brought my 3 feet by 4 feet blow-ups of the main exhibits, and placed them on two trial tri-pods that they placed directly behind me for the jury, judge, and ol' BJ to see. The blow-ups are boards of the best evidence. The blow-ups stare at the witness. And, Billy Joe Hollister, sitting there in the witness seat, to the left of the judge, twitched in his seat for a *second* time. Louder than the first.

In those early days of my Christian walk, I didn't know that God spoke to you, or in this case, me. The night before this second day of trial I was so scared, that when I went to pray, my heart was desperate, and therefore open to the still quiet voice of the Lord—*shouting* to me what to do: which was to speak to my problem and cast it into the sea in Jesus' name. Thank God, I was desperate, too desperate to question God, to analyze God, to wonder if that was really him I heard from. I *had* to do something. So, I trusted God and *spoke* to my problem. It wasn't until later that the Lord was simply telling me about what he had said in Mark 11:22-25. These are Jesus' words:

> "Have faith in God," Jesus answered. "I tell you the truth, if anyone says to this mountain, 'Go, throw yourself into the sea,' and does not doubt in his heart but believes that what he says will happen, it will be done for him. Therefore I tell you, whatever you ask for in prayer, believe that you have received it, and it will be yours. And when you stand praying, if you hold anything against anyone, forgive him, so that your Father in heaven may forgive you your sins."

The night before, when I prayed, I knew that the Lord was saying speak to your problem. Your problem is the "mountain," and say to your mountain be gone in Jesus' name, be cast into the sea in Jesus' name, and don't doubt in your heart that it will happen, but believe that what you say will happen, and it will be done for you.

And the next day it was done for me. I felt it when I asked my first question of Billy Joe Hollister, that God was with me, that he was already moving my mountain and casting it into the sea. From 2:00 p.m. to 4:30 p.m., I drilled Billy Joe Hollister. The questions flowed, and Billy Joe Hollister crumbled. He was nothing more than one big bully that crumbled fast under the weight of an amateur's questions, led by a God that is not an amateur. I felt like Moses must have felt when God told him what to say. So many of my questions I hadn't prepared, but they just flowed until the big bomb of that first day hit: under my grilling of ol' BJ of who owned Knoll Radio Company, it turned out that Hollister's lawyer, Brendan Jones, was a 5 percent owner. His own lawyer was an owner of the company, and was pushing this case because, in a nutshell, if he won the case, his 5 percent interest in the company would be worth a cool million, roughly speaking, and ol' BJ had to admit it. This was not some contingent fee situation, Jones was an owner from day one and part of the scam from day one to take Harry Goldberg's radio stations.

Their case was in serious trouble by the time I finished with my last question, at 4:30 p.m., when the judge ended the day. Hollister could barely get out of his seat.

I walked back to counsel's table and sat back down next to a beaming Harry. I was so happy to see that he was happy. He looked at me, put his arm around my shoulder and said: "Make sure you talk to that counselor again tonight." And he winked at me. He knew. He saw me glowing with a new faith —that I would never go back on. I would be steadfast forever.

That was the start of *ddarssa*. My little acronym for the set of tools the Lord gave me that I would use the rest of my life. You've got to have your tools. Customized just for you, by the Lord.

But more on that later.

T+

The Take Away 4
One set of tools: ddarssa.

1. The Lord doesn't like self-sufficiency. Many people have dependency problems, drugs, alcohol, other dependency problems. Instead, **depend on the Lord**. He wants you to.

2. You simply can't win a trial, and you can't win an important battle in life without getting right and staying right with God. "Woe to the obstinate children," declares the Lord, "to those who carry out plans that are not mine, forming an alliance, but not by my spirit, heaping sin upon sin; who go down to Egypt without consulting me . . ."

3. Ask the Lord to give you a set of tools so that you get right, and stay right with Him. One set of tools the Lord gave to me a long time ago, I summed up in an acronym I called **ddarssa**: ddarssa stands for seven words: **1. Desire; 2. Decision; 3. Ask; 4. Receive; 5. See; 6. Speak; and, 7. Act.** I know I have to have the *desire* to accomplish something, or to settle a matter or a problem; I have to make the *decision* in that regard; I *ask* God to help me; I *receive* it; I *see* it; I *speak* it; and I *act* on it. And I do not waver. Period. *ddarssa.*

4. The problems in your life are like mountains, and Jesus shows you how to handle the mountains, which are the problems in your life:

"Have faith in God," Jesus answered. "I tell you the truth, if anyone says to this mountain 'Go, throw yourself into the sea,' and does not doubt in his heart but believes that what he says will happen, it will be done for him. Therefore I tell you, whatever you ask for in prayer, believe that you have received it, and it will be yours. And when you stand praying, if you hold anything against anyone, forgive him, so that your Father in heaven may forgive you your sins."

If They Know You're a Peacemaker

They should know they're in trouble

The Lord stepped in

I became a Christian in November 1984. I had already been a lawyer for five years. I was living the good life. I was working with well-known lawyers, had big-name clients, had a big salary, had a big office, lived in Malibu, was dating pretty women, was running my life pretty well and already scouting to buy my first Porsche. This was the 80s in Los Angles, *LA Law*. So, I also remember—craziness, lots of lawyers doing cocaine, lots of office affairs and sex, fast cars with the first mobile phones (called car phones in those days) hard work and wild living. After a hard day at work, we would all go down to the little pub on the first floor of the building and engage in some sort of ritualistic quasi-party that bordered on insanity. It was somehow expected that you would attend these "get-togethers." I had lots of lawyer friends.

But now, I can't think of even one that is still standing.

Still, I don't have a bad story to tell. I didn't do drugs, never even tried cocaine, (which in those days was miraculous), I didn't mess around, was dedicated to my job, disciplined, set goals, and accomplished them. At law school, I did well, made the Law Review, had an article published, and was already sitting through trials at the firm I clerked at. I wanted to be at the top of my profession. I joined all the right lawyer associations, was on the court improvements committee, and after five years of lawyering, was already sitting as a judge pro-tem in the Los Angeles Superior Court and publishing law articles. I didn't have a bad story to tell. I don't even remember a certain level of discontent. I didn't feel "lost." Heck, I actually felt "found."

So, why did the Lord step in? In one word, "mediocrity." If I had not been rescued by the Lord, I would have led a life of mediocrity: an unfulfilled life with no purpose. In early 1984, I had started my spiritual journey. From my perspective, the New Age movement was in full swing, and I was reading all the books, hanging out at the Bodhi Tree on Melrose, going to Buddhist meditations, going to the Self-Realization Center on Sunset, and dating "spiritual" women. I even went to Paris in October 1984 as part of my search for God. I hung out with "international" spiritual people. There I was, on the Champ Elysees in Paris, sipping coffee, hanging with my spiritual friends and thinking "great thoughts." What a joke. But, *I was* searching for God. And he found me. In November 1984, God intervened, sent an angel, I was saved. But, more on that later.

The battles started after I was a Christian

At least for this one warrior, my battles started *after* I was a Christian, not before. . . .

I love my church, the Dream Center, Pastors Tommy and Matthew Barnett, and all my friends there. The Dream Center is such an amazing outreach church in downtown Los Angeles. It reaches out to the lost and broken-hearted. There is four hundred thousand square feet of ministry space at the Dream Center, and through their programs they take people off the street, let them live on campus for at least a year (or more), and change their lives. And, of course, for the most part, they find Jesus. On a typical month in 2009, the Dream Center had seven hundred people living on campus. The numbers continue to grow.

Pastor Matthew often asks one of the teens or adults living at the Dream Center to give their testimony on stage to the whole congregation.

Usually, the teen or adult will start with a comment such as "before I was a Christian, I was a heroin addict," or, "before I was a Christian, I was a prostitute," or, before I was a Christian I was homeless and lost," or something like that, and often worse than that. My story is not like that. Before I was a Christian, life was good, I was winning my cases, building a little estate, climbing the ladder, "a rising star," one of my senior lawyer friends called me. Challenges were easy to knock down.

And then I was saved. There I was, the very end of November 1984, saved, and no idea what to do next. This was new to me, *not knowing what to do next?*

So, I did what any brilliant lawyer would do: I made a list. And before long, every morning I got up early, *very early*, and made a list. And before long it wasn't my list, it was God's To Do List for me that day. And that day only. It was later I learned that Jesus said: "*Therefore do not worry about tomorrow, for tomorrow will worry about itself. Each day has enough trouble of its own.*"[1] When I read that verse, I knew in my heart that God's To Do List for me was God's idea, not my idea. That

1 Matthew 6:34.

was pretty cool, because since I wasn't running my life anymore, even though *I thought* I had done a pretty good job, Jesus was now running it. I just had to get out of the way. So the list helped. And, very early on he told me to put on the list—*to be a peacemaker*. And then, he started showing me how to do it. Which was good, because I was headed for some serious battles.

And the battles came.

God's To Do List (GTDL)

My goal as determined by the Lord was to lay my sword down and retire from litigation by July 2009. As it turned out, my last case settled the week before trial in late April, and I laid my sword down on May 1, 2009. And then, just like that, I stopped making my morning list—God's To Do List. That lasted two months, the months of May and June 2009. That hiatus was a mistake.

I had forgotten what I always knew in my heart: *At the end of each battle, the vigilance begins anew.* We are the Watch and Pray Generation. So, on the morning of July 1, 2009, I was back to the list, with or without my sword. I felt totally under attack during May and June 2009. On July 1, 2009, I was back to vigilance, back to my list. The battles I had fought for the last thirty years weren't over—they had just changed. There would be new battles. Looks like I'm going to need my list until I die here on earth. I believe that if you get up early every morning like Jesus did,[2] roll onto your knees, and ask God what he wants you to do that day, he'll tell you. You might as well go for it—make and keep a list. God's To Do List.[3] And, oh, if you ask him to use you—he will. But that's cool, no more mediocrity, that's for sure. God doesn't do *mediocrity*. In the end, you will have led a successful life, because success is finishing the purpose God has laid out for you.

A peacemaker is seriously prepared

In the early days of my early morning takedown of God's To Do List, he told me to be a peacemaker. One thing he made clear to me is that peacemakers are seriously prepared for the battle, much more so than the other side. At first that seemed counterintuitive to me, but I went along with the List, and what God told me to put on it. And after that, I was always prepared, very prepared. Because generally speaking, those that are ready to make the peace, to be a peacemaker, to resolve the problem, etc.—think there is no longer any reason to prepare for the battle.

That is a huge mistake.

Deciding to be a peacemaker in the litigation, in the fight of your life, or in any dispute whatsoever means you are going to be prepared.

2 Mark 1:35.
3 GTDL. Believe me, this is God's To "Do" List. Not God's To "Try" List. This is a list of things to "do," not "try." God doesn't *do* "try."

If you have made the Lord the Senior Partner of your law firm (and your life), you will be incredibly prepared to win. And if the other side sees your peaceful tendencies as weak, he will be in serious trouble. And, here's the reason: don't even think about being a peacemaker unless you, taking the Lord's lead, are always seriously prepared for the fight of your life, the battle, or whatever challenge you are facing, or may face. I'm a lawyer, God chose me to be a lawyer. After I was saved, I learned that God was preparing me . . . to prepare.

When you spend time with your Senior Partner, Jesus, and you are in the battle of your life, and you have decided that God is a list maker and will give you a God's To Do List, you will find out that you are going to be seriously prepared for the battle, like no other. While all of that is happening and you are studying the Bible to understand the concept of Godly preparation, you will find that our God is a God of preparation. From Genesis to Revelation, our God is a God of preparation.

Because of that, if the other side knows you are a peacemaker, they should know that they are in serious trouble.

The settlement letters

And back in May 1985, on a Wednesday, the alarm went off at 4:30 a.m. and as soon as my feet swung off the bed and hit the floor, I launched into the use of my first tool. I spoke out quite verbally to my mountain and cast it into the sea in Jesus' name. *I speak to the plaintiffs, and in particular to Knoll Radio Company, and to Billy Joe Hollister, and to the plaintiffs' lawyers, Brendan Jones, Bruce Jenson, Philip Rawlings, and Ann Davis—and I cast them into the sea in Jesus' name. I speak to the plaintiffs, and in particular to Knoll Radio Company, and to Billy Joe Hollister, and to the plaintiffs' lawyers, Brendan Jones, Bruce Jenson, Philip Rawlings, and Ann Davis—and I cast them into the sea in Jesus' name. I say it again, I speak to the plaintiffs, and in particular to Knoll Radio Company, and to Billy Joe Hollister, and to Brendan Jones, Bruce Jenson, Philip Rawlings, and Ann Davis—and I cast them into the sea in Jesus' name. Cast them into the sea in Jesus' name. Cast them into the sea in Jesus' name. Cast them into the sea in Jesus' name. I take authority over them in Jesus' name. I have faith in you Lord. And throughout this trial, I will put all my faith in you Lord. This is your trial, and I put my full trust into you. Period. Amen!*

Then, I made a list. This was in the early days of my walk with the Lord, so I made a list, but it was still somewhat "my" list. The first item on the list was: "1. Destroy Billy Joe Hollister . . . ."[4]

Was that very Christian of me?

Yes.

And, here's why.

The Lord had already been working on me. Early on in the case I had begun the process of sending settlement offers to the lawyers for 'ol BJ. I addressed the

---

4 Psalm 143:12. Perhaps I should have been more poetic, like King David: "In your unfailing love, silence my enemies; destroy all my foes, for I am your servant." See also, Psalm 54:5. "Let evil recoil on those who slander me; in your faithfulness destroy them."

letters to BJ's main lawyer, Brendan Jones. The letters were conciliatory, and in eight pages of well thought-out ideas, I proposed multiple ways to settle the case. Over sixteen months of hard-core pre-trial litigation, I had sent eight letters. But what Brendan didn't seem to pick up on was that I didn't cite Evidence Code section 1150, which would have made the letters privileged and confidential, therefore not to be used at trial. Instead, the letters ended stating that they were *not* intended to be privileged and confidential.

Which meant they *could* be used at trial.

But Brendan certainly didn't think I would use them at trial, because he thought they made us look weak, as if we had the weak case and therefore were looking for ways to settle the case. He never even responded to the eight letters. No written response whatsoever. I often asked him why I hadn't heard anything from him in response to my settlement letters, and he would say something like they had a good case and were going to win. Or, if we had a settlement conference, we could talk settlement at that time. Or, that the offers weren't good enough, keep trying.

On Wednesday morning, item one of my list, actually said: "Destroy Billy Joe Hollister, put the letters in front of him and question him about each and every one of them." Item two on my list said: "I'll give you the questions." Whoa, the Lord was going to give me the questions? Yes, he was. By the third day of trial, I loved 4:30 a.m. in the morning, I loved Mark 11:22—and I didn't even know the verse yet, and I loved the beginnings of God's To Do List for me.

ddarssa was just beginning.

I put on my khaki suit, a white button-down shirt, a striped tie, fresh for the day. To the jury, I would look exactly like I did yesterday, and the day before that. I packed up my briefcase and headed down to court. I was at the little coffee shop outside the courthouse by 7:00 a.m.

Harry was already there waiting for me. He looked at me, "Did you talk to your counselor last night?"

I looked back: "My Counselor is always there for counseling at night."

Harry nodded, seriously: "Good."

Harry and I sat there until the courthouse opened, sipping coffee and preparing. When we entered the courthouse, I received my first "tell."

At 8:00 a.m., the courthouse opened up and Harry and I started to move through a line to get in. Just behind us, swooping in, in perfect synchronization were the Blue Angels with Brendan Jones in the lead. He looked majestic is his blue pinstripe suit, matching tie and handkerchief, beautiful belt and shoes, everything so crisp looking. One lock of his hair fell out of alignment as he dropped his head a little to catch me and ask: "How much longer do you expect to take with Mr. Hollister?" That was *the* "tell." The third day of trial and Brendan was already nervous. I looked at Jones, realized I'm anything *but* crisp looking, and my hair was totally unruly, and I said: "I hope to be done with him —when I'm *done with him.*" I just told "Mr. Confident" that I was going to drill his star witness, the owner of the company, the plaintiff, all day. Imagine that. His suntanned face somehow went ashen.

And I did drill Billy Joe Hollister all day long. From 8:30 a.m. until lunch break at 12:00 noon, I drilled him on the eight letters I had sent to his lawyer. I had blown every single page of each letter up to the size of 3 feet by 4 feet, and page by page I went through each one, each proposal, each attempt to reach a reconciliation, each attempt to get a response, each attempt by me, and technically my client, to settle the case.—And Mr. Hollister had no answer. Even worse, his lawyer, good old Brendan hadn't prepared him for this line of questioning. He came across like a man that had no fiber of reconciliation in him. He looked like a man just out to take Harry's stations from him, period. By lunchtime, the jury's body language was sending very nasty messages to Hollister and his flock of lawyers.

God chose the words

That night, out of the blue, I got a telephone call at the office where I was sitting preparing for the next day in trial. The caller was Beth Norquist. She needed advice. She was crying. She said her eighteen-year-old daughter, Annie, just told her she was moving in with her boyfriend the coming weekend. Beth was devastated. The only concession Beth could get from her daughter was that she and her daughter have dinner on Friday night and talk about it. The daughter finally said yes, but she wasn't going to change her mind. I said to Beth, here's what you do: First, prepare. Get up early tomorrow morning, preferably about 4:30 a.m. Ask the Lord to help you prepare for Friday night. Make a list of what he tells you to do, and then do it. Call me Saturday morning and tell me how it went.

Beth called me Saturday morning. She said she got up at 4:15 a.m. Thursday morning. She prayed and asked the Lord what to do. The Lord told her to take some notes. First, speak to her problem —the problem being Annie's pot-smoking boyfriend, and cast him into the sea in Jesus' name. Second, write a letter to Annie about how much she loves her daughter and wants the best for her, wants her to go to college and study to be an architect like she'd always spoken of, why drugs are bad, but that if forced to, she will accept Annie's decision. Annie found the letter from her mother on Thursday afternoon.

By Friday night, Annie had broken up with the boyfriend, had applied to three colleges, and was not moving out.

On Thursday morning, I put on my khaki suit, a white button-down shirt, a striped tie, fresh for the day. To the jury, I would look exactly like I did yesterday, and the day before that, and the day before that. I packed up my briefcase and headed down to court. I was at the little coffee shop outside the courtroom by 7:00 a.m.

I was a warrior by then.

On Saturday morning after Beth Norquist told me the story about her daughter Annie, I could just hear the excitement and peace in her heart. She and her daughter also seemed totally reconciled. I couldn't help asking Beth just one quick question.

"Beth, was it hard to write the letter to Annie?" I politely asked.

"Oh no. I wrote the letter, but God chose the words," Beth said.

"No further questions," I said.

T+

The Take Away 5
Peacemakers are always seriously prepared for battle.

1. Peacemakers are seriously prepared for battle.

2. Deciding to be a peacemaker in the litigation, in the fight of your life, or in any dispute whatsoever means you are going to be prepared.

3. From Genesis to Revelation, our God is a God of preparation. Because of that, if the other side knows you are a peacemaker, they should know that they are in serious trouble.

4. To be prepared is simple: Get up early, *very early*, and make a list, ***God's To Do List (GTDL)***. Ask the Lord for His list of what He wants you to do that day, to be prepared. GTDL will be your list of how to prepare to win the battle and ultimately, to be a peacemaker. And through the process of using GTDL to go through and win the battle He will also show you how to lead a successful life, because success is finishing the purpose God has laid out for you. And God won't let a battle, a dispute, or a problem in your life deter you from His purpose for you in life. He has a purpose for you, He wants you to accomplish it.

   As for the battle you are going through—*the battle belongs to Him.*

Prepare...

And do it abundantly

The ability to face up to the battle is sometimes the hardest thing for a person to do.

But, as soon as you see it as the hardest, that is the moment that you must realize—you are trying to do it on your own strength.

Which you can't do.

Go back to the basics: You must do it on the Lord's strength.[1]

When you're in the fight of your life.

The fight of your life is the fight for your life.

Even King David cried out to God: "Preserve my life."[2]

It's a good thing to fight for your life. God gave it to you.

War mode

One day in the spring of 2005 my client Mike Harrison called me. His software and internet company was in big trouble and he needed help. That's what he told me, but it was more than that. He actually called me from his cell phone; he was already parked outside my offices in Santa Monica—he "needed to see me." He told me he should have called me months ago. I told him to come up. It was 8:00 a.m. It was going to be another sunny day in Santa Monica.

My Santa Monica "offices" are two contiguous lofts with high ceilings, lots of glass, open windows, lots of light during the day, and open to moonlight at night. I did a lot of moonlighting. I didn't have normal law offices. The lofts are big open spaces, designed for creativity. Godly creativity, as I saw it. Designed for godly solutions, as I saw it.

---

1 Philippians 4:13 (NKJV). "I can do all things through Christ who strengthens me."

2 Psalm 143:11. "For your name's sake, O LORD, preserve my life; in your righteousness, bring me out of trouble." Psalm 119:88. "Preserve my life according to your love, and I will obey the statutes of your mouth."

Mike sat down at my glass conference table. Many a war strategy had been plotted out there. My trial tri-pod easels were standing at one end of the table, as if calling me for a new attack plan. Mike had been served with a lawsuit by a big company out of the State of Washington, and he felt he and his business were in a life-and-death struggle. He didn't know what to do, couldn't hear clearly from the Lord, couldn't get a breakthrough, was in despair, had started drinking, was ignoring his wife, she had threatened to leave, and his children were in disarray. Even his skin had broken out in shingles. His body was in pain. It wasn't good. I listened quietly. But something was off. I didn't know what it was.

I would find out.

Eventually.

To win the fight of your life you must have a clear conscience.[3]

When Mike has finished talking, I stood up, walked to my two trial tri-pods, affixed my two big 3 feet by 5 feet trial pads to the tri-pods, grabbed the Magic Markers, and got ready. Within a few moments, we were in *war mode*. Whatever the problem is, a trial, a business problem, life problem, a drinking problem, a drug problem, a financial problem, a relationship problem, something to conquer, there comes a time: to go into war mode. I felt like I had lived a life, at least thirty years of it, in the middle of Ecclesiastes 3:8. There really *is* a time for war. And it comes far more often than you would ever want to believe.

There *really* are many times in your life when *the Lord* wants to see you go to battle over something in your life. You *must* go to battle.

The world can be such a comfortable place for the timid ones. Those timid ones are just one step short of the tunic collectors,[4] the lukewarms. Those that are spit out. Timidity doesn't come from the Lord, it comes from somewhere else. And that somewhere is *somewhere* you don't ever want to be.

So there was Paul, in his last letter, knowing his journey would soon be over sending out his last words of encouragement and instruction, and making it clear when he said: "For God did not give us a spirit of timidity, but a spirit of power, of love and of self-discipline."[5]

So, going forward, make the decision: are you going with the spirit of timidity, or the spirit of power, and love, and self-discipline?

There is nothing passive about war mode. There is only one thing you can be passive about: *things you don't care about.*

A time for war

"There is a time for everything, and a season for every activity under heaven: . . . a time for war and a time for peace."[6]

---

3 2 Timothy 1:3. "I thank God, whom I serve, as my forefathers did, with a clear conscience . . . ."
4 See Chapter 12 for a discussion of "the tunic collectors."
5 2 Timothy 1:7. Instruction given A.D. 66 or 67 from a prison in Rome. Nothing's changed since then. Instruction still necessary.
6 Ecclesiastes 3:8.

A good trial warrior knows, you will be destroyed if you don't know when it is time to go to war. If you don't have a relationship with the Lord and you are trying to go it alone, the problem is—you don't even know when it is time to go to war. You don't even know when you are under attack. You need a relationship with the Lord to know three things: first, that you are under attack; second, that it is time to go to war; and third, how to fight the battle. A trial warrior will know what to do; but not every trial lawyer will. If you don't have a relationship with the Lord, you are on your own—that's not a good place to be.

There's a difference between skill-set battles and spiritually-set battles. Skill-set battles leave you open to an earthly conclusion, spiritually-set battles leave you open to a heavenly victory.

An earthly skill-set, but no spiritual skill-set—that's not a good place to be.

There is an eternal element to every battle.

Forty days

Forty days is *the* number, not some other number, not twenty-one, not thirty, but forty. That is the number—when you are in the fight of your life. When you are in the fight of your life, you go into serious war mode for forty days of planning and prayer. If you don't want to win the battle, if it is *not* that important to you, then be nebulous about the number, pick any old number: but you could lose. If you are a veteran of many *war modes,* you know the number is forty.

If you are in trouble, and a warrior like me tells you that you must go into war mode for forty days, just do it, because you must start right away. Later, when you have time, you can study the great significance the Bible places on the precise number forty. The number forty is used by God to represent a period of time of testing, trial, probation, or chastisement and ends with a period of restoration, revival or renewal. In your studies, you will find that it rained for forty days and forty nights in Noah's day. After the deluge, Noah was on the ark for another forty days. Moses was with God on the mountain for forty days and forty nights. Forty years was the length of time that the Israelites wandered in the wilderness. "Forty Years" represents a generation. Jesus fasted in the wilderness for forty days and was seen on the earth for forty days after his crucifixion. There are at least ten instances in the Old and New Testament where "forty" occurs, either in days or years. It takes *forty.*

Enough on that. It works.

Always remember, the devil can fight hard, but he can't fight long.

I think everyone should have trial tri-pods (known as easels to some)—something that becomes the place to lay down the battle plan, that can be referred to over and over again. The nice thing about the tri-pods is they're in your face. You can ponder them from afar, or close up.

War mode is war mode.

Mike and I agreed that he would go into war mode for forty days and that I would be by his side for the effort. That was number one at the top of the tri-pod pad. We were planning the amount of time that he would be in war mode. Forty days.

Everybody's war mode is different, but the structure is relatively the same:

1. Forty days of concentrated effort and planning;
2. What book of the Bible will be the foundation for your effort (which includes *lectio divina*[7] on a critical verse, Mark 11:22-25, for example);
3. How to restructure your life during war mode;
4. What are your tools; and,
5. Preparation and tactics.

> Remember, the Lord will guide you.
> *Trust* will be redefined in your life.

Our God prepares

Don't you sometimes feel that God always has you in his hands? That he was always looking out for you. That he has a plan for you and has prepared a way. I've always felt that I had a heart for the Lord, that he placed that in my spirit. That he looked after me long before I paid him much attention. That he had a plan for me and was preparing a way just for me. He knew that I would be open to him when he spoke to my heart in November 1984. Why, at that time was I so sure that it, *it*, was real? That God was real, and that I could have a real relationship with him? As soon as he spoke to my heart, I was sure I was saved and that I could have a personal relationship with the Lord. This was early in my walk with the Lord. It was later that I learned that God "knit me together in my mother's womb,"[8] and that "all the days ordained for me were written in your book before one of them came to be."[9] This was before I knew the words of Jeremiah[10]: "The word of the Lord came to me, saying:

> 'Before I formed you in the womb I knew you,
> before you were born I set you apart;
> I appointed you as a prophet to the nations.'"

When this started to sink in early in my walk with the Lord, I felt this was intense stuff. I'm not a theologian. I'm no great scholar or thinker. But, clearly, I felt God was interested in me. If you are a trial lawyer, you see that this is a God

---

7 *Lectio Divina* is Latin for "divine reading," "spiritual reading," or "holy reading," and is an ancient Christian practice intended to foster communion with God. In *Lectio Divina* we turn to Scripture, knowing that we must listen for the voice of God, knowing that he often speaks softly, and knowing that we must learn to be silent. We want to meditate on the Word of God, and seek his revelation as to what we should do. Remember Psalm 46:10 (KJV): "Be still, and know that I *am* God . . . ."

8 Psalm 139:13.

9 Psalm 139:16.

10 Jeremiah 1:4-5.

who is the master of planning, and the master of being prepared. If you are close to God, you realize that he plans things out, in fact he is the Master planner.

So, you plan too.

By the time I was saved, by the time I was in that trial for Harry Goldberg, I was so *in the war*, that I had no time to really study the Bible, go to Bible classes, join a Bible study, or anything like that. I was already in the trenches, the bullets were flying at me, there was *incoming* fire of all types. The war was in full progress. Then I was saved. When my personal relationship with God started, I really had to say, "okay, please speak to me Lord, because I need to hear you, *quick*." And he did speak to me. Most of the time God had to speak to me in the crowded noisy busy halls of courthouses, or in the messy challenging hallways of rehab centers where I volunteered. But he did speak to me. And I did listen. Yet it seemed to me that he sometimes spoke to me in a normal voice, and sometimes he seemed to yell at me. But it was good. Later I learned that God speaks to us "in a still small voice."[11] Really? I thought I was weird because often, I felt God was yelling at me to get this done, or get that done, or take this tack, or use this strategy, or attack this way, or go that way. I don't think God saw me as a "still small voice" kind of guy. God seemed to speak to me rather directly, sometimes loudly. Most often, loudly. It wasn't long before I counted on hearing from God every day. The louder the better.

There was one particularly strong thing that God spoke to me about, or should I say *told me to do*, and that was: *prepare*, and *do it abundantly*. So I did. I did it for Mike Harrison on that day he showed up at my lofts in Santa Monica, and I did it for Harry *in the spring* of 1985, *at the time when kings go off to war.*[12] I'm definitely not afraid to *go off to war*. Neither should you be. I don't hang around with the guys that *go off to picnic*. Frankly, I'm not aware of the middle ground between the two. And I don't hang around with the guys that are aware of that nebulous middle ground.

We're the *watch and pray* generation.

We're not going to let down our guard.

"Be on your guard."[13]

The 8-to-3 rule

Do something extraordinary for the Lord, and expect his intervention on your behalf. That's what I told Mike in the spring of 2005, and that's what I did without telling Harry Goldberg, in the spring of 1985. In the early years, I just did it; much later, I sometimes enlisted my client in the process. If you are in the battle of your life, you must remember that it is axiomatic: That the best way to settle the case, is

---

11 1 Kings 19:11-13 (KJV).

12 2 Samuel 11:1.

13 2 Peter 3:17. Peter's last words to us: "Therefore, dear friends, since you already know this, be on your guard so that you may not be carried away by the error of lawless men and fall from your secure position." Instruction given A.D. 67. Nothing's changed since then. Instruction still necessary.

to seriously prepare for battle, and do it abundantly. The huge cases that I settled, I settled because I was abundantly prepared. Abundantly prepared for everything that had anything to do with the case, abundantly prepared for meetings with opposing counsel, abundantly prepared for all court appearances, abundantly prepared for depositions, abundantly prepared for meetings with witnesses, abundantly prepared for mediation, abundantly prepared for the settlement conference at court, abundantly prepared for anything and everything. And, of course, abundantly prepared for the battle if necessary, the battle called "the trial." I can assure you that when a case settled, one thing the other side had figured out was that I was totally prepared for the battle. And, I was. And I still am. If you are under attack, don't ever expect the other side to want to settle and give you a good settlement if they think they are going to beat you at trial. It doesn't work that way. Be prepared, and that means you and your lawyer. Prepare. Prepare to fight hard. Be in war mode, and stay in war mode. And don't be wandering about on rooftops.[14] Roof wanderers abandon their purpose.

There is a time when kings are to go off to war.[15]

One morning in early January 1985, I got up at 4:30 a.m. I was still five months away from trial in the Harry Goldberg case. I needed a breakthrough, I was getting clobbered in pretrial discovery, the four lawyers and all their associates on the other side were slamming me with depositions, written discovery, investigations, motions before our judge, everything they could imagine. Whether in required meetings, in depositions, or court hearings, they belittled my khaki suits, white button-down shirts, or joked about my tendency to stammer or stutter when under stress. If I started a sentence and got stuck, they would finish it off with a flourish and punctuate it with syntax and diction not quite a part of my language skills. Harry noticed, but couldn't afford to hire any more of our firm's lawyers to help me—so I was dead. I asked the Lord what to do. And he told me at 4:35 a.m. He said: *Spend 7 days going to bed at 8, and getting up at 3, and I will tell you everything you will need to know to beat the plaintiff and their army. You will be prepared.* Period. In my life, I came to call this the 8-to-3 rule. I still use it today, and I used it right up until my last trial in 2009. The Lord gave me the 8-to-3 rule to take down the other side in whatever battle I was in, personally or professionally. Or, to settle cases.

The Lord likes to settle cases. The Lord likes to resolve problems.

The Lord wins battles.

The 8-to-3 rule can be tough—at first. Going to bed at 8:00 p.m. knocks out most evening activities. Getting up at three for the nebulous reason of hearing from the Lord also presents problems and mid-afternoon drowsiness. Doing it seven days in a row is tough. And doing it for added-on days because you feel led

---

14 2 Samuel 11:1-5. David was supposed to go off to war. Instead he remained in Jerusalem. One evening while walking on the palace roof, he saw Bathsheba bathing. And the rest is history. David's wanderings had far reaching consequences, including murder.

15 2 Samuel 11:1.

to do it, is also hard. But the rule is: you will hear from the Lord, and he will tell you what to do, and you must do it. And ... in twenty-five years of using it, I always *received* a breakthrough. Amen. Godly challenges lead to Godly blessings.

Like it, when the Lord challenges you.

He wants to bless you.

Let him.

That evening was a Tuesday night. I was in bed at 8:00 p.m. My first thoughts, of course, were what am I doing here? This is crazy. It took me until 11:00 p.m. to fall asleep, and it was a rough sleep. A painful sleep. My head knew the alarm was going to go off at 3:00 a.m., so my sleep was shallow and painful. It was tough, but—I got up at 3:00 a.m. It was Wednesday morning. I prayed and listened for about thirty minutes, and the Lord started pouring ideas into my head. After thirty minutes he said: "stand up." And I went to work. I had five solid working and talking hours with the Lord before another person arrived at the offices. And, I prepared. For those five hours I worked my butt off. The Lord poured ideas into my head, I responded to discovery, the attacks from the other side, and better still, by Friday morning, two days later—I was moving into attack mode. By Monday, I had gone from defense—to offense. By Friday of the next week, the other side was sure Murray Katz had sent in skilled reinforcements to back me up. But Murray hadn't. I stuck to the 8-to-3 rule for forty days. And preparation of the case was complete. I was prepared, months early. All additional preparation thereafter was on the offensive. The other side was impressed, but never backed down. Too bad for them.

I still stammered on occasion after that, but it was from passion, not stress. And they never commented on it again—except once.

I have set my face like flint

Five months later, on a Thursday morning in May 1985, the fourth day of trial in the Harry Goldberg case, I felt the 8-to-3 rule was killing the other side. I was so prepared that William Joseph Hollister, "Billy Joe Hollister," and his band of Blue Angels, were falling fast. And I felt so fierce, so focused that there was no way they were going to beat me. A lot had changed by the fourth day of trial. At 4:30 a.m., when I put on my khaki suit, I realized this was the suit I wore Monday. Khaki suits wrinkle quite badly in hot courthouses. And coffee stains don't magically go away while hung in the closet. But the khaki suit rotation was every three days, so I had to wear Monday's suit. However, my Brooks Brothers white button-down shirt was clean, so was the tie. And my fingernails were pretty clean and trimmed. During the pretrial discovery I was impressed with how nicely trimmed the Blue Angels kept their nails. Even the blue angel men went to nail salons—and had nail polish on their nails. Shiny clear nail polish. In the courtroom, the fingernails of the Blue Angels shined and glittered. Things would change by the end of the trial.

All that glitters is sometimes cold.

Cold, at least to the juries I've seen in action. And, I went to the garment district the following weekend and added a few more khaki suits to the lineup. That way I could have a few at the cleaners while the others were in battle. Only so many coffee stains could be sustained on a khaki suit. . . . I would say that by the fifth year of trying cases, with a good Senior Partner to work with, I was getting into it. And by the fourth day of the trial to defend Harry, I had my game face on. I had "set my face like flint."[16]

The 8-to-3 rule developed slowly in those early years of practicing law. I had almost a year to prepare for the trial of Knoll Radio Partners vs. Harry Goldberg. After that first time I did the 8-to-3 rule for forty days, I would do it on occasion after that to sharpen up on what the Lord wanted me to do, and to just simply stay on top of things. Since you're not in trial during the pretrial phase, you have the time to arrange your life so you can go to bed really early and get up really early. It was harder when actually in trial, because often I had to stay up late to get my client and witnesses extra ready for the next day. And, in any event, if I did the 8-to-3 rule properly, by the time the trial began, I was ready, the rule had already served its purpose. And my *purpose* by then was to win the trial.

I learned early on, that if you really want to hear from the Lord, and really prepare abundantly, get up at three in the morning. And watch out. It turns out that Jesus is also an early riser.[17] And I wanted to go more than just the extra mile. I'd get up at three in the morning and think, *Lord are you awake?* And he was up. Every time. Go figure. But if you want to beat the other side, you will do it every time with the 8-to-3 rule. You must go a minimum of seven days in a row, the creation length of time. The seventh day is on the same schedule, but restful. Seven is the most sacred number for the Hebrews. Seven symbolizes perfection and completion. Be willing to go for additional days if the Lord tells you to.

"I rise before dawn and cry for help; I have put my hope in your word."[18]

The history of conflict is the entire history of man

It is 3:00 a.m. right now as I write this. I'm asking the Lord, exactly what I can tell you, what will be received by you in the spirit so that you can achieve victory against whatever has attacked you: a lawsuit, a business problem, a relationship problem, an addiction, anything. As you will see, and will find out, winning the battle with the Lord by your side is easy. You will face a lot of conflict in your life, so prepare, and do it abundantly.

---

16 Isaiah 50:7. "Because the Sovereign Lord helps me, I will not be disgraced. Therefore have I set my face like flint, and I know I will not be put to shame."

17 Mark 1:35. "Very early in the morning, while it was still dark, Jesus got up, left the house and went off to a solitary place, where he prayed." On your way to being a contemplative, you will discover the power of secret prayer early in the morning, "while it is still dark." As my friend Brad Reed says, some secrets must be caught, not taught.

18 Psalm 119:147.

The Bible is a story of conflict—from the beginning, Genesis, to the end, Revelation. In Genesis, there is the account of Creation in chapter one, but by chapter three there is the story of Adam and Eve and the first sin. By chapter four there is the story of Cain and Abel, with Cain killing his brother Abel. The descendants of Cain were ungodly, with Lamech marrying two women and boasting about killing a man who had only wounded him.[19] Then Lamech arrogantly swears that anyone who takes revenge on him, will pay a far greater price than the penalty established by God for anyone who would kill Cain. The generational curses of Cain had set in, the hearts of his descendants had hardened, and they fell further and further away from God until—Cain and all his descendants, and his entire bloodline are wiped out in the Flood.[20]

In the meantime, while the fate of Cain and his descendants is being played out, Adam and Eve give birth to another son and they name him Seth, for Eve said: "God has granted me another child in place of Abel, since Cain killed him."[21] "Seth also had a son, and he named him Enosh. At that time men began to call on the name of the Lord."[22] So, the descendants of Adam and Eve's third son, Seth, worshiped and followed God. Indeed, one of Seth's descendants, Enoch, stands out as only one of *two* of whom the Bible says: "walked with God."[23] The other person that "walked with God,"[24] was Noah, *another descendant of Seth*, and, we know the rest of his story. Seth and all his descendants were saved from the flood. Cain and all his descendants were wiped out in the flood.

The lesson is simple: walk with God. The Amplified Bible says that Noah walked in habitual fellowship with God. Noah made mistakes; you will make mistakes. David made mistakes. God understands that you will make mistakes. Still, he wants you to walk in close relationship with him.

Before, and after, the mistakes.

If you're in the fight of your life, get back to walking in close relationship with God.

Be on God's side.

It is many years later when I'm writing this. And, I still want to know more about this "still small voice" stuff. Sure, I have heard the Lord's still small voice. But I can't help but think of all those times he actually spoke to me rather loudly. I think he was yelling at me. He had to take a bat to my head on occasion. But it was good. I now know that each person's relationship to the Lord is different. I am so thankful that he could tailor one just for me. I'm more of a "bat to the head" kind of guy. You just have to love the Lord we have, one who would actually tailor a communication method just for me.

---

19 Genesis 4:23-24.
20 Genesis 6.
21 Genesis 4:25.
22 Genesis 4:26.
23 Genesis 5:24.
24 Genesis 6:9.

So, what exactly would the Lord tell you, that would be received by you in the spirit, so that you can achieve victory against whatever has attacked you: a lawsuit, a business problem, a relationship problem, an addiction, anything. He would tell you this: prepare, and do it abundantly, and don't be afraid to go into battle, and don't be afraid to win the battle, and remember that the Lord is the "King of glory . . . the Lord is strong and mighty, and the Lord is strong in battle."[25] *You also*, need to be strong and mighty, and strong in battle, and know that you are on God's side.

Lastly, remember that, once you have prepared abundantly, run quickly toward the battle line.[26]

The biblical conflicts go right up to the end in Revelation. In Revelation 19 and 20, two huge forces of evil, those of the beast and the kings of the earth and their armies,[27] and of Satan whose army was like the sand on the seashore,[28] unite to do battle against God. The Bible uses just a few verses to describe each battle— the evil beast and his forces are captured and thrown alive into the fiery lake of burning sulfur,[29] and fire from heaven devours Satan and his attacking armies and throws them also into the lake of burning sulfur.[30]

As the Bible confirms, and as many warriors have experienced: For God—*it's as easy as that.*

There is and will be nothing to worry about, no reason to have any doubts, and certainly no reason for second thoughts by believers as to whether they have chosen the right side. If you are with God, you will experience this tremendous victory with Christ.

So, on the fourth day of the Harry Goldberg case, I remember the feeling of walking around that courtroom, pacing in front of that jury, pacing in front of the judge, pacing and pacing, and attacking the plaintiff, Billy Joe Hollister, ol' "BJ", over and over again with round after round of the ammunition of questions under which he withered and twitched. And the jury watched ol' BJ squirm, and nervously twist a gold ring with a huge diamond on his left ring finger. With his right hand, Hollister would twist the ring on his left ring finger, as his own nerves betrayed him. And then it happened . . . I started a question, and I couldn't finish it, my stuttering took hold, my lips pursed tightly . . . the judge, the jury, and the spectators paused. I stopped my pacing while behind the chair of opposing counsel, Brendan Jones. "Let him finish his own damn sentence," I heard Brendan mutter, with some delight. I heard it; the jury heard it. And, after the pause I finished the question to Hollister. His answer came before Jones could even think to object. His answer killed him.

---

25 Psalm 24:8.
26 1 Samuel 17:48. In his attack on Goliath, David ran quickly toward the battle line. We all have Goliaths in life.
27 Revelation 19:19.
28 Revelation 20:8.
29 Revelation 19:20-21.
30 Revelation 20:9-10.

"Do you even for two seconds think that this collection of concocted letters and memos constitutes a . . . [my long pause] . . . binding contract?"

"No," Hollister answered, while Brendan hunkered down after mocking me and before he could even think of an objection. Ol' BJ apparently forgot the question.

"No further questions Your Honor," I said and rushed to drop my body in my chair. The record was made. Harry couldn't resist grabbing my hand to shake. I had my exhibit "A" testimony for my closing argument. Didn't Brendan know?

If you mock—the jury takes stock.[31]

The judge recessed for the day.

Later that night, a Thursday night at 9:00 p.m., I got a call at my office from Hollister's lead lawyer, Brendan Jones. They wanted to talk settlement early in the morning, before the start of the fifth day of trial. Would I meet them at court at 7:00 a.m. the next morning? They would even meet me at my favorite coffee shop.

It was only four days into the trial.

Twenty years later, my friend Mike Harrison spent forty days in intense preparation for the battle he was going to wage against one nasty group of people. He did the first week with the 8-to-3 rule. By the end of that forty days, with my help, he had a serious battle plan and we were ready for further and effective action. On the forty-first day, I drafted and sent a very reasonable business-like resolution proposal to Mike's adversary. On the forty-second day, I sat down with Mike. We discussed the plan in detail. We decided to study Mark 11:22, and Revelation chapters 19 and 20, the last two battles in the Bible. I remember that meeting well. We studied, prayed, and turned it over to the Lord. We expected to win. We knew and came in agreement, that with the Lord: *it's as easy as that.* Mike left upbeat. His only concern: could he patch things up with his wife and family? I reminded him of Ecclesiastes 4:12. He was thankful.

"Though one may be overpowered,
two can defend themselves.
A cord of three strands is not quickly broken."

But, I had to admit to myself. Mike wasn't telling me something. But it *was* "Mike." I doubted myself.

The next day again started at 4:00 a.m. Thank God, his mercies are new every morning.[32]

I count on them.

T+

31 See, Proverbs 1:22. "How long will mockers delight in mockery and fools hate knowledge?"
32 Lamentations 3:22-24. "Because of the Lord's great love we are not consumed, for his compassions never fail. They are new every morning; great is your faithfulness. I say to myself, 'The Lord is my portion; therefore I will wait for him.'"

The Take Away 6
Prepare . . . and do it abundantly.

1. The ability to *face up* to the battle is sometimes the hardest thing for you to do. But you must do it, not on your strength, but on the Lord's strength. The fight of your life is the fight for your life. **It's a good thing, if you fight for your *life*.** God gave it to you. Even King David would cry out to God: "Preserve my life."

2. *War mode.* There really is a *time* for war. There are many times in your life when *the Lord* wants to see you, indeed, calls you, to go to battle over something in your life. You must: *go to battle.* Don't be timid! "For God did not give us a spirit of timidity, but a spirit of power, of love and of self-discipline."

   There is nothing passive about war mode. There is only one thing you can be passive about: *things you don't care about.*

3. Winning battles takes commitment. When you are in the fight of your life, you go into serious war mode for *forty days* of planning and prayer. God is the master of planning, and the Master of being prepared. The God, "who knit you together in your mother's womb," will help you plan your victory. Use your **GTDL**, and do it for *forty days*.

4. There is a time when kings go off to war. There is a time for you to go off to war, and to do so, ***prepare, and do it abundantly.*** Do something extraordinary for the Lord, and expect His intervention on your behalf. **The 8-to-3 Rule:** *spend 7 days going to bed at 8, and getting up at 3, pray, and the Lord will tell you everything you will need to know to win the battle. You will be prepared.* You must go a minimum of seven days in a row, the creation length of time. The seventh day is on the same schedule, but restful.

   The Rule is: you will hear from the Lord, and He will tell you what to do, and you must do it.

   Expect your breakthrough.

   The Lord wins battles.

   Lastly, once you've prepared abundantly, run *quickly* toward the battle line.

The Cost of The Battle

The practical side
The spiritual side

When you're in the fight of your life, you want to win. But you still have to ask the question: What is the cost of this battle? To me, as an old warrior, the answer is simple.

As to the practical side: Measure the cost and complete the battle.

As to the spiritual side: Measure the cost and be prepared to give up everything.

You must be willing to do both.

If you agree to do both, you will establish two important things, among others: First, you are not a lukewarm. Second, you realize you are in the fight of your life and you want to win.

In reality, no matter what battle you are in, you must care enough to look at the practical side and the spiritual side. Because that's what the Lord wants you to do. There is victory in that approach. Time-tested victory.

Usually when a client asks me, "what is the cost of this battle?", I pause as long as I can to discern the sincerity of their commitment. Similarly, when a friend, neighbor, or someone asks me what is the cost of this battle, or what it will cost to resolve the problem, the challenge, or the burden, I still give them basically the same answer.

The same answer over and over again.

If I'm blessed and I have a client or friend that has spiritual discernment,[1] I can simply direct them to Luke 14, verses 25-35 and tell them to read those verses, pray about those verses, and meditate on those verses. All of these verses are

---

1 1 Corinthians 2:14-16. "The man without the Spirit does not accept the things that come from the Spirit of God, for they are foolishness to him, and he cannot understand them, because they are spiritually discerned."

about the cost of being a disciple. And on a practical level: measure the cost with the intention of completion; and on the spiritual level: measure the cost with the intention of preparing to give up everything.

And then perhaps, let an old warrior like me tell you what years of battles have confirmed.

As to the practical side: Measure and complete

As to the practical side of the battle, your goal is to *measure and complete*. You are called to measure the costs of the battle, the project, or the challenge. And you are called to complete what you started, or what you're defending, or what you're protecting.

"*Suppose one of you wants to build a tower. Will he not first sit down and estimate the cost to see if he has enough money to complete it? For if he lays the foundation and is not able to finish it, everyone who sees it will ridicule him, saying, 'This fellow began to build and was not able to finish.'*"[2]

Never underestimate the significance of Jesus' use of the word "tower" in this verse. In biblical times, in particular, a tower meant security, safety, and protection for the people around it. And, indeed, the Lord as our "strong tower" is part of our spiritual inheritance which we share in when we live a life of faithfulness to God. "The name of the Lord is a strong tower; the righteous run to it and are safe."[3]

And what good is a tower for you, or those that are counting on you, if you don't complete it? Our God is a God of completion. On the grandest scale of all, Jesus said: "It is finished."[4]

I do not remember any time that even one of my clients, when they were in the fight of their life did not commit to completing whatever task or battle they were facing. Ultimately, I suppose it was because they had a cheerleader like me to stand beside them and help every step of the way. And, they would know that they had to get right with God, because he was and is and always will be my Counselor, so, they had to make him their Counselor. It's not complicated to figure out how to be a person of completion.

In one of my last big cases in 2009, I represented a wonderful corporation that had been sued for something that involved a very sad and tragic accident. Still, it wasn't the company's fault. In reality is wasn't anyone's fault. Yet, the plaintiffs and their lawyers went on the attack and a very long and protracted litigation was anticipated. A potentially crippling judgment was also anticipated. (We anticipate challenges, but ultimately, we *expect* the Lord.[5]) The president,

---

2 Luke 14:28-30.

3 Proverbs 18:10. See also, Psalm 61:3. "Hear my cry, O God; listen to my prayer. . . . For you have been my refuge, a strong tower against my foe."

4 John 19:30. " . . . Jesus said, 'It is finished.' With that, he bowed his head and gave up his spirit." God's history-long plan of redemption for man was complete.

5 See chapter 10. Psalm 31:24 (AMP). "Be strong and let your heart take courage, all you who wait for *and* hope for *and expect* the Lord!"

Richard Winslow, knew he was in the fight of his life. Because of the severity of his situation, Winslow was open to getting God on his side, and on the side of his corporation. I was pleasantly surprised when early on in the case he told me that he had at least twenty people in his corporation doing the 8-to-3 rule. With the 8-to-3 rule they came to realize the spiritual disciplines of solitude and silence. Three "ante meridian" in the morning will do that to you. Some of them hadn't had "quiet" time in years. They were transformed. So was the company. So were a few marriages.

The combination process of the *fight* of your life and the personal transformation that can come from the redemptive resolution of *it*, is powerful to witness over and over again. The case settled early, at the first mediation, and very favorably for all concerned. We put the settlement on the record before the judge who was on the case. On the way out of court, Winslow looked at me and thanked me for my help and told me that he had gotten back into reading the Word. What else could he do at first; he was up at 3:00 a.m.!

He looked at me as we walked down the long hallway. Off in the distance I saw a little crowd of people waving to him.

"Tom, at 3:00 a.m. in the morning by the third day, I got back into reading the Bible, and one verse stuck with me, and it also stuck with that crowd of people waiting for me down the hall."

"Yes?" I said.

"'No one who puts his hand to the plow and looks back is fit for service in the kingdom of God.'"[6]

"I know it well," I said.

As we approached his fellow employees waiting for him, he stopped me and said: "My little prayer team keeps growing week by week."

The crowd was on us by then; it wasn't so little.

All Winslow could do was look at me and say: "We put our hand to the plow, and we didn't look back. Indeed, we are never going to look back. We are just getting started. Tom, we really learned something through this process. We get it—we know what it means to be co-laborers."

Then we were swamped by people.

This is what spiritual life in the trenches looks like. No one took a Bible class. No one took a seminar. No one called in a pastor, priest, minister or Rabbi. They prayed. They prayed hard. They got into the Word. They changed *their* routines. God responded.[7] Period. The transformation is continuing.

As to the spiritual side: Measure and be prepared to give up everything

Tragedies cause intensity. They cause you to prioritize. Perhaps they force you to prioritize. A life lesson is that oftentimes, tragedies force you to get your life

---

6 Luke 9:62.
7 Matthew 18:20. "For where two or three come together in my name, there am I with them."

back to where it should be . . . on a permanent basis. The proper prioritizing of your life is the realization of everything good that will come out of your life. If it seems daunting to you, then just be faithful with a few things, and eventually you will be called to be faithful with many things.[8]

You cannot be lukewarm. When you're in the fight of your life, you want the Lord to go out in front of you, and also to be your rear guard.[9] And to have that, you have to be willing to *give up everything*—as Luke wrote:

"Or suppose a king is about to go to war against another king. Will he not first sit down and consider whether he is able with ten thousand men to oppose the one coming against him with twenty thousand? If he is not able, he will send a delegation while the other is still a long way off and will ask for terms of peace. In the same way, any of you who does not give up everything he has cannot be my disciple."[10]

The nice thing about spending thirty years helping people with the battles in their lives is that you see a lot of miracles. You see a lot of victories. And you see a lot of lives transformed. Courtrooms and rehab centers are good places to see people who realize that they must get God on their side and turn the battle over to him. And you can't be lukewarm about that decision. You need a miracle. You need God to intervene.

As an old trial lawyer, I can relate to a God that seems to exaggerate on occasion. Or is he really exaggerating? Jesus' introduction to these verses about building a tower, and about a king who is about to go to war are as follows: "If anyone comes to me and does not hate his father and mother, his wife and children, his brothers and sisters—yes, even his own life—he cannot be my disciple."[11] I feel like saying to Jesus, "That's a little intense."

And yet, I know that the entire Old Testament ended with these words: "See, I will send you the prophet Elijah before that great and dreadful day of the Lord comes. He will turn the hearts of the fathers to their children, and the hearts of the children to their fathers; or else I will come and strike the land with a curse."[12] And with that, the Old Testament ended.

The bottom line is that Jesus knows how to drive home a point.

In a different context, Jesus said things like:

"And if your right hand causes you to sin, cut it off and throw it away. It is better for you to lose one part of your body than for your whole body to go into hell."[13]

---

8 Matthew 25:21. "His master replied, 'Well done, good and faithful servant! You have been faithful with a few things; I will put you in charge of many things.'"

9 1 Chronicles 14:15. See Chapter 22. And, Isaiah 52:12. "But you will not leave in haste or go in flight; for the Lord will go before you, the God of Israel will be your rear guard."

10 Luke 14:31-33.

11 Luke 14:26.

12 Malachi 4:5.

13 Matthew 5:30.

"Why do you look at the speck of sawdust in your brother's eye and pay no attention to the plank in your own eye?"[14]

"Again I tell you, it is easier for a camel to go through the eye of a needle than for a rich man to enter the kingdom of God."[15]

It is truly when you are in the fight of your life that you have the opportunity to get your priorities in order. For some people, it takes a crisis. Telling someone *living the good life* to do the 8-to-3 rule, to get on the Eight-Step Program, or to give up everything and follow the Lord, seems akin to casting your pearls before swine. "Do not give what is holy to the dogs; nor cast your pearls before swine, lest they trample them under their feet, and turn and tear you in pieces."[16] I have the benign view of this verse in the sense that, those living the good life, living in the comfort of geographical location and prosperity, aren't ready to hear the good news of the Gospel, or ready to hear how their lives could be immensely improved. Their lives, centered around the vortex of satisfying earthly decisions, are not in need—yet—of Godly decisions. So they think. But that changes when the earthly decisions run aground. And the sooner that happens the better. As I've found: A lesson learned early is a great blessing, a lesson learned too late is a great punishment.[17]

I've learned over time, that it is God's favor if you learn a lesson *early*. He knows when you are ready, and he knows when you are obstinate. You simply do not want to *ever* be obstinate: "'Woe to the obstinate children,' declares the Lord, 'to those who carry out plans that are not mine . . . .'"[18]

As to the spiritual side, measure, and be prepared to give up everything. Now that I look back on decades of warfare, I can promise you that you won't regret it. I still haven't witnessed someone who regretted giving up everything. I've witnessed many people who wished they had been prepared to give up everything, and wished they had done so. That's a terrible place to be in.

This isn't that complicated. Those that give up everything have everything to gain. When the decision is made and the peace sets in, you will know: you made the right decision.

Try it. Show a little courage. *"Any of you who does not give up everything he has cannot be my disciple."* Ultimately, all of us, after we have committed to give up everything, realize that "we are labourers together with God,"[19] and that everything we do takes on eternal significance. Once that feeling gets into your soul, there's no turning back. When you are blessed like me, and called to help someone in trouble, the first thing I often want to say, sometimes want to shout

---

14 Luke 6:41.
15 Matthew 19:24.
16 Matthew 7:6 (NKJV).
17 See, Chapter 18.
18 Isaiah 30:1.
19 1 Corinthians 3:9 (KJV).

is: "Do not falter in times of trouble. Show your strength! Do not—shrink back, for God will be displeased with you."[20] "Do not throw away your confidence; it will be richly rewarded."[21]

I will guide thee with mine eye

Sometimes you can't believe the sheer audacity of an attack by the other side. If you are the one attacked, you will be shocked, or you will be hurt, or both, and more. You can't believe it. As I discuss later, evil plots early and evil plots long. That's the worst evil out there—and the hardest to defend, and the hardest to launch a counter-offensive against. But, it's doable. It's done all the time. Evil attacks pay off quite often—unless aggressively defended. I believe God wants you to defend these attacks, and win. I believe God thinks you're a bad steward of his gifts if you don't defend. Indeed, God may want to raise you up to defeat the aggressor. He, most likely, wants you to go on the counteroffensive. He may be asking you to attack. He has given you the tools to attack. Remember, no weapon formed against you shall prosper.[22] Do you *receive* that? God wants to preserve your life. God has promised you, if you trust him, that: "I will instruct thee and teach thee in the way which thou shalt go: I will guide thee with mine eye."[23]

You can get there. Just ask him.

When Mike Harrison left my offices after our meeting in the spring of 2005, he had the blueprints for the battle with him. He and I had spent two hours at my conference table, and our battle plans had been written out on the big trial pads attached to my tri-pods. Mike tore off the pages, rolled them up and went home. The plan was there, including all the elements of spiritual warfare with the 8-to-3 rule and forty days of war mode. The procedural plans were also there, including all of my legal strategies. And, lastly, with my help, Mike had measured the cost of the battle, the practical side and the spiritual side. In reality, the battle started on that day, day one, at my offices—start day. There always needs to be a start day if you're going to battle, because you have to concentrate, pray, and stay focused for forty days. The battle could last longer of course, but you need those first forty days to effectuate a God-given plan. Remember, you want to win. The bottom line was that Mike and his company, Harrison Interactive had been sued; Mike had no choice but to defend, and strike back. *Blackdog vs. Harrison Interactive* was about to begin.

On that very day, I received a telephone call from an old client, Marc Brewer, who ran a major medical supplies company, TAS Medicals. Marc told me he had to sue a group of hospitals, HealthWays, Inc., who owed him almost $1,000,000

20 Proverbs 24:10. "If you falter in times of trouble, how small is your strength!" Hebrews 10:38. "And if he shrinks back, I will not be pleased with him."
21 Hebrews 10:35.
22 Isaiah 54:17 (NKJV). "No weapon formed against you shall prosper, and every tongue *which* rises up against you in judgment you shall condemn. This *is* the heritage of the servants of the Lord, and their righteousness *is* from Me," says the Lord.
23 Psalm 32:8 (KJV).

for medical supplies they hadn't paid for. HealthWays, had always paid a specific amount monthly that had led Marc to let the balance grow so big it was jeopardizing his company. Now, HealthWays was criticizing his products to justify not paying. Marc told me that despite his requests and demands, HealthWays was refusing to pay. HealthWays had changed to a different supplier. TAS Medicals vs. HealthWays was about to begin.

And on the very same day, in the late afternoon, I received a telephone call from Sarah Bleu. She owned a chain of weight loss clinics, forty-five of them to be exact. She calmly, and in a matter-of-fact voice, told me that she had a wonderful day so far. She had visited three of her clinics, taught a course in nutrition at one, exercised in her favorite park with her dog Chelsea, picked flowers and arranged them in her beautiful home as she contemplated what healthy dinner she would cook for her husband—when the doorbell rang. It was a process server. She had just spent a few moments studying the papers. Her husband had filed for divorce. Oh, and she thought she should tell me, that just last year, after ten years of marriage, she had transferred ownership of her clinics from just her, to her and her husband. He was the love of her life, they would be married forever. Sarah had done her best to hold on during her call to me, until the end. Then she said: "Tom, umm, last week (her voice was cracking) I was diagnosed with breast cancer. I was wondering if . . . you could pray for me." I told her I would drop everything and drive over to her house. She was going to hear about the 8th Row Prayer Team. Sobbing, she said, "Tom . . . could you pick up Emily (her nine-year-old daughter), she has practice 'til 4:30, . . . she'll be out front of her school."

"I know where she'll be, I'll pick her up."

"I need some time . . . to patch myself up," Sarah said apologizing.

"I'm on my way."

Bleu vs. Bleu was about to begin.

I'm not sure why I'm still a sober man after all these years.

Oh yes, I remember.

The Co-laborers

The co-laborers are an impressive group. They are completion oriented. Because of course, if you are a co-laborer with God, you are going to complete whatever you start. Even as I get older, and spend time with co-laborers that know they are close to the end of their lives, close to *completion*, the longer they have been a co-laborer, the happier and more peaceful they are. They are just getting ready for their transition, to life eternal. On the other hand, I've represented those that are not co-laborers. Perhaps, just perhaps, the fight of their life will change that.

It often does.

"For we are God's fellow workers; you are God's field, God's building."[24] The co-laborers, or "God's fellow workers" that I have worked with in the trenches of conflict, are Scripture simpliciter people. They aren't "deep." Let the relaxed pundits ponder this verse and determine whether the simple people have it wrong. Are we co-partners laboring with God to the same effect, the same end, or are we fellow-laborers more in the sense of under his direction or employment but not actually working *with* the master? Scripture simpliciter people read the verse and find great comfort knowing in their heart that God is working with them, that it is his power at work within us.[25] You and I are "God's field," the place where God wants to bestow his blessing, the place he wants to produce fruit. Let him. You are, we are, "God's building," the house he wants to build, the house he wants to dwell in. Let him. Why would anyone put off the work of the great Architect?

The co-laboring process that sometimes has to begin with the fight of your life, continues on after the victory. You see that his yoke is easy and his burden is light.[26] But even co-laborers dealing with an attack, such as a lawsuit filed against them, must do an assessment, a measuring of the costs, because, whatever the battle is, you must complete it. Ultimately, most of the measuring has to come from you. You are measuring the cost of the battle, how much you can afford, how you will measure it out over time, how you will manage to complete the battle, whether it's a lawsuit, rehab for your high-school daughter, or something else. As a lawyer, I will help you. That's what your earthly counselors are for.

I acknowledge, that sometimes it is very hard to estimate the costs of a battle, such as a courtroom battle. There are so many unknown factors such as what kind of discovery and attacks you will get from the other side, how much discovery and attacks you determine is necessary from your side, how much work will the judge make you do, what will you find out in your own discovery and investigation that you will have to follow up on, how many months, or even years the case will drag out. The list goes on and on.

As the years went on, and the cases and the trials mounted up, I was in a better position to say something like this to a client: "I just finished a similar case like yours. I use the word 'similar' in a very general sense, because not too many cases are actually 'similar.' Still, in a somewhat similar case, that I worked on with my excellent associate Susan Chen, and which she and I litigated aggressively, and settled in the eighth month, the final bill from my firm was (and I tell the client the amount). It was a multi-million dollar case like yours. In another similar case, despite our best efforts, and constant efforts, the case did not settle, and went

---

24 1 Corinthians 3:9.

25 Ephesians 3:20-21. "Now to him who is able to do immeasurable more than all we ask or imagine, according to his power that is at work within us, to him be the glory in the church and in Christ Jesus throughout all generations, for ever and ever! Amen."

26 Matthew 11:28-30. "Come to me, all you who are weary and burdened, and I will give you rest. Take my yoke upon you and learn from me, for I am gentle and humble in heart, and you will find rest for your souls. For my yoke is easy and my burden is light."

all the way through a court trial, no jury, and the final bill, which included my time, my associates, paralegals, witness fees, and costs of a fourteen-day trial, was about *four times* the amount of the case that settled. We won the case. There was an attorneys' fees provision in the contract between the parties, so we won a judgment that gave us all our attorneys' fees, and we were successful in collecting those fees. Nonetheless, you have to pay my fees as we go, otherwise I would be out of business."

"In *another* somewhat similar case the fees all the way through trial with the same backup help, were about (and I tell the client the amount), which again, was about four times the amount of the case that settled, and there was also an attorneys fees provision in the contract between the parties, so we won a judgment that gave us all our attorneys' fees. *But*, the other side appealed, and even though I was sure (you never really know) we would win the appeal, at a settlement conference at the appellate level in the case, my client, who was so happy to have won the underlying case against a really nasty plaintiff, waived his company's rights to the attorneys' fees in exchange for the plaintiff dismissing the appeal and a full and final mutual general release of all claims under the sun including those that were litigated at the trial. The case was over. My client won, and won his attorneys' fees, but waived them at the appellate level (against my advice) so he and his company could move on with their life. He was happy, so I decided I should be happy."

That is about the best you can do to estimate the costs of litigation with or without a trial. A good mediator will always tell you that you should settle your case because the case will be way too expensive to litigate, you can never be sure how much the case will cost to litigate, you don't know whether you will win, you could have a big judgment against you, and you may be hit with the other side's attorneys fees if provided for by law or contract. All of these statements are true. If a mediator doesn't tell you words to that effect, he or she is not a good mediator. In a city like Los Angeles, there are many excellent mediators. I prefer the mediators that are retired judges. I very much appreciate their background, experience, and legal knowledge. A well-chosen lawyer on your part will know the good mediators and the best mediation organizations. If he or she doesn't, he or she is not a good lawyer.

The best lawyers, the top five percent, will actually try and give somewhat of an estimate of your potential fees and costs as I noted above. But they could honestly be wrong. If the case is a serious case, you need and better get one of the best lawyers. You must do your homework, ask your most successful friends, interview several lawyers, maybe more. Do your best to find the best, and preferably a good old-fashioned work horse Christian lawyer. Some do exist. In Los Angeles there is a small contingent of great, truly top quality, Spirit-led lawyers. And in court, the other side will not want to mess with them. They all have the best Senior Partner you can imagine.

All these years later I realize, I've worked with about every problem imaginable out there in the world, whether imposed by an adversary like a lawsuit, or self-imposed, like a drug addiction or adultery. So, I can assist in measuring the cost of the battle.

But, in the end, you have to measure the practical side and the spiritual side for yourself. That's where the growth is.

Run quickly to the battle line

Attack. As a lawyer, there is something simple about knowing, simply, when it is time to *attack*. Attack simpliciter. There will come a time when you *know* that it is time to attack. It is the same for a person who is trying to quit a drug problem, a drinking problem, a sin problem. There comes a moment when you must know, that—it is time to attack, and pursue your enemies. "You will pursue your enemies, and they will fall by the sword before you. Five of you will chase a hundred, and a hundred of you will chase ten thousand, and your enemies will fall by the sword before you."[27] If you have a relationship with God and the Holy Spirit, you will *know* the time. The toughest part for a Spirit-filled lawyer is to see a wonderful person who "knows" that it is time to attack—but doesn't. That is not a good place for a person to be. That simply is not, I repeat, *not* God's plan. When you *know* it is time to attack, *attack*. And when you study God's battle plans throughout the Bible, from Genesis to Revelation, you know that with God on your side—your army is big enough.

In the spring of 2005, when Mike Harrison left my office, he went on the attack. He had me to help, his prayer partners at church, and . . . God. Marc Brewer filed his lawsuit against Healthways. And Sarah Bleu . . . she also went on the attack. I learned so much watching God work in her life. Sarah needed no fury with God on her side. God would go before her. She was and is the quintessential co-laborer. She was at peace. And way back in May 1985, in the first years of developing my working relationship with God, I already knew as a young Christian, that sure feeling, that sure *knowing* when it was time to attack. It was a good feeling to know *when*. If you know it, if you know *when*, do not, I repeat, *do not* hesitate. Run quickly to the battlefield.

"As the Philistine moved closer to attack him, David ran quickly toward the battle line to meet him."[28]

In one of the first battles of the Bible, when the time came to attack, that's what Abram did. This was Abram, before he was "Abraham," the father of nations, before God told him to: "Look up at the heavens and count the stars—if indeed you can count them . . . . So shall your offspring be."[29] When Abram went on the attack, it is hard to find any evidence, and there are no verses, that would indicate that he hesitated.

---

27 Leviticus 26:7-8.
28 1 Samuel 17:48.
29 Genesis 15:5.

What Abram did was simple: first, prepare; second, pursue; third, attack; fourth, refuse the spoils of war; and fifth, be blessed for doing the right thing. In Mike Harrison's case, the enemy attacked first. Mike's response was necessary, attack back. Mike and I didn't hesitate. We expected the war to last a while, and it did. In an early battle in the Bible, described in Genesis 14, Abram also attacked. There was no hesitation, and Abram was obviously prepared. His men were already trained. A Mesopotamian king, Kedorlaomer and his allied kings attacked Sodom and Gomorrah, seized all the goods of the two cities and all their food, and also carried off Abram's nephew Lot, and his possessions, while he was living in Sodom.[30] I suppose there are some uncles that would *not* have been too concerned about Lot because of his prior history with Abram,[31] in which Lot chose his own self interest when he made the decision to take the whole plain of the Jordan, well watered like the garden of the Lord, like the land of Egypt, toward Zoar (well before the Lord destroyed Sodom and Gomorrah), and by doing so did not defer proper respect for his uncle, Abram. Lot's selfish decision put himself and his family right in the middle of the two most sinful cities in the world.

Still, when Abram heard that Lot had been taken captive, he called out the 318 trained men born in his household and went in pursuit of Lot's captors, going as far north as the city of Dan, north of the Sea of Galilee. Genesis tells the story of how, during the night, Abram divided his men to *attack* the enemy and he routed them, pursuing them as far as Hobah, north of Damascus. Abram recovered all the goods and brought back his relative Lot and his possessions, together with the women and the other people.[32]

Some would consider Mike Harrison's *attack*, and Abram's *attack*, as "counterattacks." The Bible doesn't call them "counterattacks," and neither do I. There's a difference only the enemy learns.

Always more blessings than you think

Certainly, the actual dollar costs of a major lawsuit, whether you initiated it, or the other side did, are almost always more than you thought they would be. But, by now I've had the chance to see how battles and godly decisions play out over the long haul. And I think of Abram. Immediately after Abram returned from defeating Kedorlaomer and the kings allied with him, Melchizedek, King of Salem brought out bread and wine. "He was priest of God Most High, and he blessed Abram, saying:

Blessed be Abram by God Most High,
    Creator of heaven and earth.
And blessed be God Most High,
    who delivered your enemies into your hand."[33]

---

30 Genesis 14:12.
31 See Genesis 13.
32 Genesis 14:14-16.
33 Genesis 14:18-20.

And then, "after this, the word of the Lord came to Abram in a vision:

Do not be afraid, Abram.
  I am your shield,
    your very great reward."[34]

Poor Abram. After all of this, he was worried that he had no heir and that his eldest servant, Eliezer, would be his heir. But the Lord took Abram outside and said, "Look up at the heavens and count the stars—if indeed you can count them . . . So shall your offspring be."[35]

Blessings upon blessings. All these years of being a Christian warrior, I keep wondering why, when people do the godly thing, do they always get blessed, and the blessings are more than would ever be expected. It takes time to see the blessings of God. You might settle a case, give up more than you thought you should have, and not see the blessings until five years later, or more. For a lawyer and mediator like me, it is impossible to think of a case that was settled, that for some reason later, shouldn't have been settled. Part of the reason for me, but better still, for the client to do the 8-to-3 rule, and spend that time with the Lord, is to make sure that God wants you to take a certain action. If He does, then, you have to do it. God would never let greed or advantage be the reason to take a certain action. He wants you to store up treasures in heaven, not here on earth. I have certainly seen many of my godly clients experience tremendous financial success in their business life. But, they always gave back, and much more than a simple tithe.[36]

And then, God blesses them even more.

Eternal significance

In a typical week for a lawyer like myself, in addition to all the other work you are doing as a lawyer, plus teaching, writing, pro-bono clinic, etc., you will get a call like I did one night. It was my friend Phil. It was 9:00 p.m.. He had just caught his sixteen-year-old daughter with heroin in her bedroom. *Heroin*, in her bedroom! She said she got it from classmates at her private school in Santa Monica. She was a user. His daughter, Jennifer, had been spiraling down for the last year; it was obvious. Phil was done with a passive approach. He was ready to attack the problem, not the person, his beautiful daughter. We spent some time on the telephone, with pads in hand measuring all the options, from an outback wilderness treatment and rehab center in Utah at approximately $20,000 a month for a six-month stay, to rehab at the Dream Center in downtown Los Angeles which would be free for one year, and all other options in between. It took about

---

34 Genesis 15:1.

35 Genesis 15:5.

36 Malachi 3:10. "'Bring the whole tithe into the storehouse, that there may be food in my house. Test me in this," says the Lord Almighty, 'and see if I will not throw open the floodgates of heaven and pour out so much blessing that you will not have room enough for it.'"

two hours of planning, and some prayer. Phil decided on the rehab center in Utah. He felt he had to get his daughter as far away from Santa Monica as possible.

Phil walked into his daughter's room at about 1:00 a.m. in the morning, with his wife, the daughter's older sister, an aunt and uncle, and their pastor's assistant. They gathered Jennifer up, loaded her and her necessary possessions in a car, and drove her for hours and hours straight to the outback rehab center in Utah, where she was forced to stay for 6 months.

Jennifer is nineteen now, and just finished her first year at college, top of her class, studying to be a lawyer, interested in constitutional law, teaching and politics. I had coffee with Phil recently, and he credits it all to finally, and fortunately, not too late, taking serious action, on that particular night. He told me that his business was really hurting at the time. He paid the first four months of Jennifer's treatment on his credit card, and was getting close to the end of his rope. But, in the end the money was there, his business bounced back, and it was all worth it. Phil said, looking back over the last three years, he and his wife see nothing but the blessings.

Phil reminded me that since he became a Christian, he only wanted to do things that have eternal significance. On that one late night with Jennifer, he knew what to do, confirmed the decision with his wife and Counselor, and did it. When Phil and I were having coffee, Jennifer caught up with us and sat down.

She looked at me and said: "Tom, you don't have to tell me, but I know my daddy called you that night. . . . Thank you."

I was happy to hear that. But, I guess it's in my nature, I was also sad. And I had to look away for a minute. Because I know of some that got away from us. That slipped through the radar. And I can still lose it if I think about it, because one of them was my brother.

After that I would tell my clients: always run quickly to the battle line.

God wants you to measure the costs, but he doesn't want you to hesitate.

T+

The Take Away 7, (part a.)
Measure the cost and complete the battle.

1. **What is the cost of the battle?** What is the cost of what needs to be done to resolve the dispute, or solve the problem, for someone else, or yourself?

   As to the practical side: Measure the cost and complete the battle.

   As to the spiritual side: Measure the cost and be prepared to give up everything.

   You must be willing to do both.

   If you do both, you will establish two important things, among others: First, you are not a lukewarm; Second, you realize you are in the fight of your life, or a fight or a cause worth fighting for, and you want to win.

2. **On the practical side:** Measure the cost with the intention of completion. Compare your fight, or your cause to a *tower*.

   "Suppose one of you wants to build a tower. Will he not first sit down and estimate the cost to see if he has enough money to complete it? For if he lays the foundation and is not able to finish it, everyone who sees it will ridicule him, saying, 'This fellow began to build and was not able to finish.'"

   Never underestimate the significance of Jesus' use of the word "tower" in this verse. In Biblical times, in particular, a tower meant security, safety, and protection for the people. Indeed, the Lord as our "strong tower" is part of our spiritual inheritance in which we share when we live a life of faithfulness to God. "The name of the Lord is a strong tower; the righteous run to it and are safe."

   What good is a tower for you, or those that are counting on you, if you don't *complete it*? Our God is a God of completion. On the grandest scale of all, Jesus said: "It is finished."

   "No one who puts his hand to the plow and looks back is fit for service in the kingdom of God."

The Take Away 7, (part b.)
Measure the cost and be prepared to give up everything.

3. **On the spiritual side**: Measure the cost with the intention of preparing to give up everything.

You cannot be lukewarm. When you're in the fight of your life, you want the Lord to go out in front of you, and also to be your rear guard. And to have that, you have to be willing to *give up everything.*

"Or suppose a king is about to go to war against another king. Will he not first sit down and consider whether he is able with ten thousand men to oppose the one coming against him with twenty thousand? If he is not able, he will send a delegation while the other is still a long way off and will ask for terms of peace. In the same way, any of you who does not give up everything he has cannot be my disciple."

"Any of you who does not give up everything he has cannot be my disciple." Ultimately, all of us, after we have committed to give up everything, realize that "we are laborers together with God," and that everything we do takes on eternal significance.

4. Work on the practical side and the spiritual side of measuring the costs.

Know, that God wants to preserve your life. God has promised you, if you trust Him, that: "I will instruct thee and teach thee in the way which thou shalt go: I will guide thee with mine eye."

You can get there. Just ask Him.

When you study God's battle plans throughout the Bible, from Genesis to Revelation, you know that with God on your side—your army is big enough. Still, remember *again*, always run quickly to the battle line. God wants you to measure the costs, but He doesn't want you to hesitate.

8

Journal Entry, June 18, 1989

Sunday morning, 4:30 a.m.
Lord, get me out of this

Lord, I'm tired. I've been at this for ten solid years now. Litigating, trying cases, arbitrations, mediations, teaching, serving as a judge pro-tem, and so much more. And, so much less. I'm exhausted. My mind and body are worn out. It's my birthday. I'm thirty-five years old. It's 4:30 a.m. I'm alone as usual. Is this what you want for me?

I spend so much time in the courtrooms of life, in hospitals where sad or bad things happen to people, in counseling sessions where the train wrecks of life are strewn out before me, in rehab centers where I take my friends with their addictions, and Lord, they look to me for answers. Do they know . . . that I look to you?

That I look *only* to you? Most people don't need to know; most people don't want to know. The look of desperation on their faces says it all. A few of my friends and clients know that I look to you. Some don't. That's also lonely at times.

Lord, you fight for me

Lord, I've had a working relationship with you since November 1984. Thank you! Thank you again for coming into my life. Thank you for working with me. You've been an incredible Senior Partner. But, at 4:30 a.m., alone here sitting in my room, my inadequacies weigh on me. Am I at least an "okay" junior partner? I have to tell you, you make me feel so wanted by you, so cared for by you. I can actually hear you here in my heart.[1] Lord, I wouldn't

---

1 John 10:27. Jesus said: "My sheep listen to my voice; I know them, and they follow me. I give them eternal life, and they shall never perish; no one can snatch them out of my hand."

give that up for anything, nothing in the world compares to those moments when I hear you in my heart. You have taught me to be like Nehemiah. So often in my legal work, I have little time to think. But, in those circumstances I pray immediately, just like Nehemiah. Nehemiah prayed even while talking to others; he would pray quickly, even in the toughest of situations.[2] Lord, you fight for me, I know that. As Nehemiah said: "Our God will fight for us!"[3]

Lord, in those courtrooms I see so much pain. Sometimes I see the pain as a good thing. If there's pain, if there's at least some feelings, there's humanity. I see hope in those situations. When there's no pain, I see inhumanity and no hope. Sometimes people can attack others and feel no pain whatsoever. They seem to have the devil as their senior partner. They can attack with no remorse, no feelings. The attack is simply for gain. All gain seems to mean no pain. It emboldens them. Those cases are so hard to settle, Lord. The bad guys, the opportunists, are easy to spot. Thanks to you Lord, I can *see* it, I can see them. Those are the ones storing up their treasures on earth. They have sat back, with *supposedly* good lawyers, have assessed their chances of winning, and have already measured their potential for gain. Their lawyers are the same. I can see it; they also have "counselors," but not *the* Counselor, not you Lord.

Now strengthen my hands

I know that you know those moments in my heart when I want to tilt my head up, and look up to you and say, or request, or cry out, or even scream— *Lord, get me out of this!!* Perhaps even Nehemiah, when he was under such attack while he went about his mission of rebuilding the walls of Jerusalem, thought the same thing. But, he stopped and prayed to you Lord: "Now strengthen my hands."[4] And he would not be deterred from carrying on his work.

And neither will I be deterred. So, I carry on. Lord, I'm thirty-five years old today. I will carry on. Stay close. I love your verse for me tonight: *The Lord is my portion, saith my soul.*[5] I know that you, Lord, are my all-sufficient portion. And, I have such peace knowing that I have been *called* according to your purpose for my life.[6]

---

2 Nehemiah 2:4; 4:4-5, 9; 5:19; 6:14; 13:14, 22, 29. I also remember: "A short prayer pierces the heavens." *The Cloud of Unknowing*, referencing St. John of the Cross, *The Living Flame of Love*.

3 Nehemiah 4:20.

4 Nehemiah 6:9.

5 Lamentations 3:24 (KJV).

6 Romans 8:28. "And we know that in all things God works for the good of those who love him, who have been called according to his purpose."

I still have a lot of walls to rebuild. I know that the joy of the Lord is my strength.[7] And, I know that you are a forgiving God, gracious and compassionate, slow to anger and abounding in love.[8]

I pray that like Nehemiah, someday, after I have rebuilt the walls you have asked me to rebuild, I can say: "Remember me with favor, O my God."[9]

Let me kneel by my bed now, and say a prayer. I'm looking forward to a day of rest with you.

"Rest," I admit I'm not so good at resting. But—today, I will *make every effort*.[10] I learned that from my old friend Harry Goldberg.

It's Sunday.

Amen.

T+

---

7 Nehemiah 8:10.
8 Nehemiah 9:17.
9 Nehemiah 13:31.
10 Hebrews 4:8-11. "There remains, then, a Sabbath-rest for the people of God; for anyone who enters God's rest also rests from his own work, just as God did from his. Let us, there, make every effort to enter that rest . . . ."

The Take Away 8
Be assured of your calling.

1. This was my journal entry on my birthday in 1989. I've journaled my entire law career. I've journaled every challenge and every victory. It has been my conversation with God for over thirty years. Through all the battles and victories, all the blessings and challenges, I've tried to record everything the Lord has told me and taught me.

2. Journaling is the only way I know to *really build* a working relationship with God, recording everything He tells you, learning to listen to Him in your heart. This is how I learned that the Lord will fight for me. As Nehemiah said: "Our God will fight for us!"

3. Jesus said in John 10:27: "My sheep listen to my voice; I know them, and they follow me. I give them eternal life, and they shall never perish; no one can snatch them out of my hand."

4. Learn, learn, learn to listen to the Lord. Record what he tells you and teaches you. And thereby you will be assured that you are *called* according to His *purpose* for your life. *We know that in all things God works for the good of those who love him, who have been called according to his purpose.*

PART
II

Settle It!

Settle all the "its" in your life

9

Settle All the "Its" in Your Life, *part 1*
Even God had an "it"

By the time you finish this chapter, Part 1

By the time you finish this chapter and skip ahead and finish chapter 15, you can decide to do something that will completely change your life forever. It doesn't take that long. And, you will be so blessed for doing so. It only takes a moment, or a few minutes, or approximately the time it would take to finish reading two chapters of this book. That's how I've seen the biggest and best changes made in peoples' lives. That fast. That permanent.

With God, *it's as easy as that.*

And, of course, for all of us, there is, most certainly, at least one "it" each one of us must resolve. One momentary decision . . . that will last for eternity.

I've never seen a longer fight land less wounds, Part 1

Early in my career, when I was younger, I would volunteer my time as a mediator at the Los Angeles Superior Court. The judges would send each volunteer three or four cases and we would try to settle them. Basically, especially in those early days, the courts were logjammed with too many cases, and if most of the cases didn't settle, the system would break down. It remains pretty much the same way today.

I remember one day when I had four cases sent to me all at once. The morning started at 8:30 a.m. I settled two of them, and we walked into the courtroom and put the two settlements on the record with the judge presiding. The parties were equally *disappointed*, but relieved, so I had two successes for the day. It was 11:00 a.m. As mentioned earlier, a mediator's cliché is: the best settlements are the ones where both sides leave disappointed. If one side believes they "won," then, most likely, this is not a good settlement. He or she probably sacrificed nothing. *The one that sacrifices nothing, is the one that learns and discerns nothing.* Accordingly, there is a higher likelihood the dispute will return. Or, he or she will create the dispute elsewhere. It's important that both sides sacrifice something. Your heart follows your sacrifice. And if it's settled in your heart, it's settled.

One would think that the person that sacrificed nothing would be happier with the settlement.

It doesn't work that way. Their "happiness" will be fleeting. It's delusional.

The third case didn't settle; that's the way it goes sometimes. You can drive yourself to despair trying to get those that won't compromise—to compromise; trying to get those that won't sacrifice—to sacrifice. One of the litigants, a woman named Lydia, kept emphasizing how hurt and "wounded" she felt by the conduct of the other parties. Her lawyer used a typical easy exit excuse to terminate the mediation: "It is too early to settle the case, we need more time to do discovery, depositions, investigation, etc." That's just an excuse, but it often works, and it allows the lawyers to make more money, and the litigants to fight longer. You can drive yourself to despair trying to get those that want to fight to stop fighting.

Still, if a case I'm trying to settle doesn't settle, I feel defeated. But, every defeat has a message in it.

Indeed, as I was wrapping up my failed effort to settle that third case, Lydia, the "wounded" one, smirked, and spit out words to one of the other parties, "I guess we get to keep on fighting now."

I could see that Lydia's words really hurt the other party, a woman named Zoe. She really looked crushed, and I think she muttered, "I guess we do."

And I said, "I've never seen a longer fight land less wounds."

Lydia stopped—in her tracks.

Did she really want to keep on fighting?

The other parties left. I don't think Zoe's head could have hung any lower.

"Lydia, perhaps you should study the Prayer of Saint Francis." I said.

She looked at me, rolled her eyes and said, "I don't pray."

More "wounds" were to come.

But it was the fourth case in particular, that I had juggled with the other cases all morning, that got to my heart. So, although as a volunteer, I had only committed to a half day, I decided to stay on and see if I could settle this last case, one that looked like it was going to be a very difficult case. The case involved a family-owned business, a chain of art and framing stores, and the partners, three brothers, wanted to sell it, or split it up, or arrange a buy-out between the brothers, or run it into the ground to spite each other. The Moretti brothers case: Giovanni Jr., the eldest, and the one that ran the family business full time; Francesco, the middle brother, a lawyer in private practice and counsel to the family business; Paolo, the youngest, an artist and free spirit; and, I can't leave out a fourth party, their father Giovanni Moretti Sr., the patriarch of the family, who was *dead.*

Giovanni Jr. would yell as if with dagger thrusts: "If Papa were here he would tell you—I run this business full-time and always have, I should get half of it, at least—both of you have your *jobs*. This business has been my life."

Francesco would yell back with professional aplomb: "Papa would tell you it was my business and legal skills that caused the business to prosper, not your *administrative* abilities," further inflaming his older brother.

Paolo would say nonchalantly, "Papa loved me the most, my painting is my work, he told me I didn't have to work, 'pursue your art!' But, I should still get my fair share, one-third."

Those were the *nice* things they said; the juicy stuff they screamed in Italian.

I expected a fistfight to erupt in the halls.

Giovanni Sr. had died ten years before, leaving no will; the lawsuit was filed nine years ago. Yes, *nine years ago*. They hadn't stopped fighting in all that time. They would simply take breaks from the fighting, and then get back to it when time allowed, between weddings, funerals, and other family get-togethers. They had even waived important statutes of limitations so they could carry on with the fighting. It's much harder to do that these days; the courthouses are much less lenient with those that want to drag on their fighting.

That's a good thing.

The six-hour man

As a mediator, I sometimes thought of myself as the six-hour man. For the really tough cases, I couldn't seem to get anything really substantial done with the disputing parties in less than six hours. If the mediation started at 8:30 a.m., the first three hours were taken up with the various sides telling their story, what they are demanding, why they were going to win, etc. They always had to submit briefs in advance, so I already knew a lot about the case. But, I just had to give them the time to tell their story or they just didn't feel right about the process. People want to be heard. They want to make sure you understand their side of the story. Most of this storytelling and legal positioning is done in caucuses, when the mediator meets with each side separately. If the Moretti brothers were in the same room, they just yelled at each other while simultaneously threatening to walk out—which they would have done if the judge hadn't ordered them to go through the process. They were about to start a long trial against each other; neither side wanted to upset the judge. They each had lawyers, and I actually felt that the lawyers were more than ready to turn the case over to me to settle, they were not looking forward to a long drawn-out jury trial between three fighting brothers. Even if it meant more fees for them.

This was a classic "no win" situation, as most cases are.

This is the only place I am

At 12:15 p.m., sandwiches were brought in and we called a truce over lunch while I ate with the Moretti brothers in the same room. They sat in their corners, eating quietly. Curiously, Giovanni Jr. mused with his lawyer about bringing in a thermos with a very special coffee that he had found in Italy on a recent trip. He would share it with his lawyer, and no others. Then he talked about some special desserts he had brought in. He would share them with his lawyer also, and no others. Then he complained incessantly about the sandwiches ordered from the little coffee shop outside the courthouse—the one I loved. In disgust, he tossed them into the trash can, trying to get a huge "thud" from his efforts.

Lunch burned up time until 1:30 p.m.; my attempts at congeniality over lunch were mocked. These guys were biding their time, talking "settlement," but only because the judge ordered them to stay with me until the end of the day.

But the lunch together told me all I needed to know as to how to settle this case.

After lunch, I went back to caucusing with each side. It was Paolo's turn, so I met with him separately. This was the third time I had met with Paolo. Basically, he believed that the business should be sold and he just wanted his "third," which is what he said Papa would have wanted. I suspected that Paolo was about thirty-seven, and totally dedicated to his painting. So, I got him to talk about it, which he did in detail; how he got his inspiration, what music he listened to, where his studio was, what did he like about his studio, everything I could cover in about a half hour. Then, toward the end I asked him: "Paolo, when this case is over, and let's say this business is sold, and you get your hoped-for one-third, what are you going to do?" I already knew the answer.

"Paint, what else," he said, bubbling over.

"But, what will Giovanni do?" I asked.

"I don't know, that's his problem. He'll have plenty of money, he can do nothing if he wants."

Paolo didn't seem to care.

It was 2:00 p.m. Next up for a caucus was Francesco, the counselor for the family. He'd been in practice over ten years. He was thirty-nine and the most confident. As the lawyer, he predicted that the jury would have no choice but to split the business up into thirds. He'd get his third. That was the bottom line. His brother, Giovanni Jr., was being incredibly unreasonable. Indeed, he told me that for the longest time Giovanni wanted the whole business, but would give each brother 10 percent. Giovanni's reasoning was simple, the business had directly or indirectly supported both Francesco and Paolo as they pursued their individual interests. The business had sent Paolo to art school, and Francesco to law school, among other things. But, Francesco and Paolo would argue that Giovanni was highly paid, and had enjoyed a privileged expense package.

Then, toward the end of the caucus, I asked Francesco: "Francesco, when this case is over, and let's say this business is sold, and you get your hoped-for one-third, what are you going to do?" I already knew the answer.

"Practice law! What are you an idiot!?" he said.

"But, what will Giovanni Jr. do?" I asked.

"I don't know, find something else to dabble in I suppose. He'll have enough money, why should I care?"

I almost expected him to say, *am I my brother's keeper?*

After a short coffee break, an important restroom prayer stop, and reporting back to the judge about our lack of progress, it was getting close to 3:00 p.m. The Moretti brothers believed they were beating *me*. They were determined to show me: this case could not settle. I have to admit, by that time of the day, I can sometimes feel drained by the emotions, the legal ramblings, the jousting, and too much coffee.

It was Giovanni Jr's. turn. I sat there alone with him for a few minutes and asked him about the coffee I overheard him brag about at lunch. He told me about it, and poured me a cup. I felt honored, like I had been admitted to some type of inner circle. The Inklings. I felt that Jack Lewis would pull up a chair at any moment and sit next to us. Good coffee does these things to me. I let a few minutes pass as I savored the coffee . . . and wondered if Giovanni thought I had run out of gas. Not much gas left, but lots of spirit.

Then I looked over my cup at him and said: "Sometimes I have that feeling that this is the only place I am, where I feel like I shouldn't be somewhere else." Inside, I felt that right then. *This is where God wants me to be, no place else, at this moment. Like the great I Am was right here with me. With us.*

A few more moments passed, then Giovanni spoke. He blinked.

"I know, what you mean. But, I've only had a glimpse," he said.

"Giovanni, you spoke of a recent trip to Italy. Have you ever gone to Italy with your brothers?" I asked.

"On no, not since long before Papa died," he said with a sigh confirming that he doesn't get along with his brothers.

"What do you do while in Italy?" I asked.

"I visit the cafés, I meet with old friends, I meet new friends, I eat, drink, you know, nothing special," with his voice trailing off.

"How old are you?" I asked, trying to sound like it wasn't important.

"Forty-three."

"You're young."

"I feel like a hundred," he said, sipping his coffee.

I looked at my watch. I couldn't figure out how a half hour had already gone by. I looked at Giovanni; I have to admit, for a second there, he looked like a hundred. I didn't want to say it, but we were running out of time. Judges like to close up shop at 4:30, so if we were going to get a deal done, get it on the record, and settle this case, something had to happen.

So, I asked: "Giovanni, what is the *it* of your life?"

"What?" he said, no longer in the mood to talk.

"What is the one thing you've always wanted to do with your life?" I asked.

Mercy, I thought hours went by, although it was just a very long moment. "Well," he started to say, looking so tired, "I suppose I've always wanted to open a little Italian café, right here in America, but old school, just like in Italy, where my father was born—with white tile, small petite tables, blue tablecloths, blue shirts, a special menu, with outdoor seating, blue umbrellas—a certain type of chairs, plants, photography . . . you know—large windows, plenty of sunlight at day, moonlight at night, in a neighborhood, where people think it's their place . . ." He had his handkerchief out.

"What would you call it?" I asked.

"Giovanni's, an Italian café," he said, catching my eye, wondering if he was displaying too much ego.

"Nice," I said. "So, what do you think it would cost to set it up?"

"Well . . . ."

And there it was. From his back pocket, he pulled out two pages of detailed worn-out notes on both sides of the pages, which I couldn't read. They were in Italian. But I could see the details, with the numbers by each line item.

"It's a lot, I want to do it right. It *has to be* right. $398,548.25," Giovanni said.

" . . . and 25 cents," I asked, chiding him.

"It has to be right," he said.

"Can I borrow your notes? Please?"

"Okay," he said, as he *slowly* handed me his two sacred documents.

I suppose he knew what I was going to do. He didn't specifically approve it, but I think he knew.

It was 3:50 p.m.

I took the notes and headed down the hall to meet with Francesco and Paolo.

Ten minutes later, Francesco, Paolo, with me in distant tow, barged into the room where Giovanni and his lawyer sat alone, waiting for me to return. Francesco launched into Giovanni: "Gio, Gio—why? Why? did you never tell us of this dream?"—he grabbed Giovanni and squeezed him. "Why, my brother, are you crazy, that you keep such a thing as this from us, we're your brothers!"

Paolo joined in the hug: "Gio, we love you, you shall have this dream. This is your dream!! You shall have it."

Then Francesco and Paolo argued with each other, Paolo going first: "We shall sell the business and Gio shall have $398,548.25 right off the top first, before we get a dime."

Francesco jumped in, yelling at Paolo: "You cheap, ungrateful . . . (I didn't understand the Italian, but it sounded quite colorful), we shall give him $450,000 off the top, before we get a nickel."

"It should be $450,000, plus interest! Gio should have done this a long time ago," yelled Paolo.

"What time is it?" yelled Francesco. "We must see this judge right away. We have no further disputes. We have nothing to argue about. We are brothers again."

"It's 4:15, we'd better hurry," I said.

I heard the other lawyers in the background, saying they weren't exactly sure what happened, or what the settlement was, but . . . as they hesitated, the two brothers were already heading out the door to go see the judge, with all of us playing catch-up.

But, Giovanni Jr. grabbed me, and threw his arm around my neck, which I remember was a certain kind of intended stranglehold hug. I think. But I think he was happy.

We were in the second floor attorney conference rooms of the LA courthouse. It was 4:17 p.m. We all had to walk down the long second floor hallway, take two sets of escalators up to the fourth floor, and then walk back down the long hallway of the fourth floor to get to the courtroom where the judge on the case presided. The entire way, Giovanni Jr. had his arm around my shoulder telling me in half-English half-Italian he had seen me in the men's room earlier muttering something, a prayer or something, and how bold I was.

"Tommaso, at the coffee break, I walked into the men's room. I heard you: *'Lord, I speak to my mountain, my mountain is this case Lord, I cast all barriers to settlement—into the sea in Jesus' name, into the sea in Jesus' name. Lord, I have faith in you, please settle this case.'* Tommaso, you sounded like an idiot. Such boldness.[1] I laughed at the time. I thought, this case can't settle, we need to just battle it to the end and be done with it. But—you settled it."

"All glory to God," I said.

"You know Tommaso, I believe in God too, but I thought about what I heard in the men's room, and I did some of my own talking to God." He stopped, took his arm off my shoulder, and looked at me: "Tommaso, thank you for talking to God."

"You're welcome," I said, rubbing my neck.

Just outside the courtroom, Giovanni Jr. stopped me again.

"Do you always speak out like that to God, Tommaso?" he asked.

"Only when I think no one is listening," I smiled as we pulled open the courtroom doors and walked in.

"Oh! But thank God, he was listening," Giovanni Jr. said, laughing.

This time I stopped him.

"He's *always* listening."

Giovanni Jr. nodded at me in agreement.

When we arrived at the specific courtroom, our judge was waiting for us. He was still planning to end the day at 4:30 p.m., he had a busy late afternoon and

---

1 Acts 4:29. *Now, Lord, . . . enable your servants to speak your word with great boldness.*

early evening, as most judges do when they prepare for the next day. We lined up in front of counsel's table. The judge asked us: "What's the status of your discussions counsel?"

"Your honor, I believed we have settled the case and we'd like to put the settlement on the record."

"Please proceed, counsel," said the judge, nodding in approval. Judges love it when cases settle. He looked over at the court reporter to make sure she was ready to go. She was.

"Your honor, here are the terms:

First: The partners, the three brothers, have decided to sell their chain of art and framing stores.

Second, once the stores are sold, off the top, before any distributions, the two younger brothers, Francesco and Paolo have agreed that the first $450,000 shall go to the eldest brother, Giovanni, Jr., dedicated to opening his beloved Italian café."

"Plus interest!" Paolo blurted out. "Plus interest!!"

That started Francesco and Paolo arguing again, and the judge cutting them off: "Counsel, control your clients!"

"Your honor, I'm the mediator," I said. "But the parties and their counsel have agreed that I could put the settlement on the record."

The judge confirmed this with the brothers' lawyers in the courtroom, and they agreed. "Well, carry on."

"Anyway, after the business is sold, and (I looked at Francesco and Paolo) — *now* the two younger brothers have agreed that Giovanni Jr. shall receive the first $500,000, which shall cover some interest that would have accumulated if Giovanni had had the money several years earlier.

"Third, after, Giovanni gets the first $500,000 off the top from the sale of the business, then the remaining money realized from the sale shall be divided in thirds, with a third going to each brother.

"Fourth, the brothers will agree to sign mutual general releases all around, dismiss the lawsuit between them, and that will end the case.

"Fifth, they already know of a broker they want to list the business with; they trust the broker."

Paolo again blurted out: "And Mr. Tommaso shall decide if the price offered for the business is reasonable, and whether we should take it."

As the lawyers and the judge jumped to again admonish Paolo for blurting out, while simultaneously debating the issue, Francesco shouted: "Agreed!!"

After that, the judge took care of formalities, making sure that each brother was in full agreement, making sure that each of their lawyers was in agreement, and then making housekeeping decisions, such as who would be filing the dismissal of the case and when.

The case was over . . . nine years had gone by. I was led from the courtroom in a conglomeration of hugs and strangleholds. Then, I was invited to Giovanni's house for a dinner celebration.

Later, Giovanni stood up at the dinner table where three large families were seated and said: "Tommaso, you settled it. But more than that, you settled a few other things. I'm thankful, that I know I can realize my dream now. You have restored our three families. We are thankful."

Francesco: "But . . . more importantly, we thank God for Tommaso, and for using him to help us . . . to you, Tommaso!!" and the glasses went up.

All I could think was *Lord, why me?*

We are called to settle conflicts, not solve them.

It is done

Later, Giovanni invited me into his private little library, poured us both a small glass of Chianti, raved about the vintage of the Chianti, which this non-drinking lawyer sipped, and then said to me: "You know Tommaso, that was such a simple question you asked earlier, but when I heard it, I have to tell you, in my heart, for the second time, I heard God say to me, 'Giovanni, it is done.'"

"What question, Giovanni?" I asked.

"You said, 'Giovanni, what is the *it* of your life?'—Such a simple question. But, I knew the answer almost before you asked."

"When God says 'It is done,'[2] then it *is* done," I said. "And it happens in an instant. Our Lord planned it, and this one he planned for you, Giovanni."

"You know Tommaso, I just love good endings, in a movie, a song, a love affair, a dream, anything. I just love a good ending. . . . My Mamma, may she rest in peace, would read the Bible to me as a young man, and she would make me memorize verses. Well, I'm an idiot and I could only remember the short ones. And, my friend Tommaso, my new favorite, because it will be so easy to remember is: 'It is done.' The ending is good. I know that. . . . The ending is good Tommaso. The ending is good. Never forget that."

Do you talk to God? Part 1

A year and a half later we were all sitting outside at *Giovanni's, an Italian café.* Family, friends, former litigants, neighbors, and strangers. The restaurant was packed.

Paolo was shouting at Giovanni, Jr. "What do you mean, you were talking to God, and he told you to put the restaurant on this corner? Are you crazy?"

"That's what I said," said Giovanni Jr.

Francesco chimed in, "What? You just called him up and asked him, 'hey God, where should I put my restaurant?'"

---

2 Revelation 21:6. "It is done."

They were all laughing at Giovanni, Jr.

"Of course I talk to God, everyone should talk to God. Who else can you trust? I certainly can't trust you bums. —Look at Tommaso, he talks to God, and look at him!"

Paolo said, "Hey Tommaso, do you talk to God?"

"Of course I do," I said.

"When you talk to God, how do you know he listens?" Paolo said with a laugh.

And I felt that old familiar feeling of being told what to say.

So I said: "I can prove it to you."

Now they were all laughing at me.

I looked at Giovanni, Jr. and I said, "Giovanni, on that day we settled your case with your brothers did you talk to God?"

"Yes," Giovanni Jr. said.

"And, what did you say?"

"I said, 'Lord, it's time, please help me out.'"

"And did he?"

It was getting quiet with the group.

"Yes," said Giovanni Jr., taking his time to answer. "I asked him, 'Lord God, my friend, please now, bring my plan for this restaurant, the plan I have in my back pocket, to life.'"

"And, what did God say?" I asked.

"He said, 'Giovanni, *it is done.*'"

Everybody was dead quiet.

"Giovanni, how long had you had that plan in your heart?"

"Since I was twelve, I had this *desire in my heart.*"[3]

"Giovanni, how long had you had those plans, or a draft of those plans, in your back pocket?"

Giovanni Jr's eyes welled up.

"Twenty-five years."

"Was that day the very first time you asked God to bring those plans to life?" I quietly asked.

"Yes," he said.

Then I looked up and noticed something on the wall. Giovanni had framed the two pages he had pulled from his pocket the day of the settlement. The two pages with writing on both sides, with the details for *Giovanni's, an Italian café*. And I could see from where I sat that the two pages were framed in such a way that you could flip the frame and see both sides of the pages.

And at the top of the frame was written: *"It is done."*

---

3 Psalm 37:4. "Delight yourself in the Lord and he will give you the desires of your heart."

Paolo stood up. "Papa, you told us all to pursue our dreams. To that we say: *'It is done.'*"

The two other brothers stood up.

And then they reverently toasted their father, Giovanni Moretti Sr.

And I remembered a thought my pastor, Tommy Barnett, implanted in my heart a long time ago: When God has given you a dream, remember,

"Delay is not denial."

T+

The Take Away 9
What is the one thing you've always wanted to do with your life?

1. ***What is the one thing you've always wanted to do with your life?*** Why is
it that underlying so many disputes, and so many conflicts, is someone's
unfulfilled dream? So often, if you resolve that issue, *and determine to
have your dream,* you resolve the conflict.

2. A mediator's principle is: The best settlements are the ones where both
sides leave disappointed. In a *worldly* sense, this is true. If one side believes
they "won," then most likely, this is not a good settlement, or a good
resolution. He or she sacrificed little or nothing. ***The one that sacrifices
nothing, is the one that learns and discerns nothing.*** Accordingly, there
is a higher likelihood the dispute or conflict will return. Or, he or she will
create a dispute elsewhere.

3. A godly principle is: The best settlements are the ones where both sides
leave *blessed.* In a *godly* sense, this is true. There is still sacrifice, but
sacrifice turns into blessings. ***We are called to settle conflicts, not solve
them.*** Settle it first, and the solving will follow. In Matthew 5:25 Jesus
said, "Settle matters quickly," not *solve* matters quickly. Proverbs 3:5 tells
us to lean not on our own understanding.

4. Delay is not denial. When God has given you a dream, remember, delay is
not denial. But why delay? As I lay out in Chapter 15:
     Take out a simple standard issue, cafeteria-grade white paper
napkin. Put a "T" at the top, and a "+" next to it. "T+" ("Trust the Lord").
Take a moment, put out all the fires in your mind, and remove all the
distractions. Let the one big thing in your life come to mind that you
would like settled quickly, or a goal you'd like accomplished quickly. Write
that on the napkin somewhere under the "T+". After you write down that
one big thing, go ahead and add a few other things you'd like to settle, or
accomplish. That's "your list." Ask God to help you settle the matters on
your list and receive in your heart the victory. Date your list and sign your
name. Fold the napkin and put it in your pocket. Read Chapter 15. You
will be amazed at what you can accomplish in forty days, with God's help.

Delight yourself in the Lord and he will give you the desires of your heart.

Your Life Is But a Mist

Small droplets suspended in the air

An open vessel, not a sinking vessel

It was Friday morning, May 1985, 6:45 a.m., and I was sitting in my favorite coffee house next to the courthouse with Harry Goldberg. It was the fifth day of the Knoll Radio Company vs. Harry Goldberg case. The other side, not me, not Harry, but the other side, and in particular, the main plaintiff's lawyer, Brendan Jones, had asked for this meeting at 7:00 a.m., to talk settlement. That's a "tell." They were, *somewhat*, concerned. But, they figured a "tell" to a young inexperienced guy like me was worth the small perceived risk.

I was thirty-one years old and I was already a stoic, a Christian mystic, a warrior. Well, in my own mind anyway. But, I was seriously talking to God by then, and I already had a strong sense that I had so, so, so much to learn, but, in time of war, which I was always in, I was an *open vessel*. God knew I was an open vessel. That's why He yelled at me on occasion. Better to keep me from being a *sinking vessel*.

I sat there sipping coffee with Harry. It was now close to 7:00 a.m. And I was thinking of small droplets of water suspended in the air. Then I saw plaintiffs' lawyers first appear walking up to the coffee shop. Brendan Jones, Bruce Jenson, Philip Rawlings, and Ann Davis swooped in like clockwork at about 6:59:59 a.m., with precision accuracy. They had their matching navy blue suits, the Blue Angels. I almost expected them to have their arms out like wings as they rounded the corner toward the coffee shop. Dipping to the right as they sailed to the front of the coffee shop.

And I was thinking of small droplets of water suspended in the air.

That's what mist is.

And mist vanishes so fast.

I took a sip of my coffee as I saw the Blue Angels talk amongst themselves just outside the coffee shop. And I was thinking, what did James mean when he said in the Bible: "You are a mist that appears for a little while and then vanishes"?[1] I looked at the Blue Angels and thought, don't they see they are a mist? They are here for such a little while and then—they will vanish. It was nice in those days being so new in the faith; I tended to take things literally. Harry and I had to be there. The Blue Angels and their clients didn't. They opted to take a shot at Harry and, hopefully, get his radio stations at a bargain basement price. But they were going to lose. I had faith. I knew not to worry; I did anyway. And I, by then, had basically memorized Micah 6:8, and personalized it: *What does the Lord require of me? To act justly and to love mercy and to walk humbly with my Lord.*

And then bash their heads in.

Figuratively speaking, of course.

Brendan peeled off from his band of barbarians, *blue* barbarians, and came and sat next to me. He suggested that just he and I go to the counter and talk. No others present. I was trying to be tough, so I said, "okay." At the counter, Brendan looked at me and said: "Look, it's Friday, why don't we try to settle this thing before the weekend, the weather's perfect, we could all *enjoy our weekends,* put this thing behind us. What do you think?"

I truly was a stoic. I had read Marcus Aurelius by then and, in particular, *Meditations.* I had read Aurelius because I was reading the Christian mystics. At that time my favorite was Bede Griffiths whose early life was influenced by Aurelius. By Roman standards, Marcus Aurelius was conservative and just, and a phenomenal warrior. Believe me, *enjoying my weekend* was not going to appeal to this young warrior, I was a stoic, "endure" and "abstain" were my two words for the moment. I wanted to be a mystic, a Christian mystic.

I looked at Brendan and said: "I gave you a 'walk-away' moment, and you turned me down."

"Just hear me out," he requested, and looked over his shoulder to make sure the Blue Angels' engines were idling appropriately. They signaled back. Brendan looked back at me: "We are prepared to 'up' our pretrial offer by $300,000 to settle this case. That gives Harry a nice chunk of additional money for his two stations, and no matter how you look at it, that's a fair price. Okay? That's close to the amount of money you offered to take at the settlement conference a month before the trial. That should do it," he said, looking convinced. "You can be the *hero,*" he added.

Brendan really knew how to tie a necktie. How did he get that dimple so perfect under the knot? His name and picture was in the local law journal that day; a judgment had come down in his client's favor and it had made the local and national press. I didn't know that until the end of the day. He had the same

---

1 James 4:14. See also Psalm 78:39. "He remembered that they were by flesh, a passing breeze that does not return."

tie on in the picture; same tight knot. He was superstitious. Another "tell." This trial was getting in the way of his press interviews. I didn't know that either until the end of the day. I went and sat back at the table with Harry and repeated Brendan's offer. Harry's swift reply is not printable. Which is why I still can slip and cuss on occasion. It gets in your head. Poetic words are spoken quite often in courthouses. I went back and sat next to Brendan at the counter.

"Brendan," I said, looking at him relatively directly although I was sitting next to him. "Take your piece of crap settlement offer and shove it.... Those are Harry's words, not mine. We gave you a *walk-away moment*, and you didn't take it." I stood up. "See you in court."

I walked away thinking, I only have one *hero*, and apparently Brendan doesn't know *him*.

Clearly, I had much more work to do with Micah 6:8. My version of walking humbly with the Lord needed some polish. Lots of polish. Stay on the path, and let him polish.

Expect the Lord

There are so many times in life when the train has left the station and it's too late. Sometimes some of us will even tell the train to leave the station and realize later, that it's too late. This case was just a game to those guys. I had tried everything under the sun to settle with them. Now—in trial, my business settlement letters, and piles of evidence were already stacking up against them, and they were getting beat. And it was only day five. So, *now*, they wanted to settle. Gee, thanks a lot. That's pleasant of you. But Harry had rallied, he was in good spirits, he felt something so new, so powerful inside him, so reaffirming, so good. It just felt good. It just felt right. Harry felt, in the right. He wanted to keep his stations. He didn't know how. He still had the same financial problems that had sent him down this path, that got him in trouble, but he had a new *fight* about him. My client, Harry, saw that I had a Senior Partner. He saw how I counted on him. Harry decided he was going to keep his stations. They were no longer for sale. He was no longer for sale. We are going all the way to the end. "Be strong and let your heart take courage, all you who wait for *and* hope for *and expect* the Lord!"[2]

As for Harry and I, we *expected* to win.

We would end up in trial for three more weeks.

A *walk away* moment is very simple. You make an offer and then—there's the moment that you look opposing counsel and his client in the eye and say something like: "Okay, this is it, this is the moment when you either take our best and final offer, or you walk away. If you walk away, that's it, it's off the table forever. So, I'm going to stop talking in a second, and unless you say something

2 Psalm 31:24 (AMP).

fast, like, 'we are going to accept the offer,' then that's it, the offer is gone, and we go to trial. So, here it is." At that point you stop talking and look them in the eye again. If they pause just ever so long, and they say nothing, you say: "Okay, that's it. Done."

And walk away.

And don't look back.

At a settlement conference one month before the trial, I did just that to Brendan Jones and his client. They didn't take Harry's offer. They were regretting that now.

I've never seen a longer fight land less wounds, Part 2

At lunch that day, Harry and I went up to the ninth floor cafeteria at the courthouse. It's a big cafeteria, with plenty of room to spread out. Even I, by now, saw some old friends from law school, or just the other trial lawyers you always see downtown in trial. We'd say hello, and once in a while introduce ourselves. Harry and I sat down and started preparing notes from the morning session of the trial. Eventually, Brendan Jones and his band of blue barbarians also came into the cafeteria and I could see there was a commotion around him and he seemed to be holding court on something else, but definitely not on the Knoll Radio Company case. I could see his client, William James Hollister ("Ol' BJ"), in the shadows, while Brendan answered questions from reporters on another case. I knew the look on his face. It said: *Hmmm, my lawyer is obviously famous, well-known, and he obviously had some sort of victory on a previous case—but is he focused on my case?* I actually felt a tad bit sorry for Ol' BJ.

The mist was fading.

And just at that moment, a woman walked up to me. "Tom?"

"Yes," I answered as Harry brought us some trial food: turkey on wheat, nothing else on it, a hard boiled egg, no salt allowed, and green tea (only for lunch), and an apple for desert. Harry splurged, he got cheese on his turkey sandwich, and, god forbid, mayonnaise. I hate mayonnaise; unnecessary fat.

"Do you remember me?" she asked.

"Yes, of course. I was disappointed I didn't settle your case last February. You were my third case."

"Thank you, for remembering," Lydia said. And both Harry and I saw how sad she was. When she sat down, we knew that was the right thing for her to do just then, despite our need to focus on our trial. But, it was Friday afternoon, and then we'd have the weekend to prepare. No sweat.

"We're still fighting. Four more months of fighting. I remember what you said that day: 'I've never seen a longer fight land less wounds'." A long moment passed. Harry and I could see the fresh wounds. "We had some kind of big pre-trial court proceeding this morning; things are rough. The actual trial will start soon. The worst part is . . . (she started to cry) I've lost two friends. I miss my friends. I've hurt them so much."

"You weren't concerned about their feelings last time. You were only concerned about your own," I said.

"I know," she said.

"I remember your case. You're an author, you've written three books toward a five-book contract. You have a co-writer that was expecting to receive co-authorship credit on the fourth book. You refused. There is a dispute as to whether you ever made that promise. There is nothing in writing. Furthermore, you feel your publisher hasn't done a good job marketing and selling your books, and therefore you want out of the remainder of your contract. You haven't written and turned in your fourth book because you're in conflict and you've lost your blessing. Now you're all embroiled in a lawsuit. Something like that. And, you go to trial soon, or tomorrow, I think you said."

"That just doesn't matter anymore. I've hurt my co-writer, Zoe. And my publisher has an editor, Francie. I've hurt her also. This fighting has wiped me out. I only now realize how much I have hurt them, and hurt myself."

"You haven't accomplished much since our settlement conference?" I said.

"Well, we've spent a lot more on lawyer's fees. I haven't written one word in four months, and, I miss my friends," she said. "But, I did read that prayer."

"I was hoping you'd pray it, eventually," I said.

She nodded. But I couldn't tell if that meant she agreed.

She was still crying: "What are you doing here?" she asked.

Strange question I thought. It would take me about twenty years to learn why she asked it. But, right then I said, "Well, I live here."

And Harry said with a grunt: "I was forced to come here."

I could see, Lydia was really hurting.

"Okay, let me tell you what to do, and then I have to get back to Harry here (Harry nodded on cue), and you have to get back to your case."

"Yes, we decided to talk settlement one more time this afternoon. Informally."

"Don't waste another day on this case," I demanded. "So, grab a napkin."

She grabbed a standard issue, cafeteria-grade white paper napkin, the ultimate paperwork for a good settlement. I continued: "At the top put a capital "T" and a little plus sign next to it. T+.

"Number 1: On the fourth and fifth books, Zoe gets co-authorship credit. She deserves it. Second, you made a promise, stick to it and finish your five-book commitment to the publisher, and stop complaining. Third, the publisher agrees that Francie will carry on as your editor and see if you can get her a raise, even if it comes out of your portion. Fourth, all parties walk away and drop their claims against each other. Fifth, all parties attorneys' fees are paid off the top from royalties, to help put everyone back to where they were before this case started. Before *you* caused this problem. That's it. Now go. And be blessed!"

She furiously wrote everything I said down on the napkin.

"Okay. Tom, what's the T and the + at the top of the napkin stand for?"

"The T is for 'Trust' and the + is for the Lord. 'Trust the Lord,'" I said as she started to walk away.

"But I'm an atheist," she said.

"Not today," I said firmly.

I turned back to Harry and she vanished.

"She can go back to being an atheist tomorrow if she wants," I said to Harry as we got back to our notes. That's what I said, but not what I was thinking. Somewhere down deep, her spirit is still alive.

"You did that to Brendan Jones, at the settlement conference last month. It was early in the day," Harry said.

"You know Harry, I haven't been doing this too long, only since I was fifteen years old when I started working for the Santa Barbara law library." I smiled, trying to get credit for my years of snot-nosed running around for lawyers and the law librarian. "But, so far, I haven't seen a case, or situation, or a problem, or an addiction, that couldn't be settled on the back of a standard issue paper napkin. If the parties will only just try. Or, if even one person will only—just try."

"Tom, I kept the napkin you pushed across the table to Brendan that day. When he rejected the offer, and pushed the napkin back. I kept it. I was just plain hoping we could beat it in trial." Harry reached into his back pocket, and there it was. He looked at it. And with his index finger tapped the top of the napkin, where the T was, and the +. He tapped it several times.

"How's your faith now, Harry?" I asked.

He thought for a second. "It's good Tom, it's good," and folded the napkin back up and put it back in his pocket.

"Harry," I said, looking him in the eye. "If you have the napkin, you don't need the gun."

He looked back at me. "Okay."

Two guys, at peace, in that cafeteria, on that one day, finished their lunch, and went back to war at 1:30 p.m.

Numbering your days

In the northern hemisphere and, of course, the United States, the first day of summer is the day of the year when the Sun is farthest north (on June 20th or the 21st). It's also the longest day of the year in the sense that the length of time elapsed between sunrise and sunset on this day is the maximum for the year. This is the Summer Solstice. And on that day in 2005, a Tuesday, Mike Harrison returned to my office after spending forty days in hard-core war mode. Under his arm he had the "blue prints," the large pages from my large trial pads attached to my large trial tri-pods. Everything is large about trial work, and war mode. The blueprints are three feet wide and four feet long. There were seven pages of Mike's and my big letters from our strategy session forty days ago. But now they had lots of Mike's smaller notes and Bible verses. He got the picture, there really is a time for everything, including a time for battle.[3] He was ready. Mike and I started toward my *large* glass conference table, but diverted toward the coffee brewer.

"Tom, today I hit the big '11,315,'" he said.

I knew what he meant. "Congratulations . . . that's nothing, I'm in the '18,250' range," I said as we each got large cups of coffee.

"And if we make it to seventy years old, we will have been on the earth 25,550 days. As of 2004, the average American male's life expectancy hit a record 75.2 years or approximately 27,448 days on the earth. I suppose I still have a way to go," Mike concluded.

Coffee in hand, we sat down at the conference table. My large trial tri-pods stared at us from the other end of the conference table. I looked at Mike and said: "When I've had problems, and I've had many, I've also gone into war mode for forty days. And one thing that happens every time, is I end up counting my days. 'Teach us to number our days aright, that we may gain a heart of wisdom.'"[4]

As Mike unrolled the seven pages of blue prints I saw the big words at the top: "Battle Blueprints," and the logo I put there last time "T+."

Mike said, "'Show me, O lord, my life's end and the number of my days; let me know how fleeting is my life.'"[5]

I looked at Mike's battle plans. There were our detailed notes from our meeting forty days ago, the things we had already accomplished (we had answered the complaint, and filed a cross-complaint), Bible verses everywhere to support his work and our strategy, and the expectation notes at the end—we *expected* to win. And at the end, I saw his wife's notes and both their signatures They had both signed off on the plans. They were in agreement.

Mike looked at me and said, "you see these battles all the time don't you?"

"Yes," I admitted.

"I don't know exactly how to say this, but these plans . . . I think they are saving my marriage, and my family."

Mike and I worked hard that day on his case, Blackdog vs. Harrison Interactive. He left my Santa Monica offices just after lunch. On the way out the door, he turned to me and said: "Tom, it is really painful to be sued, and to have to go through this. But, I can't help but think that this may have been what it takes to bring me back to life, to realize all the blessings I have, to realize the incredible value of just one, just one, day in my life. What a gift that is. I don't know how to put this in words, so anyway. . . ."

I nodded. We shook hands and he left.

If you have been a trial lawyer for a long time, you realize the incredible amount of time that people burn up fighting each other. You realize the incredible waste

---

3 Ecclesiastes 3:8.

4 Psalm 90:12.

5 Psalm 39:4-5. "Show me, O lord, my life's end and the number of my days; let me know how fleeting is my life. You have made my days a mere handbreadth; the span of my years is as nothing before you. Each man's life is but a breath." And see Job 7:7. "Remember, O God, that my life is but a breath."

of resources. Some people, like Mike, are forced to go through it. Others choose to go through it, even enjoy it if they are evil enough—they simply like to attack people. If you are a Christian trial lawyer, and filled with the Holy Spirit, you see and discern a lot of evil in the world. And one of the great vortexes of evil is being played out in the courthouses of the world. The courthouses—that last bastion of warfare, the last resort before actual warfare, the kind with guns, bullets and bombs. The blessings, grace and mercy of God are so real to me. But, so is evil. And there is only one way I know to fight it, and that is with God on your side, and with His suggested tools.

One set of *His* tools he gave me is *ddarssa*.

Mist

When Mike left that day of the Summer Solstice, I was pensive. I chatted with the Lord. *Lord, am I doing a good job with my days? Mercy, this is such hard work, I'm always tired, I drink mountains of coffee and I'm always lonely. What else can I say?* Maybe I was feeling sorry for myself. Probably. Anyway, at that moment, I remembered that Friday, back in 1985, and my lunch with Harry Goldberg, when Lydia walked up to me, distraught that she was going to trial, and my suggestion to her as to how to settle her case, written of course, on a standard issue cafeteria-grade white paper napkin. On that particular day, I remember most of the facts of the case, and I remembered a prayer I suggested to her.

At the end of that very day in 1985, at about 4:30 p.m. in the afternoon, when court usually ends for the day, Harry Goldberg and I walked out of the courtroom, and began the process of walking down the long courthouse hall, out the door, and on to the long sidewalk on Grand Avenue, where the trial lawyers with their rolling carts of trial boxes gather out front. Basically, a choreographed exit from the courthouse includes the moment when your associate pulls up to the curb, and you, the other lawyers, and the clients load their boxes into the SUVs to take home for the evening, or, in this case, for the weekend. That's what Harry and I, and my associates were doing when—I heard the woman's voice. And there she was running up to me and Harry.

She was out of breath as she ran up to me. "Tom, do you know that this courthouse has nine floors and a 'million' courtrooms? I looked for you everywhere for the last hour." She caught her breath. "The case settled," she said, and tears were in her eyes. Harry and I went into stoic tough guy mode. "Just like you suggested. I had to thank you. I just had to. I have to admit, it was a miracle running into you at lunch. I have my friend Zoe back. I also have Francie back. And I heard the most beautiful words I've ever heard. They forgave me. I can't wait to start writing again. My head is bursting with ideas for the fourth book, *co-written* with Zoe. But—I had to find you."

She said some more nice things, and gave Harry and me more details. But, she eventually saw that we were tired and we began our pleasant goodbyes.

"Do you believe in miracles?" I couldn't help but ask her.

"You'll have to give me more time on that one. But, I have to admit again, I read the Prayer of Saint Francis."[6]

"Why don't you try praying it sometime?" I asked, as Harry and I started loading boxes into my car. I could see the internal fight with her atheism.

"I'll think about it," was all she could muster.

"Don't think too long, you will need him again, I promise."

"You think so?" she asked.

"Yes. And besides, you owe him one."

"I guess I do, don't I?"

"Yes, you do."

As she walked away, she waved at me—with the standard issue cafeteria-grade white paper napkin (the ultimate paperwork for a good settlement) from our lunch meeting earlier.

Harry and I turned around. He slung his arm around my shoulder and muttered something like: "I think you've got a hot one there, Tom."

I looked down at Harry's shoes. Harry is a tall guy, maybe about six feet four inches. His shoes were so big they reminded me of aircraft carriers.

"Tom!" I heard Lydia shout to me.

"Yes," I sort of yelled back.

"Can I take you to coffee sometime? To thank you," she called.

"I suppose," I yelled.

She stopped to make a point.

"You know, we are a mist, we're here for a little while, and then we are gone—I know that now. I will never waste another day in my life," she called back triumphantly, spun around, and kept walking.

Hmmm, I thought. Where did that come from!?

Did she know she was quoting the Bible?

Somebody else laid that on her heart. It wasn't me. As the years went on, I knew who it was.

T+

---

6 Prayer of Saint Francis. "Lord, make me an instrument of your peace.
   Where there is hatred, let me sow love;
   where there is injury, pardon
   where there is doubt, faith;
   where there is despair, hope;
   where there is darkness, light;
   and where there is sadness, joy.
   O divine Master, grant that I may not so much seek to be consoled as to console;
   to be understood as to understand;
   to be loved as to love.
   For it is in giving that we receive;
   it is in pardoning that we are pardoned;
   and it is in dying that we are born to eternal life."
   Amen.

The Take Away 10
We are a mist, we're here for a little while, then we are gone.

1. Take this moment and number your days. Multiply your age by 365 days in a year. How many days have we spent so far on this earth? Each of us need that sense of how fleeting our life is, and therefore how important is each day of our life. *Show me, O Lord, my life's end and the number of my days; let me know how fleeting is my life.* If we ask Him, the Lord will *teach us to number our days aright, that we may gain a heart of wisdom.*

2. I haven't seen a case, or situation, or a problem, or an addiction, that couldn't be settled on the back of a standard issue cafeteria-grade white paper napkin. And yet I've witnessed the incredible amount of time that people burn up fighting each other, or failing to settle a personal problem or addiction. They are wasting their days, there is no *heart of wisdom.*

3. Blessed are those that reach that simple place in life when they can take a standard issue cafeteria-grade white paper napkin, put a T+ (Trust the Lord) at the top of it, and ask the Lord for a simple list of things they will do *quickly*, to settle the case, the problem in their life, an addiction, or a dispute, or, better still, to reach a goal or a dream.

4. How you get there (the place of peace, and being a peacemaker) is between you and the Lord. For some, just praying the prayer of Saint Francis brought the needed change in their life:

Prayer of Saint Francis.   "Lord, make me an instrument of your peace.
Where there is hatred, let me sow love;
where there is injury, pardon;
where there is doubt, faith;
where there is despair, hope
where there is darkness, light
and where there is sadness, joy
O divine Master, grant that I may not so much seek to be consoled as to console;
to be understood as to understand;
to be loved as to love.
For it is in giving that we receive;
it is in pardoning that we are pardoned;
and it is in dying that we are born to eternal life."
Amen.

Why Did You Strike Me?

Evil plots early and evil plots long

Peace for everyone who does good

I haven't enjoyed life a whole lot, I admit that. I suppose I'm one of those who "groan inwardly."[1] You may be one of those who groan inwardly. It's okay, I find that to be a good sign. You are, most likely, going about the Lord's work. "We ourselves, who have the firstfuits of the Spirit, *groan inwardly* as we wait eagerly for our adoption as sons, the redemption of our bodies."

Groan inwardly, but be at peace.

Peace. That I know. John 14:27 has been with me since shortly after I became a Christian. "Peace I leave with you; my peace I give you. I do not give to you as the world gives. Do not let your hearts be troubled and do not be afraid." That's my verse for a lifetime, one lifespan. My lifespan. I never discovered lasting joy in the midst of all the courtroom battles, but I've known the peace of the Lord that surpasses all understanding.[2] I have tried to always do good, having the sense that God would give me peace if I did good.

He did.

Indeed, there is peace for everyone who does good.[3]

---

1 Romans 8:22-23. "We know that the whole creation has been groaning as in the pains of childbirth right up to the present time. Not only so, but we ourselves, who have the firstfruits of the Spirit, groan inwardly as we wait eagerly for our adoption as sons, the redemption of our bodies."

2 Philippians 4:7. "And the peace of God which transcends all understanding, will guard your hearts and your minds in Christ Jesus."

3 See Romans 2:10. [There is] glory, honor and peace for everyone who does good.

The peace I know is peace with God, and peace in my conscience.[4]

I never accomplished that chirpy, happy person thing I've seen other people display. No, I've been a warrior, a fighter, one that is usually surrounded by hostile forces bent on destroying my client and me. I live in a world of fighting words, cussing, sometimes screaming: judges, lawyers, clients, witnesses, percipient witnesses, expert witnesses, hostile witnesses, rebuttal witnesses, direct-examination, cross-examination, opening statements, closing statements, words, words, words, fight, fight, fight. I didn't find, see much of, or experience much happiness or joy in the midst of all that.

But I did ask the Lord to *send me* and . . . He did.[5]

And, I'm blessed, and I did know and still have: peace, that peace that transcends all understanding, that peace that guards your heart and your mind, and keeps you close to Jesus.

No matter how you see it, or experience it, worldly joy and happiness are fleeting, episodic, they come and go, and have been for me: not reliable, not consistent. For me, peace has had different characteristics, it has been consistent, reliable, and ever present. And on those occasions, when I lost it due to sin or selfishness, I wanted it back, I couldn't live without it. Only God can bring me the type of peace I've had, and still have; it was and is a great gift. It has kept me close to Jesus; nothing else has. A foundation of godly peace, is a good foundation to do battle against: evil. And evil is not something to fear. As a trial lawyer, I had to face down evil (and other things) constantly, and I *felt* fear, lots of it, but I never ran. I stood firm, I could not be moved, budged, or shifted. And if you were my client sitting next to me—I wouldn't let you move either. The d*evil*, the one with the word "evil" built right into his name, wanders the halls of the courthouses, right there along with the lukewarms. But he's just a big bully, and all bullies can be brought down.

In the end, everyone of them is brought down.

Your "one" significant lifespan

A lifespan is an interesting thing. Our lives truly are a mist. And we know that to gain a heart of wisdom we are to "number our days aright."[6] But these verses are never in any way meant to convey a message that would suggest that our lives are "short" and therefore not significant. Quite the contrary, the biblical value of each one of our lives is beyond our comprehension. And, the process of getting closer and closer to God is also a process of realizing just how much he values each

---

4 C. H. Spurgeon, *Spiritual Peace*, A Sermon, No. 300, February 19, 1860. "Peace with God is the treaty; peace in the conscience is the publication of it. Peace with God is the fountain, and peace with conscience is the crystal stream which issues from it. There is a peace decreed in the court of divine justice in heaven; and then there follows as a necessary consequence, as soon as the news is known, a peace in the minor court of human judgment, wherein conscience sits upon the throne to judge us according to our works."

5 Isaiah 6:8. "Then I heard the voice of the Lord saying, 'Whom shall I send? And who will go for us?' And I said, 'Here am I. Send me!'"

6 Psalm 90:12.

one of our lives and how our *one* lifespan is so important to God. In thousands of years of human history, millions of years of other life and earth history, and galaxies of space and time beyond our comprehension, planets and solar systems spreading out far beyond our puny eyesight, great expanses of time, space, nature and science—God chose just *one* lifespan to make his imprint on our lives, an imprint that would last our lifetime and for all eternity, the one lifespan of . . . Jesus. Just one lifespan. Clearly, God values one lifespan. It can all be done, all be finished, and all be blessed, in one lifespan.

It doesn't get more important than that.

That is how important your lifespan is.

Sometimes I think it would be nice to live a life of comfort, going from happiness to happiness, joy to joy—and then get indignant when your happiness or joy is impinged upon. Even famous pastors display that life of outward pretense of the "life is good" hoax. Sorry, I've been the go-to guy when the proverbial stuff—hits the fan. Thirty years of helping people through their most public battles, or their most intimate battles, has led me to know that you simply must seriously discount, or in some cases, toss out any belief that those outward appearances are always real, or even sometimes real.

The acuteness of the developing need to be more and more aware of the presence and risk of evil from without or within should be prominent in your mind.

The toolbox of weapons is in order, and it never changes

I love to do battles alongside fellow warriors. In 2005, when Mike Harrison and Mark Brewer had good cause to do battle with their enemies, they picked up their spiritual weapons first, and with my help, tacked on the procedural weapons including abundant preparation and thereby—they were a force to be reckoned with. They were going to win.

Among other things, I remember Mike and Mark getting their tithing in order.[7] These guys would kneel down and ask the Lord to search their hearts to root out any sin or offensive way in their own lives, before thinking they could presume to have God's power on their side to do battle with their enemies. They would meditate on Psalm 139:23-24.

"Search me, O God, and know my heart;
   test me and know my anxious thoughts.
See if there is any offensive way in me,
   and lead me in the way everlasting."

Mike Harrison and Mark Brewer had both been blessed by God. Their businesses had prospered. They were both good family men, involved in their local communities and were under good pastors. They were, and still are, God's mighty

---

7 Malachi 3:8.

warriors.[8] But they were still hit. Right smack in the face. When I first looked at Mike's case, it looked to me like the enemy had stolen Harrison Interactive's software, formed a huge company, were planning on making a lot of money—and were alleging that Mike had stolen *their* software. That was Blackdog vs. Harrison Interactive.

Mark Brewer ran a major medical supplies company, TAS Medicals. Mark had to sue a group of hospitals, Healthways, Inc., who owed TAS more than $1,000,000 for medical supplies they hadn't paid for. Healthways new defense was to complain about TAS's medical supplies and disparage TAS in the marketplace. Mark felt his company was on the line. They could go bankrupt from the combination of money they were owed, and the negative comments Healthways was making in the marketplace and with TAS's other customers. The Healthways strategy seemed to be that they would stop the disparaging comments if TAS would walk, or significantly reduce the amount of money owed by Healthways. Default and distort was the Healthways' strategy. That was TAS Medicals vs. Healthways.

Both Mike and Mark had, by all outward appearances led good lives, and things were going well—but they were hit. And they had to call me. And even Mike and Mark eventually asked me: Why did they hit me? They are stealing from me, why? They are lying, why? Sometimes there is simply no discernable reason. The victim is an innocent victim.

And sometimes you yourself let the door open and the devil comes roaring in. With one of these guys, that was the case. But it would take me a while to find out.

But, it is particularly hard when wonderful, honest good people get attacked unjustly, for no reason, and for nefarious reasons. And the innocent person says, why me? Even the somewhat innocent person says, why me?

Why did they strike me?

I have to remind them that a greater person than them asked the same question.

Why did you strike me?

Why did you strike me? Even Jesus asked this question. So many times over the years a client or friend would ask me: why did a certain person attack them, or hit them, or abuse them, or divorce them, or sue them, or steal from them, or hurt them in some way? Most of my clients have eventually asked that question or a similar one. The bewilderment or astonishment on their face said it all. Even Jesus asked the same question. Often, my clients already knew the answer, but had to ask the question anyway. Even Jesus knew he had to drink the cup the Father had given him.[9] Jesus had said: "My food is to do the will of him who sent me and to finish his work."[10] *Still*, Jesus asked the question. Even my clients who

---

8 Judges 6:12.
9 John 18:11.
10 John 4:34.

are well-known pastors, went to the best seminaries, still preaching into their seventies, have asked the question. Because, it hurts when someone strikes you. And it hurt Jesus. That's just one of the many reasons I've been able to relate to him all these years. He's real, he does exist, he can be hurt, and he did go through this life experience just like me.

And just like you.

Jesus' first preliminary hearing

After Jesus was arrested, he was taken to a preliminary hearing before Annas who, in the eyes of the Jews, still held the office of high priest because that position was—for life. The Romans had deposed Annas, so the current high priest, Caiaphas, Annas's son-in-law, would make the final decision as to whether Jesus should be tried. Annas questioned Jesus about his disciples and his teaching.[11] This is what happened next:

> "I have spoken openly to the world," Jesus replied to Annas. "I always taught in synagogues or at the temple, where all the Jews come together. I said nothing in secret. Why question me? Ask those who heard me. Surely they know what I said."
> When Jesus said this, one of the officials nearby struck him in the face. "Is this the way you answer the high priest?" he demanded.
> "If I said something wrong," Jesus replied, "testify as to what is wrong. But if I spoke the truth, *why did you strike me*?" Then Annas sent him, still bound, to Caiaphas the high priest.[12]

And that is how so many of my clients felt over the years. If you've been a good person, or a good business partner, or a good spouse, and if you've been honest and spoke the truth, you want to know, why did someone hit you? Oftentimes this is a hard question to answer, and it takes time to find the motive, but so often, the answer is simple: the person is self-seeking, he (or she) rejects the truth, and follows evil. Not too complicated.[13]

When you're a trial lawyer and you have such a heart to settle matters, and settle them quickly, the reason you have that heart is because you know it is in the best interests of your client, and really in the best interests of both parties. Or, if you are just one person trying to resolve a personal problem, it is in your own best interests to settle it quickly. Either way, a quick resolution will be the springboard to moving on with your life, carrying on with your mission, your purpose in life, or—to find a purpose if you don't have one. Resolution is peace. Resolution gets you back to the passion in your life, or puts you in the place to find it.

You can't pursue your passion in the middle of your conflict.

---

11 John 18:19.
12 John 18:20-24.
13 Romans 2:8. "But for those who are self-seeking and who reject the truth and follow evil, there will be wrath and anger."

But, there are those times when you still have a heart to settle matters, and settle them quickly, but you have that heart for a very different reason. You want your client out—*now,* away, as far as possible, from something that you see, something that you recognize, something that is hard to deal with easily. You see something that by its own design is not meant to be seen. That something is *evil.* Evil is present when the driving principle behind the other person is the devil's one and only commandment: *do as thou wilt.* To see it, to understand it, and to combat it, you need to have serious discernment. *For our struggle is not against flesh and blood, but against the rulers, against the authorities, against the powers of this dark world and against the spiritual forces of evil in the heavenly realms.*[14]

So what do you do? We live in a world that does not even believe that evil exists. It's not fun living the life of a trial lawyer, mediator, counselor, and fighter who has looked in the face of evil so many times that he knows it's real—he doesn't have any doubts. It's real, it exists and to fight evil, you better have a whole different skill set. You fight evil with good, and only God is good, the kind of "good" you need to fight evil.

"Do not be overcome by evil, but overcome evil with good."[15]

Jesus' second preliminary hearing

After the first farce of a preliminary hearing, Annas sent Jesus to Caiaphas for a second illegal "hearing," also at night and also in secret. This second hearing went like the first, only worse. Caiaphas the "high priest" said to Jesus: "I charge you under oath by the living God: Tell us if you are the Christ, the Son of God." It's hard being a trial lawyer and reading about someone being so abused liked this. Jesus was treated like scum, he was being tried in the middle of the night, in a secret hearing, with no defense counsel. And, for the most part, he remained silent.

Except when this question was asked, Jesus answered Caiaphas by saying: "Yes, it is as you say. But I say to all of you: In the future you will see the Son of Man sitting at the right hand of the Mighty One and coming on the clouds of heaven."

Jesus would answer when it counted, and his answer has been recorded for eternity. This is what happened next: "Then the high priest tore his clothes and said, 'He has spoken blasphemy! Why do we need any more witnesses? Look, now you have heard the blasphemy. What do you think?'"

"He is worthy of death," they answered.

"Then they spit in his face and struck him with their fists. Others slapped him and said, 'Prophesy to us, Christ. Who hit you?'"[16]

Annas, Caiaphas, and later in the morning at the illegal "trial" before the Sanhedrin, all the chief priests and the members of the Jewish Council would run Jesus through a sham trial with really only one goal in mind: to condemn Jesus to die.

---

14 Ephesians 6:12.
15 Romans 12:21.
16 Matthew 26:63-68.

And that's what they did.

Annas and Caiaphas were evil, and the work of the Sanhedrin was evil. That's what thirty years of trial work will do for you: you know evil when you see it and you call it as you see it. I'm not a Supreme Court Justice, but I know *evil* when I see it, just like Associate Supreme Court Justice Potter Stewart said when he saw hard-core pornography: . . . "I know it when I see it." Annas and Caiaphas cared more about their political ambitions than about their duties and responsibilities as religious leaders, duties that should have required them to take their time to conduct *legal* hearings during the day, not at night, that should have required them to seek out honest witnesses, not false witnesses, that should have required them to insist on and allow a defense for Jesus, instead of determining Jesus' guilt from the start, and most importantly, that should have required them to consider the possible truth of what Jesus said, that he was the "Christ," the Son of God.

And after these two illegal, rushed and predetermined secret hearings at night, all the Sanhedrin did "early in the morning,"[17] was to compound the evil and rubber-stamp the decision of Annas and Caiaphas. Jesus, the most innocent defendant to ever walk on the face of the earth, was condemned to die. I've defended a lot of innocents over the years, but nobody was innocent like Jesus was innocent. He suffered and died for someone else's crime, someone else's sin. Yours and mine.

But still, evil could not and cannot win out in the end.

In this world you will have trouble

Two thousand years later, nothing has changed. And accordingly, we must and need to pray for each other fervently, especially regarding evil, just as Jesus did. John Seventeen relates the important events prior to Jesus being sent before Annas, Caiaphas and the Sanhedrin in Chapter Eighteen. In Chapter Seventeen, Jesus is praying for his disciples, and you and me. I will repeat the whole prayer here, for so many reasons, but mostly because it is Jesus' prayer, these are Jesus' words.

Would it be possible dear reader, for you to really stop and meditate on this prayer of Jesus? To stop everything in your life right now to hear Jesus pray this prayer into your heart:

"Father, the time has come. Glorify your Son, that your Son may glorify you. For you granted him authority over all people that he might give eternal life to all those you have given him. Now this is eternal life: that they may know you, the only true God, and Jesus Christ, whom you have sent. I have brought you glory on earth by *completing the work you gave*

---

17 Matthew 27:1.

me to do. And now, Father, glorify me in your presence with the glory I had with you before the world began.

"I have revealed you to those whom you gave me out of the world, they were yours; you gave them to me and they have obeyed your word. Now they know that everything you have given me comes from you. For I gave them the words you gave me and they accepted them. They knew with certainty that I came from you, and they believed that you sent me. *I pray for them. I am not praying for the world, but for those you have given me, for they are yours.* All I have is yours, and all you have is mine. And glory has come to me through them. I will remain in the world no longer, but they are still in the world, and I am coming to you. Holy Father, *protect them by the power of your name—the name you gave me*—so that they may be one as we are one. While I was with them, I protected them and kept them safe by that name you gave me. None has been lost except the one doomed to destruction so that Scripture would be fulfilled.

"I am coming to you now, but I say these things while I am still in the world, so that they may have the full measure of my joy within them. I have given them your word and the world has hated them, *for they are not of the world any more than I am of the world.* My prayer is not that you take them out of the world but that *you protect them from the evil one. They are not of the world, even as I am not of it.* Sanctify them by the truth; your word is truth. As you sent me into the world, I have sent them into the world. For them I sanctify myself, that they too may be truly sanctified.

"My prayer is not for them alone. I pray also for those who will believe in me through their message, that all of them may be one, Father, just as you are in me and I am in you. May they also be in us so that the world may believe that you have sent me. I have given them the glory that you gave me, that they may be one as we are one: I in them and you in me. May they be brought to complete unity to let the world know that you sent me and have loved them even as you have loved me.

"Father, I want those you have given me to be with me where I am, and to see my glory, the glory you have given me because you loved me before the creation of the world.

"Righteous Father, though the world does not know you, I know you, and they know that you have sent me. I have made you known to them, and will continue to make you known in order that the love you have for me may be in them and that I myself may be in them."
        (Emphasis added.)

In so many ways, when you, or a friend, or a client is facing a tough situation, it is a good thing to read John Chapter Seventeen. Pray to God, and Jesus when facing evil. Take Jesus' prayer as a lesson on how to pray. Sometimes, "we do not know what we ought to pray for, but the Spirit intercedes for us with groans that words cannot express."[18]

As Jesus said at the end of Chapter Sixteen:
"In this world you will have trouble. But take heart! I have overcome the world."[19]

After thirty years of trials, I'm a witness: Jesus has overcome the world. Any victory is possible with Jesus on your side. Are you really going to risk a battle without him on your side?

Do you have a prayer team?

In April 2006, I settled a huge case against a major computer company. A little company called Apple. I was so tired after the case that, as usual, I asked the Lord if I could be done with litigation and trial work. To my amazement, He said "yes." And further said, I would be done in the summer of 2009, July to be exact. I was a little disheartened; I had over three years to go. Three years! And, thirty-four more trials still on the books to complete. Thirty-four! I was wasted. I had no more juice. I was dead. Nothing left. Two of the cases on that list were Mike Harrison's Blackdog vs. Harrison Interactive, and Mark Brewer's TAS Medicals vs. Healthways. They were two of the small cases.

Time to really call in the prayer team.

I don't know what to suggest to those people that are in battles way over their head, if they don't believe in God, and don't believe in prayer. Earlier, I spoke about when the Lord saved me and I was born again. I asked, why did the Lord step in? In one word, "mediocrity." That's what the Lord saved me from, not drugs, not alcohol, not bad living. He saved me from "mediocrity." It has now been more than twenty-five years since I was saved, and I have the advantage of seeing how mediocrity has played out, not with me, but with my friends and colleagues that were not saved, never knew, and still don't know the Lord, and the power of prayer. Most of them are long gone to drugs, alcohol, sex addictions, mental illness, disbarment, and some of them are dead. Some of them are missing. And a few are still standing. The ones that are still standing and are thriving are Christians, and a few are Jewish. Other than that, I don't have any good examples of survivors that survived under their own power. I'm sure there are some, I just don't know them. When the Lord saved me from mediocrity, it might as well have been from alcoholism or drug addiction. From my experience of watching those that lived long lives of mediocrity, the end result is the same. So, I'm very thankful

---

18 Romans 8:26.
19 John 16:33.

to the Lord. My life has been tough, but not mediocre, and not meaningless. And I don't run around searching for meaning or a purpose.

I'm about my Father's business.

And I still have a lot to do.

So, when I was facing thirty-four more trials to do over three years, 2006 to 2009, I called on my prayer team. Because I was up against some mean people; some of whom were just plain evil. Their evil was manifested in some simple ways: they wanted what was best for them, they had no empathy for what they were doing to my client or me, there was no bounds to their deceit, there was no bounds to how they would accomplish their evil goal—and they wrapped up all their actions in a blanket of alleged respectability and an outward appearance of perfection and honesty. And, of course, they had no God in their life. They enjoyed the possibility of taking a good person down . . . just another day in their life. The truly bad guys would eventually threaten my life one way or the other because as you make inroads in exposing their deceit or crime, they would panic, and then they'd threaten me. One of my associates and I would always do the same thing when the threat came in—usually in person at the courthouse: I would look down at my watch and say something like, "Wow, it's 10:00 a.m., the first threat of the day, usually it comes a little earlier." Or I'd look at them, and then at my associate, and say something like: "Wow, it's 2:00 p.m., yours is the third threat of the day, you're a little late." And then I'd say something relatively unpleasant to them, and my associate and I would walk away. My message was, I won't be deterred, I'm going to win, and you won't stop me. I'm taking *you* down.

The 8th Row Prayer Team at my church, the Dream Center in downtown Los Angeles, is a force to be reckoned with. They had always prayed for me, as I did for them, but beginning in April 2006, I really needed prayer. I had no energy left, I was wasted, I was exhausted, I was beat up, and at times I didn't even know it. But my prayer team went to work and they prayed for me—just as fervently as Jesus did. They prayed hard. And, I could feel it. I really could. I rallied. I stuck to my guns, I fought hard, I prepared abundantly. If you have said goodbye to a mediocre life, if you have set your goals high, higher than something you could ever accomplish on your own, then you need God on your side, and you need a prayer team.

Remember, the days are evil.[20]

I got out my napkin, and I wrote down the names of the thirty-four cases. I put the T+ at the top of the napkin. And I began the final lap of my trial lawyer life. I was ready. I had three years to go.

As usual, God had other plans for me. Yes, I was done by the summer of 2009, July to be exact. Just like he said. But, there's more to the story.

---

20 Ephesians 5:15-16. "Be very careful, then, how you live—not as unwise but as wise, making the most of every opportunity, *because the days are evil.*"

Evil plots early and evil plots long

Evil plots early and evil plots long. It always amazed me in the tough cases how long and involved the evil person's plot was. In the Harry Goldberg case, the plaintiffs had planned for a very long time exactly how to take Harry down, take his radio stations and build a case that would destroy him. One memo at a time, one letter at a time, one phone call, one more piece of evidence to indicate that Harry was willing to sell his radio stations at a ridiculously low amount of money, and there was a long paper trail to prove it, the devil's paper trail. I was dealt a serious uphill battle in court. In Mike Harrison's and Mark Brewer's case, same thing. Several years in the planning, and many steps in the process, and hundreds of deceits along the way to set up a perfect "victory" in the end for their evil schemes.[21] Harry Goldberg's case laid the groundwork for many battles to come. By the time I was up to the Mike Harrison and Mark Brewer cases, I had an amazing prayer team, and a full toolbox of weapons at my disposal. And I used them seriously every day. I was going to win both cases, or settle them very favorably for my clients. Period. That's what I *expected.*

I learned a lesson very early in my career: you win the case before it even starts. If I was fortunate enough to be hired by my client as soon as he or she felt there was something wrong, I could immediately build a winning situation. The Lord, at 3:00 a.m., and for the hours thereafter would tell me what to do. I was thwarting the devil, every step of the way. So, you need to act fast if you sense that something is wrong. Don't hesitate. Everything a good lawyer will do for you before the case is started is what you will need to win it. Evil plots early and evil plots long.

Be vigilant.

Do you remember the story of the devil tempting Jesus in the desert? May I give you a trial lawyer's perspective on that? . . . Shortly after Jesus was baptized by John, he was led by the Spirit into the desert to be tempted by the devil.[22] And, every time the devil tempted Jesus, Jesus *threw* Scripture at him. I should say, Jesus *quoted* Scripture. For example, after fasting forty days and forty nights, Jesus was hungry. "The Tempter came to him and said, "If you are the Son of God, tell these stones to become bread."

Jesus answered, "It is written: 'Man does not live on bread alone, but on every word that comes from the mouth of God.'" Jesus was tempted two more times in the desert, and each time Jesus threw Scripture at the devil. And in Luke 4:13, the Bible says: "When the devil had finished all this tempting, he left him until an opportune time."

Usually at this point, the preacher, or anyone discussing this story will marvel at the fact that the devil *never* tempted Jesus again. Nowhere in the Bible is it

---

21 Psalm 83:3. "With cunning they conspire against your people; they plot against those you cherish."
22 See Matthew, chapter 4.

written that the devil approached Jesus to try again to tempt him. The power of Jesus throwing Scripture at the devil caused the devil to go away, and never come back again to tempt Jesus.

Well, I'm a trial lawyer, so the first thing I think is: *of course not, the devil wouldn't come back and try that again, he tried it three times and each time Jesus had a killer comeback.*

The devil would try something else.

Actually, I know what the devil did.

The devil called up Caiaphas and Annas, and they picked up the phone.

They picked up where the devil left off.

T+

The Take Away 11
Even Jesus wanted to know, "why did you strike me?"

1. So many times over the years a client or friend would ask me: why did a certain person attack them, or hit them, or abuse them, or divorce them, or sue them, or steal from them, or hurt them in some way? Most of my clients have eventually asked that question or a similar one. The bewilderment or astonishment on their face said it all. *Even Jesus asked the same question.*

2. After Jesus was arrested, He was taken to a preliminary hearing before Annas. Annas questioned Jesus about his disciples and his teaching. This is what happened next:
   "I have spoken openly to the world," Jesus replied to Annas. "I always taught in synagogues or at the temple, where all the Jews come together. I said nothing in secret. Why question me? Ask those who heard me. Surely they know what I said."
   When Jesus said this, one of the officials nearby struck him in the face. "Is this the way you answer the high priest?" he demanded.
   "If I said something wrong," Jesus replied, "testify as to what is wrong. But if I spoke the truth, *why did you strike me?*"

3. It is an understatement to say that Jesus faced trouble in His life on Earth, and so shall we. But, it's okay, as Jesus said: *In this world you will have trouble. But take heart! I have overcome the world.* After thirty years of trials, I'm a witness: Jesus has overcome the world. Any victory is possible with Jesus on your side. Are you really going to risk going into a battle without Him on your side?

4. **Evil plots early and evil plots long**. It always amazes me in the tough cases how long and involved the evil person's, or the devil's, plot was. So what do you do? We live in a world that does not even believe that evil exists. It's not fun living the life of a trial lawyer, mediator, counselor, and fighter that has looked in the face of evil so many times that—he knows it's real, he doesn't have any doubts. It's real, it exists and to fight evil, you better have a whole different skill set. You fight evil with good, and only God is good, the kind of "good" you need to fight evil. *There is peace for everyone who does good.*

   "Do not be overcome by evil, but overcome evil with good."
   Romans 12:21.

Striking Back

*The problem of evil is a problem for
the other side*

*Jesus was no pacifist
The tunic collectors*

On a Monday in January 2006, Dr. Ezra Ezekiel came to my offices, sat on my leather sofa and cried. Once again, I felt so deeply in my spirit, here I am *for such a time as this*. He had come to the right place; and I was going to help him. Dr. Ezra thought he was going to lose his five medical clinics, his life's work, his passion, and his dream, because of a few mistakes he made with some Russian lenders. Dr. Ezekiel is African-American. Which normally would be irrelevant, except that those that were trying to take him down were racist, and prejudiced. That was obvious, they actually had put it in writing to him. Dr. Ezra had definitely come to the right place. I was going to strike back, and they were going to lose. Period. That's what I *expected*. In April 2006, Dr. Ezra's case was one of the thirty-four cases I still had scheduled to complete before July 2009, when the Lord said I could lay down my sword. Just when the weight of thirty-four cases to go left me feeling exhausted, burned out, wasted, that God thing happened. He reminded me of my source of strength, and I was fired up again, for such a time as this.

As I've said, the Bible is a story of conflict, which is why I sometimes see it as one long trial: Genesis includes the opening statement and first introduction of evidence, and Revelation the closing statement and judgment. One long arc of resolution. And in between there is book after book, chapter after chapter, verse after verse, and witness after witness presented. As a trial lawyer, I see the Bible as the ultimate trial, the ultimate presentation of evidence, evidence stacked up century after century. Good versus evil in every possible way. And one thing is for sure, and one thing is clear, good wins in the end, evil loses, there is a God, his son is Jesus, and he is on our side. Which, in a way, makes all my challenges and trials look quite small.

This is not a discussion for the lukewarms exposed in Revelation 3:15-16. Those passionless people that inhabit the courthouses, and other places of the world, wasting their precious time on earth, devoting themselves to storing up treasures on earth: the "tunic collectors," I call them. In case you're wondering, in case you care, Jesus was *not* a pacifist. I promise you that. To call him a pacifist would, to me, be the same as calling him a "lukewarm." In the one long trial previously noted, Jesus was and is the great mediator between God and man. As I've cited previously: "For there is one God and one mediator between God and men, the man Christ Jesus, who gave himself as a ransom for all men—the testimony given in its proper time."[1] Someone who gives himself as a ransom for all men, is not a pacifist. With Jesus at your side, you know you don't have a pacifist backing you up at trial. You don't want a pacifist backing you up on whatever challenge or problem you have.

To support an argument that Jesus is a pacifist, I'm always amused when people cite to me verses such as: Luke 6:29, "If someone strikes you on one cheek, turn to him the other also. If someone takes your cloak, do not stop him from taking your tunic." Or, Matthew 5:41, "If someone forces you to go one mile, go with him two miles."

My first response is usually something like: *pardon me while I yawn.*

Then I say something like: "Are you kidding? My clients are the type that have already turned the other cheek, have already given up their tunic and much more, and have already gone the extra mile or more—and it was not enough.

And they'd still give *more!*"

I remember Doug, my friend and client who, before being sued, had already turned the other cheek to insult after insult, had given up tunic after tunic in time, money, and resources, and gone many extra miles, but it wasn't enough. The other side saw him as weak, as easy pickings, so they were going to go all out after him, his whole business, everything. Believe me, in Dr. Ezra's case, the other side also wanted everything. Basically speaking, the evil ones come *only* to steal and kill and destroy, or to put it another way: to wipe you out.[2] They are *only* coming to do that, nothing else.

My clients are peacemakers. But, as I've said, what the evil ones fail to see is that: *If they know you're a peacemaker, they should know they're in trouble.* But they don't, and the reason is simple, and it is played out in trial after trial, and throughout the Bible: the first act of deceit is to deceive yourself. Evil people don't know that they should prepare for burning coals to be heaped on their

---

1 1 Timothy 2:5.
2 John 10:10. "The thief comes only to steal and kill and destroy."

heads.[3] Doug was the type, like so many of my clients, that showed love toward his enemies,[4] and did so in many ways. But the "love" was misread, and the Lord, the great equalizer of the accounts of man, would surely step in.

The "tunic collectors." Those are the lukewarms that use the court system to extort money and other things from people that are forced to pay up so that they can get back to their lives of purpose and passion. We lawyers see good people and companies make "nuisance value" settlements all the time. The plaintiffs have no case, but the good guys pay 'em off anyway. They give up their "tunic," they "turn the other cheek," they "go the extra mile." But they, the good ones, the blessed, get blessed even more by life, and by God when they settle anyway. And, as to the tunic collectors, well, I'll bet you've seen them or experienced them yourself. These are the ones who marvel over their trite victories in court, their extortions, their swift negotiations to cheat someone out of a fair price for their goods and services. I believe there is a special place in hell for the tunic collectors, the ones that have persistently made other peoples' lives miserable on a short-term basis, possibly a long-term basis. These are the "pros" at attacking people at low range, so that even if they crash, they survive and move on to their next victim. You could erase at least a third of the pending civil cases if the tunic collectors would just apologize to their victims, and then go home.

Be careful that you are never a tunic collector, or someone that occasionally slips into tunic collection mode. I'm older now, especially in "lawyer" years; I've seen how the mediocrity of tunic collection plays out over the years. Those people are miserable, lonely, depressed souls, with no hope. One easy sign of a tunic collector is that they are hoarders. They don't follow God's principles of tithing and giving. They hoard. Believe me, you don't have to take revenge on people like that. Revenge is for the Lord, and it is not a pretty picture. As the Lord said: "Do not take revenge, my friends, but leave room for God's wrath, for it is written: 'It is mine to avenge; I will repay.'"[5] The tunic collectors are the small timers, storing up the wrath of God. If only they would heed the words of Paul, one of the Bible's ultimate repentants: "But because of your stubbornness and your unrepentant heart, you are storing up wrath against yourself for the day of God's wrath, when his righteous judgment will be revealed."[6]

And that is why I have to admit, I love courthouses and rehab centers. Courthouses are the crossroads of humanity. You can easily see those that have stored up wrath against themselves, and those that have stored up treasures in heaven. In rehab centers, it's the same thing. Because, even though someone has to fight their way through an addiction, you can see those that have stored up a

---

3 Proverbs 25:21-22. "If your enemy is hungry, give him food to eat; if he is thirsty, give him water to drink. In doing this, you will heap burning coals on his head, and the Lord will reward you."
4 Matthew 5:44. "But I tell you: Love your enemies and pray for those who persecute you, that you may be sons of your Father in heaven."
5 Deuteronomy. 32:35.
6 Romans 2:5.

little treasure in heaven, even if it is *just a little*. You can see God swoop in to help all he can. You can see the person's spirit come alive; you just want to be around people like that, they are a blessing. And, you can see the ones that have stored up wrath. I know those types well. As they come out of their addiction, and see what they've done, the fight is much harder. We put them on suicide watch. And pray hard that they find Jesus quickly.

Avoid the tunic collectors, those that slowly store up the wrath of God. They are never worth your valuable time and energy. Look at their "wealth," if they have any, and think of Matthew 6:19: "Do not store up for yourselves treasures on earth, where moth and rust destroy, and where thieves break in and steal."

And, more accurately, look at Habakkuk 2:6:

"Woe to him who piles up stolen goods
and makes himself wealthy by extortion!"

My dad's friends

My father was a physicist. He worked on a lot of missile and space projects. I'm sure I inherited a lot of his confidence, brashness, sassiness, and fondness for repartee. I've also inherited his inability to keep tabs on it. When I was a kid, his scientist friends would come over to our house and they'd all sit at the dining room table, analyzing something, talking about something, drawing equations on pads, discussing, discussing more, and smoking. I remember that they all smoked. And billowing clouds of smoke would rise up from the table, and somehow every gesture they made included a filter-less cigarette, with names like "Lucky Strike" and "Chesterfield," tucked between their two fingers as they made their point on a potential mathematical solution. Then they'd take a sip of coffee, or for some, a beer, and they'd carry on trying to figure out how to make something work. It could be the lunar rover, or a concept for a space shuttle, or how satellites would work, or missile technology.

It didn't take long for me, as a kid, to figure out that my dad's scientist friends were Jewish. Most of them. And my Dad loved them and I was impressed by how much they loved my Dad. My Dad told me everything he knew about Jewish history, with a particular emphasis on the founding of the Jewish state in 1948 and the wars that followed. We were Catholic. I wondered if I had been born into the wrong tribe. Thanks to my father, I saw the truth and evidence of Genesis 12:2-3: "I will make you into a great nation and I will bless you; I will make your name great, and you will be a blessing. I will bless those who bless you, and whoever curses you I will curse." The Jews had had every kind of challenge and evil possible thrown at them, and they still survived, and they still prospered. They were truly blessed, and I believed they were a blessing to my family and me. The sense of purpose that drove those guys sitting around our dining room table was mind-boggling to me. Everything was ultimately solvable, everything was ultimately overcome. These guys were the ultimate overcomers. The history of the Jews shows us that.

In the summer of my twelfth year of life, I decided to become a lawyer. My dad and his buddies could do the most amazing math equations right in their heads, logarithms, anything, and they certainly didn't need those stupid cheating devices that started to come out—calculators. I just couldn't do math like those guys, but mercy, could I theorize, could I argue, and could I debate. And, of course, I was always "right." And in my little Catholic head, I figured I was already about my Father's business. I had a purpose. Later, I was to find out about another twelve-year-old that was about his Father's business at that age.[7] The plan for my life certainly felt sealed long before I arrived on this earth. I was a fighter; I would fight with words and reasoning. And I would fight hard. This was about survival.

So it only makes sense that many years later I was offered a job to work for a prominent Century City law firm headed up by Max Greenberg and Herb Bernhardt. I felt right at home. I was twenty-seven years old, and all I did was litigation and trials, and help Max fight for the Anti-Defamation League. Max made me feel special. I liked working on the Anti-Defamation matters that ranged from intense conspiratorial intrigues that we solved, to pathetic small time bigots, like a bar owner that had a sign up over his microwave oven: *hotdogs and Jews only*. Let's just say, we ran him out of business. One day after our latest victory for the ADL, I was sitting in Max's office, which was a bit like a throne room and I said: "Max, it seems to me that ultimately, the problem of evil is a problem for the other side." He looked at me with a furrowed brow and said something profound like: "Hmmm." And he nodded up and down. *He agreed.*

It happened to be Purim for my Jewish friends.

Purim; Gallows built for the just are used to hang the unjust

I was thinking about Max, and Purim, when Dr. Ezra Ezekiel was sitting on my sofa in January 2006. Max would have said: Well, here we are again, evil people who have been plotting a long time, believe they have set it up perfectly, believe they can't lose, believe they will greatly prosper, are set to hang Dr. Ezra, but instead—we are going to hang them, on the gallows they built, seventy-five feet in the air. And they don't know it. But we do. And Max would have taken a long, slow breath and said by way of an afterthought, while lighting up his pipe: "Hmmm, *for such a time as this.*"

Dr. Ezekiel had already received numerous racist letters from opposing counsel, Chris Hatch. Hatch's clients, Georgy Tarasov and his Russian partners had lent the good doctor several hundred thousand dollars, but as far as I could tell, Dr. Ezra had paid it back. But Tarasov wanted more, and he had the signed documents to back him up. At least in Harry Goldberg's case, Harry hadn't signed

7 Luke 2:41-49.

an actual contract, just deal memos. But in Dr. Ezekiel's case, he had actually signed documents that gave half of his ownership in five medical clinics to the Russians, Tarasov's group. And in one contract in particular, a supposed "management contract," it did appear to give away half of the doctor's practice to Tarasov's Russian group. I did a long "hmmm," just like Max would do, looked at Dr. Ezra and told him, "Don't worry, I'll get the contract thrown out and we will beat these scumbags." We were dealing with plain evil. I saw Hatch as a snake, and Tarasov's group, the Russians, as scorpions, and I had every intention of trampling on them.

"I have given you authority to trample on snakes and scorpions and to overcome all the power of the enemy; nothing will harm you."[8]

If God gives you the authority, use it; He wants you to use it.

I have defended a lot of doctors and hospitals over the years. Did I say thirty years? You know the cliché: proper diagnosis is 90 percent of the cure. Similarly, you don't make rash decisions about who is evil and who isn't. The level of discernment needed to fight these battles is crucial. You must stay prayed up. The devil is a worthy adversary in a "worldly" sense. The devil is worthy of worldly battles, but very defeatable. So get your diagnosis right or you're not a good doctor, and certainly not a good lawyer.

For Max, and most people familiar with the story, Haman, from the book of Esther, is the archetype of evil. Haman was an Agagite, a descendant of Agag, king of the Amalekites. The Amalekites were ancient enemies of the Israelites. In 474 B.C., the Persian King Xerxes honored Haman, elevating him and giving him a seat of honor higher than that of all the other nobles. "All the royal officials at the king's gate knelt down and paid honor to Haman, for the king had commanded this concerning him. But Mordecai would not kneel down or pay him honor."[9] This enraged Haman, and he and his wife Zeresh determined to kill not just Mordecai, but to kill all of Mordecai's people, the Jews, throughout the whole kingdom of Xerxes. Haman cast the "Purim" (that is, the lots) to determine the best day to carry out his plot to kill Mordecai and all the Jews. Haman was already setting into motion the very events that would bring about his own downfall, not that of the Jews.

The story of Haman should be written on the subway walls, and especially the courthouse walls.

Haman convinces King Xerxes to issue a decree to all of the king's provinces to annihilate all the Jews—young and old, women and little children—on a single day, the thirteenth day of the twelfth month and to plunder their goods.[10] Now Mordecai was a righteous Jew, who had already earlier foiled a plot to assassinate King Xerxes. Furthermore, when Esther's mother and father died, Mordecai had

8 Luke 10:19.
9 Esther 3:2.
10 Esther 3:13.

taken Esther as his own daughter. Esther, "lovely in form and features," eventually becomes queen, replacing the previous Queen Vashti who was dethroned after an act of disrespect to the king, an act that would be considered quite tame by today's standards. In any event, God is in control, and Esther, a Jew, ends up becoming queen in a Persian kingdom.

As Haman plots, God intervenes.

When Mordecai and the Jews learn of King Xerxes decree, "there is great mourning among the Jews, with fasting, weeping and wailing."[11] Mordecai tries to get a message to Queen Esther, to go before the King and beg for mercy and plead with him for her people. But she sends back to Mordecai the following message:

"All the king's officials and the people of the royal provinces know that for any man or woman who approaches the king in the inner court without being summoned the king has but one law: that he be put to death. The only exception to this is for the king to extend the royal scepter to him and spare his life. But thirty days have passed since I was called to go to the king."[12]

When Esther's message was repeated to Mordecai, he sent back this message, a message for all time:

"Do not think that because you are in the king's house you alone of all the Jews will escape. For if you remain silent at this time, relief and deliverance for the Jews will arise from another place, but you and your father's family will perish. And who knows but that you have come to royal position *for such a time as this*?"

Esther replies to Mordecai, asks that the Jews fast for her, and tells him that she will go to the king, even though it is against the law, "and if I perish, I perish."[13]

But when Esther approached, the king was pleased with her, he held out to her the gold scepter and Esther touched the tip of it. She would not perish. The king asked Esther, "What is it, Queen Esther? What is your request? Even up to half the kingdom, it will be given to you."

"If it pleases the king," replied Esther, "let the king, together with Haman, come today to a banquet I have prepared for him."

"Bring Haman at once," the king said, "so that we may do what Esther asks."

Pride comes before the fall.[14] Haman doesn't see it coming. Haman attends the *exclusive* banquet, and indeed, gets the invitation from Queen Esther to attend another one the next day. "Haman went out that day happy and in high spirits." But, once again he sees Mordecai who "neither rose nor showed fear in his

---

11 Esther 4:3.
12 Esther 4:11.
13 Esther 4:15-16.
14 Proverbs 16:18.

presence." Mordecai refused to bow down to the wicked Haman, such an act of bowing was equivalent to acknowledging him as a god. Mordecai worshiped God alone. Haman's wife Zeresh and all his friends tell this to Haman: "Have a gallows built, seventy-five feet high, and ask the king in the morning to have Mordecai hanged on it. Then go with the king to the dinner and be happy."[15] Haman likes the bad advice, and takes it.

He has the gallows built.

For my new client, and soon-to-be-friend, Dr. Ezra Ezekiel, a still small voice told me that the Russian's lawyer, Chris Hatch, drafted the management contract that they were going to use to take away half of Dr. Ezekiel's practice, and eventually destroy it. I saw the "management contract" as the "gallows," and I intended to use it against them, *seriously* against them.

King Xerxes can't sleep at all the right times. The night after the first banquet he, by *coincidence*, decides to have a book read to him of the chronicles of his reign. He becomes aware of the time that Mordecai thwarted an assassination plot against the king. He learns that nothing was done to honor and recognize Mordecai and when Haman appears in the court the next morning asks Haman: "What should be done for the man the king delights to honor?" And, of course Haman, the prideful one, thinks to himself, "Who is there that the king would rather honor than me?"

This is the type of pride I've seen in many a litigant as they approach a trial. Booming confidence that their scam, their evil, will pay off. They have it all figured out. They continue to store up wrath.

Of course Haman, thinking the honor was for himself, describes an elaborate public display of recognition "for the man the king delights to honor." But the man is not Haman, it is Mordecai, and Haman is forced to lead the procession in which Mordecai is honored, not Haman.

At the second banquet the next day with King Xerxes and Haman, Queen Esther finally makes her request to the king, that she and her people be spared, from "destruction, slaughter and annihilation." And she identifies the man behind the plot, telling the king that "the adversary and enemy is this vile Haman."[16] The king was outraged and his attendants tell him, "A gallows seventy-five feet high stands by Haman's house. He had it made for Mordecai, who spoke up to help the king."

The king said, "Hang him on it!"

"So they hanged Haman on the gallows he had prepared for Mordecai. Then the king's fury subsided."[17]

---

15 Esther 5:14.
16 Esther 7:6.
17 Esther 7:9-10. See also Psalm 7:15-16, "He who digs a hole and scoops it out falls into the pit he has made. The trouble he causes recoils on himself; his violence comes down on his own head."

"If a man digs a pit, he will fall into it; if a man rolls a stone, it will roll back on him."[18] The Jews celebrate Purim, the day of their survival from extermination, on the fourteenth day of Adar, which is usually in March. The thirteenth day of Adar is the day that Haman chose to kill all the Jews; instead, it was both the day of the Jews' deliverance and the day that they struck down their enemies, including the ten sons of Haman.

No weapon formed against you shall prosper

It's amazing to me how a contract can be a weapon. It can be a weapon formed against someone to destroy them, destroy their livelihood, destroy their hope. I was never the go-to lawyer for someone because that person supposedly had a potential claim against someone, and even the potential chance to win some money from them in court. No, those were the cases for the lukewarms, the guys without better things to do in their lives. But, bring to me a case where you have been wronged by an evildoer, who had formed a weapon against you so that they could prosper, then I was your man, your lawyer, because I hate evil.[19] I saw those battles as needing both legal weapons, and spiritual weapons, and I felt that God gave those to me, both directly through his Holy Spirit, the Counselor, and through his God-inspired toolbox, the Bible.

When you're a spirit-filled trial lawyer, living a life in courthouses, you see the weapons formed against people. In ancient times they could be anything including the gallows. In modern times they can still be anything, including contracts. In Dr. Ezekiel's case, the weapon formed against him was the "management contract," designed so that Tarasov's group would prosper greatly beyond anything reasonable for a loan that had already been paid back, and further designed to destroy Dr. Ezekiel's lifelong professional dreams. It was a "perfect" weapon of the devil. Except that Dr. Ezekiel was referred to me for such a time as this. And that was the beginning of the end for Tarasov and his lawyer—at least with respect to their actions against Dr. Ezekiel. As the Lord declared, and still declares today: "No weapon that is forged against thee shall prosper; and every tongue that shall rise against thee in judgment thou shalt condemn."[20]

I sent my settlement letters; I did all I could to get Hatch and the Russians to settle. But no way, they wanted a huge amount of money and half of the medical practice. I took the truthful position, the money had been paid back, they, as non-doctors, could not legally own a medical practice, and the "management contract" was unenforceable and would be voided by the court. Still, Dr. Ezekiel and I continued to send our nice and pleasant business settlement offers, not privileged, that would later be introduced in evidence against them. It would

---

18 Proverbs 26:27. See also Proverbs 1:18, "These men lie in wait for their own blood; they waylay only themselves!"
19 Psalm 97:10. "Let those who love the Lord hate evil, for he guards the lives of his faithful ones and delivers them from the hand of the wicked."
20 Isaiah 54:17 (KJV).

take twelve months to get to trial. I would again, be spending a lot of time at my favorite coffee shop. It was the same story, meeting early every morning with Dr. Ezekiel before the start of the day in court, often sitting at the same place I had sat with Harry Goldberg, twenty-two years before. Same tools, same 8-to-3 rule, same Counselor helping all day and all night. I expected to beat them. I was going to use the contract to hang them.

The walk-away moment

On the day of the trial the judge did the typical thing, he sent us to mediation for one last shot at settling the case. Dr. Ezekiel was his usual good self. He made generous and fair offers, mostly to avoid the cost and pain of going through a long jury trial. Win or lose (but we don't expect to lose) a trial is expensive. But, the other side wouldn't accept the offers. They wanted cash, plus half the practice. Under no circumstances would we give them, or would they get, half the practice. That was the deal breaker. My associate, Susan Chen was with us throughout the trial. We were "abundantly" prepared, and I had spoken out Mark 11:22 many, many times against the snake and his scorpion clients.

Hatch was a racist. I've always been amazed at these guys when I've come across them. The depth of arrogance is hard to imagine, except that they are so possessed, they can't see the light. Dr. Ezekiel had made one last "best and final offer" to the other side and they actually were considering it. Dr. Ezekiel had actually offered them $250,000 to walk away. That was an amazing deal if they took it. There came a moment, when Hatch was doing his best to make a pitch that his clients deserved more, plus a "piece" of the practice. In the middle of his pitch, he alluded to my client's color, and the way he alluded to it was disgusting and unrepeatable here. And then he further suggested that because of that, they would win. You see this kind of garbage on occasion, more than you'd like. This conduct is "self-condemning." I was down the hall from our court-room when Hatch made his comments to me. I was so mad, so filled with disgust, I had to walk away fast; I figured I might haul off and hit him as hard as I could. But I had another way to hit him. Dr. Ezekiel and my associate Susan saw my demeanor as I returned. I called them over, then I walked up to Georgy Tarasov and his scumbag partners and said: "Remember this moment, you just walked away from $250,000. The offer is off the table—forever." There are all types of walk-away moments in litigation. Once the moment has occurred, I've never returned. Or, I should say, I never heard the Lord tell me to return. If he ever told me to return, I would, I would have listened. I'm a pretty good listener.

Whoever attacks you will surrender to you

A trial is no place for lack of confidence. If you've litigated enough cases you figure you can learn and do just about anything. I remember when I did medical malpractice defense. You had to know the surgical procedure inside and out; I learned it so well, I actually thought I could do the surgery. Thank God I was never put to the test. Godly confidence is a good thing because no matter what happened, I would never budge unless the Lord told me to. And he would tell me, if he wanted to. The first ten days of the Dr. Ezekiel trial went very well. On the tenth day, Hatch and his Russians finally rested. I brought a motion for a directed verdict to throw out the management contract. Just as I thought, the contract had been drafted by Hatch. And if the contract was, as I believed, unenforceable, then not only would I have gutted a major part of the plaintiff's case, Hatch would look like a fool because he drafted an unenforceable contract. He may have committed legal malpractice.

There is an interesting point in the Esther story that I see played out a lot in court, and sometimes in life. At the second banquet with the king and Haman, Queen Esther finally makes her request to the king, that she and her people be spared, and she exposes Haman as the vile man that he is. The king is so outraged that he got up, left his wine and went out into the palace.[21] As the story goes, Haman stays back with the queen, and begs Esther for his life. There is nothing to indicate that Esther responded. It gets worse for Haman as it usually does for those that eventually self-condemn. "Just as the king returned from the palace garden to the banquet hall, Haman was falling on the couch where Esther was reclining. The king exclaimed, 'Will he even molest the queen while she is with me in the house?'"[22] The next words out the king's mouth were to—hang Haman on the gallows he built for Mordecai.

"You may be sure that such a man is warped and sinful; he is self-condemned."[23]

I brought the motion with the help of my very competent associate Susan Chen. It was a very long oral argument before the judge. I argued, Hatch defended, I responded. And the judge ruled from the bench: We won, she threw out the management agreement, the whole thing. The case wasn't totally over, but a huge part of Tarasov's case against my client was thrown out. It was a huge victory, and we hadn't even started our defense, hadn't even called our first defense witness. As Dr. Ezekiel, Susan Chen and I left the courtroom late that Friday afternoon, I looked at Susan and said, "when do you think we'll get the call?" She has tried cases with me before. She knew what I meant. She said, "tomorrow afternoon, the office telephone will ring. Hatch knows *now*, that you work Saturdays." Hatch would indeed, call me Saturday and beg for his life; he would beg to settle, he would beg to see if he could get our old settlement offer out of us, or even a reduced settlement offer.

I said the usual thing: "See you in court on Monday."

"Whoever attacks you will surrender to you."[24]

---

21 Esther 7:6-7.
22 Esther 7:8-9.
23 Titus 3:11.
24 Isaiah 54:15. "If anyone does attack you, it will not be my doing; whoever attacks you will surrender to you."

I have two pastors, Tommy and Matthew Barnett. Tommy is Matthew's father. He's in his seventies. He knows from whence he came. One thing he said to me once applied right here and now: "Most men compete instead of complete." I've wondered on occasion if Pastor Tommy could appreciate the various places I would apply his quote? Well, for now, I was going to apply it to this case.

I intended to *complete* this trial. Dr. Ezekiel was in total agreement.

On Monday, I would start to put on Dr. Ezekiel's defense. I wasn't worried.

The problem of evil is a problem for the other side.

T+

The Take Away 12
The problem of evil is a problem for the other side.

1. I saw this endless times over thirty plus years of battles: the trouble a man causes another recoils on himself. Psalm 7:15-16 says: *He who digs a hole and scoops it out falls into the pit he has made. The trouble he causes recoils on himself; his violence comes down on his own head.* **The problem of evil is a problem for the other side, the one who caused it, the one who perpetrated it, the one who thought he would get away with it.** The bottom line is always the same: you are accountable.

2. **Jesus was no pacifist, and neither should you be.** The Bible is a story of conflict, which is why I sometimes see it as one long trial. With Genesis at the beginning and Revelation at the end, the Bible is one long arc of resolution. And one thing is for sure, and one thing is clear: good wins in the end, evil loses, there is a God, his son is Jesus, He is on our side, and He is on your side. In this one long trial, Jesus was and is the great mediator between God and man. "For there is one God and one mediator between God and men, the man Christ Jesus, who gave himself as a ransom for all men—the testimony given in its proper time." Someone who gives himself as a ransom for all men, is not a pacifist. Jesus is on your side, and he is *not* a pacifist.

3. You have been called *for such a time as this*. The story of Haman from the Book of Esther, should be written on the subway walls, and especially the courthouse walls. Haman, the archetype of evil, had plotted to kill the honorable and godly man Mordecai and all of Mordecai's people, the Jews, throughout the kingdom of Xerxes. But God is in control, and Esther, a Jew, ends up becoming the queen of the Persian kingdom. As Haman plotted, God intervened. Eventually, Mordecai sent a message for all the ages to Esther:
   "Do not think that because you are in the king's house you alone of all the Jews will escape. For if you remain silent at this time, relief and deliverance for the Jews will arise from another place, but you and your father's family will perish. And who knows but that you have come to royal position *for such a time as this*?" Esther chooses to put her life on the line, and through her actions Mordecai and the Jews are saved.
   Haman, the evil one, ends up being hung on the gallows, seventy-five feet high, that he had built to hang Mordecai.

4. **The problem of evil is a problem for the other side.** Psalm 97:10 says, *Let those who love the Lord hate evil, for he guards the lives of his faithful ones and delivers them from the hand of the wicked.*

The Lord Is a Warrior

ddarssa

Watch and pray

There comes a time in a trial when, surprisingly, things seem to be going so well, you wonder why you worried so much. A warrior, like me, knows why it's going so well. To us, the worst temptation would be to let our guard down. We *never* let our guard down. Our spirit *is* willing. We don't get tired. We don't get complacent.[1] We're the watch and pray generation. As Jesus said: "Watch and pray so that you will not fall into t emptation. The spirit is willing, but the body is weak."[2] And, no, we don't "worry."

Call it a focused concern. A *fierce* concern.

While I was in the Dr. Ezekiel trial, the judge would always give us a morning and afternoon break, and a ninety-minute lunch break. My team and Dr. Ezekiel would go up to the ninth floor cafeteria with lots of space to spread out and work. While I was in trial for Dr. Ezekiel, my friend and fellow lawyer, Abby Neilson, was also in trial, and he and his client would do the same thing, come up to the ninth floor cafeteria and work on their case through lunch. It was good to see Abby, because he was another lawyer that had a well-developed biblical toolbox, and he'd be working and praying all through lunch.

Abby and I were alike. We weren't passive "believers" in God that occasionally read the Bible and went to church. No, we needed serious help, and we had to work the tools, i.e. the verses of the Bible, that God meant for us to work with, so that we could have victory. We had to pray; we prayed hard. We had to listen to

---

1 Proverbs 1:32-33. "For the waywardness of the simple will kill them, and the complacency of fools will destroy them; but whoever listens to me ["Wisdom"; the mind of God revealed] will live in safety and be at ease, without fear of harm."
2 Matthew 26:41.

God; we listened hard. We didn't have an "active" faith, we had an "action" faith. We believe in the inerrancy of the Bible. Abby and I know, there is authority in those words, the words of the Bible. We relied on it. The *authority*. We had to. *We know there is authority in the Word of God and we use it with authority.³* Indeed, we believe that we are to speak the Word of God as one who commands. And we know that "the weapons we fight with are not weapons of the world. On the contrary, they have divine power to demolish strongholds."⁴

Abby's toolbox focused on Ephesians 6, *The Armor of God*. On Monday, the eleventh day of Dr. Ezekiel's trial, at lunchtime, I wandered over to where Abby and his client were hunkered down. Abby and I took a short walk. We talked about our cases, mostly what stage of the case we were in, and then reminded each other to stay focused on our toolbox, our Bible verses, so we would win. Like me, Abby had been a trial lawyer a long time. His Senior Partner was also Jesus Christ. On trial days, Abby gets up very early and prays, and then for his final preparation for trial, he meditates on Ephesians 6:10-13:

"Finally, be strong in the Lord and in his mighty power. Put on the full armor of God so that you can take your stand against the devil's schemes. For our struggle is not against flesh and blood, but against the rulers, against the authorities, against the powers of this dark world and against the spiritual forces of evil in the heavenly realms. Therefore put on the full armor of God, so that when the day of evil comes, you may be able to stand your ground, and after you have done everything, to stand."

The Lord, does not, I repeat, *does not*, let you use his tools for anything less than a totally righteous cause. I know Abby's history. He is righteous, and he has fought righteous causes. "The man is righteous; he will surely live."⁵. After meditating on those verses in Ephesians, Abby would then spiritually put on each piece of God's armor. He would take a deep breath at this point, and picture each piece of armor, in place on his body, in his life, and with the case he was fighting. First, the belt of truth, and he would buckle it around his waist; second, the breastplate of righteousness, and he would fasten in place; third, the footwear, and he would fit his feet with the readiness that comes from the gospel of peace. Abby knows, as I know, all trials come down to one word: trustworthiness.⁶ The judge and jury must trust you, your client, your witnesses, and everything said on your side of the case.

And Abby was only half done.

---

3 Titus 2:15. "Encourage and rebuke with all authority."
4 2 Corinthians 10:3-4. "For though we live in the world, we do not wage war as the world does. The weapons we fight with are not the weapons of the world. On the contrary, they have divine power to demolish strongholds."
5 Ezekiel 18:9.
6 Much credit to Irving Younger, a great trial lawyer. I remember him saying this in one of his lectures decades ago. I believe he also said: "All trials are nothing more than a complicated way of reaching a decision." That's just what I remember, but I can no longer find a reference. Any good trial lawyer I've known is well versed in Younger's "Ten Commandments of Cross-Examination."

"In addition to all this," as the Word says, Abby had three more steps to take: Fourth, Abby would take up the shield of faith, with which he could extinguish all the flaming arrows of the evil one; fifth, he would take the helmet of salvation which would protect his mind from doubting God's saving work in his life and his case; and sixth, he would take up the sword of the Spirit, which is the word of God, and with the sword, the only weapon of offense in the list of armor, he would take the offensive against his adversary.[7]

You did not want to be Abby's opponent. But he still wasn't done. He would pray in the spirit, and fearlessly let God know his requests, and "with this in mind, be alert and always keep on praying,"[8] after all, it was going to be a long day of battle. Watch and pray.

My toolbox is a little different.[9] Yours will be too. They are custom made. But you have to ask.

ddarssa

I have to admit, I didn't like Georgy Tarasov. But he would never know that. I treated him with the utmost respect. After all, I had already dealt with him and his scumbag lawyer, Chris Hatch, at 4:30 a.m. in the morning. The two co-conspirators, were going down.

Here's what 4:30 a.m. in the morning looked like for me, on the eleventh day of the trial, Monday morning:

"Lord Jesus, I speak to my mountain, my mountain is Georgy Tarasov, and his partners, and his lawyer, Chris Hatch, and I cast them into the sea in Jesus' name, cast them into the sea in Jesus' name. Lord Jesus, I speak to my mountain, my mountain is Georgy Tarasov, and his partners, and his lawyer, Chris Hatch, and I cast them into the sea in Jesus' name, cast them into the sea in Jesus' name. I say it again, Lord Jesus, I speak to my mountain, my mountain is Georgy Tarasov, and his partners, and his lawyer, Chris Hatch, and I cast them into the sea in Jesus' name, cast them into the sea in Jesus' name, cast them into the sea in Jesus' name, cast them into the sea in Jesus' name. Lord, I believe I have already received this victory. Father God, I have complete faith in You. And throughout this trial, I will put all my faith in you Lord. This is your trial, and I will put my full trust in you. Period. Amen. And, Amen."[10]

If you are a warrior, and have spent a lot of time in trial, and have counseled and spent a lot of time with people going through the trials of life, then you are very glad, and also relieved that the Lord is a Warrior.

"The LORD is a Warrior; the LORD is his name."[11]

---

7 Ephesians 6:10-18.
8 Ephesians 6:18.
9 "The method is not sacred, the *message* is sacred." Pastor Tommy Barnett.
10 Mark 11:22.
11 Exodus 15:3. See also Exodus 14:14. "The LORD will fight for you; you need only be still."

And, he is on your side.

The Dr. Ezekiel trial was twenty-one years after the Harry Goldberg trial. I was still speaking out against my enemies. But I was a new Christian in 1985, I didn't even know about Mark 11:22. The Lord just told me what to do and I did it. Later I learned of Mark 11:22, and then I *got* it. As I've said, I became a Christian in November 1984. That's when I started a personal relationship with Jesus Christ. And Jesus would tell me what to do, and how to prepare for trial, or the trials of life, and I would do it. Later, I would eventually read or hear a sermon that verified the biblical basis for the lesson the Lord had already taught me, and I had already put into practice. My Christian education was a lot like my friend Abby's. We learned in the trenches. The Lord told us what to do, we did it. And we did it, and we still do it, with passion. There's too much at stake. We don't mull things over. We don't wander around on rooftops.[12] We don't sit in classes. We're in the trenches. We listen and apply. That's about all we had time to do.

And, of course we don't defend it. "The Bible is like a lion. Who ever heard of defending a lion? Just turn it loose, it will defend itself."[13]

As the years went by, I felt the Lord was giving me a method, tailoring for me a method by which to work through my challenges, problems, and trials. I have a wonderful friend and accountability buddy, Eliseo Ovando He was very instrumental in helping me with *ddarssa*. We have thought through each of the seven elements of ddarssa. The whole point of it is to give us a reference, a quick source of critical verses in time of serious need. We use it.
Often.

I applied *ddarssa* to the Dr. Ezekiel case. Both before, and during the trial I was focused on victory. It was this simple: First, **Desire**, I had a desire, a deep desire to protect my client, Dr. Ezekiel from a malicious attack, and my desire was to win the case for him and all his employees, and all his patients that were counting on him.

Second, **Decision**, I made the decision to take on this case, to fight this case, and to win it for Dr. Ezekiel. The process of making the decision, is critical to me and I believe, to the Lord. A man cannot be double-minded. The best way to avoid that is to make a conscious decision. I'm good at that. All glory to the Lord.

Third, *Ask*, I would ask the Lord for victory. Faith is asking. I was persistent. "Persistence" is probably an understatement for me, except that I'm convinced the Lord loves a persistent servant.

Fourth, **Receive**, I would, and still do, affirm that I have already received the victory over the problem, the challenge, or victory in the case I was fighting.

12 2 Samuel 11:2. It was springtime. David was supposed to go off to war. That's what the King should have done. Instead, David remained in Jerusalem. "One evening David got up from his bed and walked around on the roof of the palace." David saw Bathsheba bathing. David was not where he was supposed to be, and the consequences were disastrous.
13 Charles Spurgeon.

Fifth, *See*, I would *see* the victory over the problem, I would see what it looks like, I would see it in my mind, that was a good way for me to put my mind to use, it was *my* mind after all.

Sixth, *Speak*, I would speak victory. As to the cases, I would speak to my mountain, and I would cast it into the sea in Jesus' name. And, indeed, that's what would happen. Maybe not literally, but certainly realistically.

Seventh, *Act*, I would act on it. I was not passive. I knew, and I know, what to do. I understand my role. I made sure I worked harder than anyone, in an earthly and spiritual sense.

Over time, Eliseo and I put together a four-page summary of *ddarssa* and all the verses and quotes that support each principle element of the acronym. It's good to have an accountability buddy. There's a reason that Jesus sent out his disciples in twos. Eliseo has a wonderful wife; a wife who likes the fact that her husband has an accountability buddy.

At least that's what she told me.

Don't sweat the war zone, it's all war zone

Monday morning. It's 7:00 a.m. I'm at the little coffee shop outside the courthouse. Dr. Ezekiel is with me. We're ready. He will be my first witness. We're talking about coffee.

"You drink too much coffee," Dr. Ezekiel said, "when this trial is over I want you to come in for a physical."

I turned up my nose and in mock amusement declared, "The coffee is baptized, leave me alone."

"Baptized?" queried my friend.

"Yes, baptized," I responded with feigned intelligence. Raising a cup of brew, I noted: "You see, it is commonly understood that coffee was originally a Muslim drink, first put to use for its enjoyment and energizing effects in the middle of the fifteenth century. However, Pope Clement VIII discovered coffee, and loved it. His draconian advisors told him to outlaw it 'as the bitter invention of Satan.' But, instead, Clement VIII, declared: 'This devil's drink is so good, we should cheat the devil by baptizing it.' Now, I know there is no way I can verify this story. However, coffee, indeed, is so good, I have come to believe it has been baptized and the blessings have carried through the generations until now. Indeed, until this very moment, and this very cup of coffee." I take another sip.

Dr. Ezekiel mused: "Pontificating to relieve stress?"

"Exactly," I responded.

The coffee shop was buzzing. It was a busy Monday morning. By 7:30 a.m., there were a lot of lawyers, their clients and others milling around, waiting for the courthouse to open. I saw Abby Neilson and his client close by. You could tell they were working hard. Just then, Mike Harrison walked up. His case had a Final Status Conference today. My associate Susan Chen, would take Mike to the courtroom with her. Mike's presence at the Final Status Conference was not necessary. But, I like my clients to be familiar with the courtroom where the case will be tried. I want them to see the judge, the clerk, the bailiff, the whole layout. And, I want to start signaling to the judge and his staff how important my client takes his case and the matters that will be before them. Susan could handle the hearing without me while I started the eleventh day of the Dr. Ezekiel trial. Besides, I knew the judge well. He would send the case out for another shot at settling the case. Mike's case was going very well, or so I thought at the time.

We were going to settle it, or win it.

Period.

That's when Janie Blyth walked up. She wanted to catch me before I carried on with another day in court.

"Welcome to the war zone," I said to Janie as she walked up.

Janie sat down.

"Should I leave?" Mike said, and moved away before I could say anything. And, I could see that Susan Chen was walking up, so she would take over making sure he was comfortable and brief him on the day.

"Should *I* leave?" Dr. Ezekiel said.

"No," Janie said. "Please stay. I'm just here to drop off some documents for Tom. I got sued. My first." She looked at Dr. Ezekiel and softly shrugged her shoulders.

I started with the introductions, "Dr. Ezekiel, this is Dr. Janie Blyth, a wonderful and very prominent ophthalmologist." They exchanged greetings. Doctor to doctor, words were not needed to sympathize. I speed-read the lawsuit against Janie. Basically, the plaintiff was suing for an allegedly botched eye surgery, with allegations of lack of informed consent and medical malpractice. I've litigated, i.e. defended, dozens of these cases.

"Janie, I have read this, but I will study it tonight and call you. Now, let me tell you something, you will win. We will either settle it or win it. Now, go back to your office, continue to take good care of your patients. They are counting on you. Don't let this worry you."

Janie stood up and surveyed all the commotion going on around us at the coffee shop. She looked up at the nine-story courthouse. "Tom, the war zone scares me."

I stood up. I looked at Janie. "Don't sweat the war zone, it's all war zone."

She hugged me. Dr. Ezekiel stood up. She nodded a goodbye to him. They shook hands. He nodded back.

Dr. Ezekiel and I sat down. He looked at me, paused, and said: "The war zone is everywhere, isn't it?"

"Yes," I said.

"I know in my case, it all happened out there," Dr. Ezekiel gestured to the world, "this courthouse is just where it all comes to a head."

"The courthouses of life are the cross-roads of human fighting—just one step before the actual wars—fought with guns and bullets," I responded.

Dr. Ezekiel hung his head in his hand. "It's hard to go through day after day of a trial that seems to highlight every mistake you ever made, and to see all the signs you missed . . . or ignored. I've learned a lot about myself in this trial. I'm not so sure it wasn't a good thing for me."

"You're one of the children of light," I said. "You didn't even come close to seeing them coming at you."

"So, then, what is Georgy Tarasov?" Dr. Ezekiel asked.

"A child of darkness," I responded.

"And he's smarter than me?"

"I'd say shrewder and wiser," I said.

"Hmmm," was Dr. Ezekiel's wise comeback.

"Don't worry, you win in the end," I said, *prayerfully*.

We started to gather up our files, as I juggled a last sip of my coffee.

Dr. Ezekiel looked at me: "Tom, I still think you drink too much coffee. You're addicted."

I looked at him, savored one last slow sip and said: "I have generally found that whatever condition my friends think I have, I have; whatever condition my enemies think I have, they have."[14]

We made our way into the courthouse. I was concerned. Not only had I not spilled my coffee yet, but there was nary a coffee stain anywhere on my khaki suit. I hoped the judge and jury wouldn't hold it against me.

My other thought was that the other side was going to be late today. Call it a gut instinct: Chris Hatch, and his client, Georgy Tarasov would be late this morning. They would have been arguing about the progress of the case to date, and lost as to what to do next. It was just a hunch.

The LORD is a Warrior; the LORD is his name.

It's all war zone.

T+

---

14 See, Proverbs 27:6. "Wounds from a friend can be trusted, but an enemy multiplies kisses."

The Take Away 13
We do not wage war as the world does.

1. Jesus was no pacifist, and neither should you be. If you are going through the trial of your life, or a great challenge, or any painful event, you must get Jesus, and the Lord, on your side. Be very glad, and also relieved that the Lord is a Warrior.
   "The LORD is a Warrior; the LORD is his name."
   And, He is on your side.

2. Remember that complacency is a trap. Proverbs 1:32-33 says: "For the waywardness of the simple will kill them, and the complacency of fools will destroy them; but whoever listens to me ["Wisdom"; the mind of God revealed] will live in safety and be at ease, without fear of harm."

3. Warriors are not passive, warriors are not complacent. Warriors use weapons, and the best weapons are the Word of God. One warrior might use Ephesians 6 and put on The Armor of God, and another warrior might use a customized set of tools, such as ***ddarssa [see Take Away 4].***

4. The bottom line is that although we live in the world, we *do not* wage war as the world does. The weapons we fight with are not the weapons of the world. The weapons we use are the Word of God. They have divine power to demolish strongholds. Don't be passive, don't be complacent. Certainly if you are going through a trial, a challenge, a painful event, or trying to overcome an addiction or other stronghold in your life, use the Word of God, speak it out, *work* it every day.

Children of Light
Versus the children of darkness

Doers of the Word

Dr. Ezekiel and I were striding down the hallway when I again ran into Abby Neilson and his client. They were in trial in a courtroom just a few doors away from us. Abby took a few steps toward me and said: "Be a doer of the Word," and he nodded.

"Be a doer of the Word, Abby," I said back. "The armor's looking real good today."

"It's a perfect fit," he said as he went back to his client. I watched as they walked into their courtroom.

Just two warriors; doing our fieldwork.

I suppose most people have their way of being a *doer* of the Word, but on that day, Abby was using Ephesians 6:10-18, I was using *ddarssa* and Mark 11:22. We were *doers* of the Word, the way the Lord told us to. For Abby and I, sound doctrine was never an end in itself. Our goal was not to know more, just so that we would know more. No way. We wanted to know more, we needed to know more, because we were the types that would be putting that knowledge into serious action on Monday morning, on Tuesday morning, on Wednesday morning, etc., etc. We were warriors. We had deadlines. I felt God called me to take down Georgy Tarasov and Chris Hatch. It would have been a sin of omission if I didn't *complete* what I was called to complete. Tarasov, in particular, was a racist, who had written and made racist comments to my client, an African-American doctor. I am an admirer of Rabbi Abraham Joshua Heschel who said: "God is either the father of all men or of no man, and the idea of judging a person in terms of black or brown or white is an eye disease." I was always on the alert for that type of disease. Georgy Tarasov had the disease of the eye; that was just an additional reason to take him down. Rabbi Heschel had marched with Martin Luther King in Selma in 1965 and is often quoted for saying, "I felt my legs were praying." So often when I walked down those courthouse hallways, *I felt my legs were shaking*, but my heart was praying.

Tarasov should have never made those unrepeatable comments to Dr. Ezekiel. I will politely say it this way: "God was not happy." And God makes known the end from the beginning.[1] My job was to get in agreement with the Lord, and see it, *the end*, also. I'm good at that. Tarasov was going to lose. Indeed, it would be worse than that for him.

"But be ye doers of the word, and not hearers only, deceiving your own selves."[2] After a long day in court, I subsequently had a young preacher tell me after a talk I gave on courtroom warfare (I call them "Opening Statements"), that "being a *doer* of the Word means to obey the message and avoid sinful conduct." Such a comment to me, at the end of a day of hard-core fighting in court is, I must say—a *serious understatement.*

I wasn't able to control my sassiness as much as I would have liked. So I said: "You'll have to forgive me, I never had a shot at going to Bible school."

"No, really, being a doer of the word means to submit yourself to the Scriptures," he chimed back at me.

I bit my tongue. "Look, get off your sofa and join me in a Federal District Court Trial sometime. I had better be doing *a lot more* than just obeying the message and avoiding sin. No wonder you guys get pummeled by the children of darkness. Jesus said: 'I am sending you out like sheep among wolves. Therefore be as shrewd as snakes and as innocent as doves.'[3] Obeying the message and avoiding sin is just the starting place. You can do that sitting on your sofa."

Jesus said: "I am sending you out . . ." Out!! Warriors don't sit around. We are *not* rooftop wanderers as David was.[4] You might end up wandering around and cultivating disaster. The enemy is the other side. Don't destroy yourself. Destroy them.

Children of this world

Ddarssa is just one of my responses to the reprove set forth in Luke 16:8. Putting on the armor of God, Ephesians 6:10-18 is just one of Abby Neilson's responses to the reprove set forth in Luke 16:8. We simply are not willing to let the "Children of this World," the Children of Darkness, either be, or benefit from, being "wiser" than us. It is not going to happen. The Lord warned us in the *Parable of the Shrewd Manager.*

---

1 Isaiah 46:10.

2 James 1:22 (KJV).

3 Matthew 10:16.

4 2 Samuel 11:1-5. In the spring, at the time when kings go off to war, David remained in Jerusalem. One evening David got up from his bed and walked around on the roof of the palace. And he saw a woman bathing, and that woman was Bathsheba, the wife of one of David's faithful warriors. David's sinful act of sleeping with Bathsheba led to an attempted cover up and murder. Eventually David's sin was revealed, and he was punished, but the ramifications of his conduct were devastating.

"And the lord commended the unjust steward, because he had done wisely: for the children of this world are in their generation wiser than the children of light."[5]

We take the warning to heart.

Somewhere around ten years ago, after twenty years of hard-core litigation, one thing set in for me: Bad people are often seriously confident people. Their self-assurance amazes me and continues to amaze me. Frankly, the power is real. *Their* power. In the courthouses of life, the *children of the world* have to really stick to their confidence, their self-assuredness, their unrelenting confidence. They are the best. They have all the answers. You, however, are a worm, and they will squish you when the time comes.

I remember Chris Hatch's confidence in his, and his client, Georgy Tarasov's case. On occasion, Hatch would take an opportunity before or after a court hearing to lecture me as to how and why he would win the case. He would have a sublime look of peace and resolve on his face. Tarasov would usually be standing next to him, proud of his lawyer, and exhibiting the same face, one of confidence and sanquinity. As a lawyer, I am often forced to listen to these diatribes because they are couched in terms of "settlement" discussions, or a "settlement" offer, and as a lawyer, I'm ethically bound to convey any settlement overture or offer to my client. On one occasion after Hatch had prattled on about his most assured victory, for huge money of course, Tarasov looked at me and said, "By the time we are finished enforcing our huge judgment against your client, his black a-- will be selling knock-off Cartier watches in the back alleys of Beverly Hills." Then he smirked, pirouetted, and walked away, with Hatch in tow. That was one of his few comments that is close to printable. Hatch and Tarasov couched all their racist comments, whether in writing or spoken, as "privileged or confidential settlement discussions," and therefore, inadmissible to the judge or jury. They felt they could insult and infuriate, with no consequences, no price to pay.

At times like that, I feel such peace, knowing that . . . *God is listening.*

Tarasov and his partners, with the help of Hatch, had *worldly* grounds for their confidence in the lawsuit they brought. Through their connivance and artifice, they now controlled six other substantial medical practices, and they weren't doctors. On a surface level it wasn't hard to figure out. As "medical practice managers," they controlled the leases, they acquired or leased the medical equipment and office furniture (which is always a substantial expense), and the doctor's employees worked for the "management company." They even controlled the patients because the patients mostly came from their marketing efforts and were loyal to the site of the medical practice, mostly for convenience and financial reasons. Then, on top of that, they "loaned" money to the doctor. The unwitting doctor racked up debt to Tarasov's group, and eventually Tarasov "owned" the doctors—at least in their minds. I was the first person to blow the whistle.

And they came at me guns ablazin'.

---

5 Luke 16:8 (KJV).

They simply had to win this case, or their whole empire would come crumbling down.

I was already visualizing the crumbling.

After one of Hatch's long harangues on why they would win the case, and why Dr. Ezekiel should pay several million dollars to settle, I would do what Nehemiah did: pray immediately, but imperceptibly, and then say or do whatever God laid on my heart. While I was praying, in the flash of a few seconds, Hatch followed up with a closing remark:

"Tom, we have six other clinic systems under our control, we've done it the same way every time, there's nothing illegal about it. We are going to win, Dr. Ezekiel is going to owe us a lot of money, and he will go bankrupt. All we will do is plunk another doctor is his place, in *our* clinic, the lease is in our name, and continue on with our business. And it's all your fault because you didn't tell him to pay Mr. Tarasov what he is owed." Hatch paused and looked at me, "You rarely say much in response to me when I make these proposals. You need to say something. WHAT do you have to say!?"

I finished my quick prayer. I quietly said, almost to myself, "What then shall I say to these things? If God *be* for us, who *can be* against us?"

"What?" Hatch shouted to me. "What are you talking about?" he shouted again, frustrated and indignant.

"Romans 8:31."

"Romans!? What the [several cuss words] are you talking about?" He shouted at me again.

I looked at Hatch as nicely as I could, nodded as nicely as I could, and said: "He who digs a hole falls into the pit he has made."[6]

Hatch looked at me: "Tom, you are one demented human being."

I looked back at Hatch: "I have generally found that whatever condition my friends think I have, I have; whatever condition my enemies think I have, they have."

And I walked away.

Hatch: with so much sin in his heart, had lost his mind. His soul had followed.

Hatch and his client are evil. They are the type that cannot sleep until they do evil; they are robbed of slumber until they make someone fall.[7] They are children of this world, children of darkness.

Children of light

Sometimes I can be so disappointed in myself. A little sin here, a little sin there. Sometimes I feel that I can never live up to what God wants from me. My body gets

---

6 Psalm 7:15-16. "He who digs a hole and scoops it out falls into the pit he has made. The trouble he causes recoils on himself; his violence comes down on his own head."

7 Proverbs 4:16 . "For they cannot sleep till they do evil; they are robbed of slumber till they make someone fall." See also John 8:42-47 where Jesus talks about the children of the Devil. "You belong to your father, the devil, and you want to carry out your father's desire."

tired, I get lonely, I get depressed, I see too much hardship and pain, I have way too much on my plate, my head hurts. I can spend time with Abby Neilson, Sam, Dave, or a few other Christian trial lawyers that go through what I go through. We all live amazingly stressful, painful, hard-fighting lives. Sometimes in a depressed moment, we'll verbally wonder why we are called to do this. Why would anyone want to live this kind of life? Sometimes we feel like shouting: "Lord, even David only slew one Goliath! I've had five just this week. I'm hurting, my body just doesn't seem to rest." And again we picture David, standing there before King Saul, with Goliath's head still in his hand, blood dripping."[8] Just another day's work for us. And then, of course, that attitude seems like a sin. "Mercy, I'm tired," I'll scream. And my buddies will hoist their cups of coffee and toast another day of warfare. After all, David, too, had many Goliaths. In many different forms.

The trials aren't the warfare. *Everything* we do is the warfare. Every conversation we have, every letter we write, every transaction we assist in, every meeting we have, and every trial we begin. We live in moments.[9] Every moment could bring a major mistake. Or, it could bring a major blessing. Just like life. It's *all* part of life. There is one palpable benefit of what I do, and what Abby, Sam, and Dave do every day: What we do forces us to be so in tune with God's power in our lives. We know it when we have it, and we know it when it leaves us. Just the slightest little sin, and we feel it in our lives. We will feel it in the power that we will need the next day in court as we battle the children of the world, the children of darkness. Abby, Sam and Dave; these guys are *not* the type to cheat on their wives; it will not happen. Mercy, the Holy Spirit will slam them, will slam me, for something much less than that. This is just our experience, our fieldwork with the Lord. I can assure you of this, the Lord loves it when you commit to fieldwork with Him. He loves it. He'll be on your side. Indeed, he will go ahead of you, he will clear the way. *The Lord will go before you.*[10] Dan, Sam, Dave and I are "believers." We *have* to be. I am so glad we have to be. We will not back down. We know the "incomparably great power for us who believe."[11]

I suppose when I die one day, all my work with the Lord will have been fieldwork. I'm in my mid-fifties now. I guess there is nary a chance that I will have had any classroom work with the Lord. Sitting in class, getting credit toward a degree, plenty of down time to analyze the deeper meanings of a particular passage of the Bible. Any pastor could criticize Abby, or Sam, or Dave, or me, and tell us how our fieldwork has caused us to misinterpret the Bible, and we would listen. We would. I promise. But we would still know exactly what it means to have a personal relationship with Jesus Christ. So, we will listen. But with us, the Bible, and the tools therein, are tried and tested in the cauldron of daily warfare.

---

8 1 Samuel 17:57.

9 I was never a day by day guy. I am a moment by moment guy. "God never gives strength for tomorrow, or for the next hour, but only for the strain of the moment." Oswald Chambers, My Utmost for his Highest, August 2.

10 Isaiah 52:12.

11 Ephesians 1:19.

Every day.

For us, "the word of God is living and active. Sharper than any double-edged sword . . . ."[12]

And we are living and active with the use of the Word.

It is sharper than any double-edged sword of our opponent.

Let your light shine

When Dr. Ezekiel and I walked into the courtroom, I was excited. On the other side of the bar, to the left, at the bailiff's desk, sat Shifty Wallace. Oh, my Lord, it was good to see him. He's a sheriff's officer, who acts as the bailiff for the judge. Shifty has been a Superior Court bailiff for a long time. And Shifty is a serious *believer*. Shifty usually works in a courtroom down the hall. Several years back, I had a long jury trial in his courtroom. It was so good to have Shifty's presence in that courtroom. Shifty sits at the bailiff's desk, and is not the least bit shy about leaving his big ol' Bible open, turned to wherever he is studying, out in full view for everyone in the courtroom. The courtroom seemed to glow with his spirit, and with the Spirit of the Lord. There was so much peace in his courtroom. Because of him, the presence of the Lord was palpable in that courtroom. You could feel it.

I walked over to Shifty. "Shifty, it is so good to see you! How are you?"

Shifty is a big black guy with this wonderful, deep, thick, *something*, of a voice. "I'm doing great, my man. Keeping the faith, you *know* it! James (the usual bailiff for this department) called in sick, so I was sent down to keep an eye on you. I'll be here for the remainder of your trial."

"Well, we will be blessed by your presence. What are you reading today?"

He looked down at this Bible. "I'm reading Ephesians 5:8-10, 'For you were once darkness, but now you are light in the Lord. Live as children of light (for the fruit of the light consists in all goodness, righteousness and truth) and find out what pleases the Lord.' Amen, brother, amen!" And we nodded our agreement.

"I receive that Shifty. Bless you, my friend."

He looked at me with his big sparkling brown eyes, "Bless you my brother."

Need I say more about Shifty?

It was definitely going to be a good day in that courtroom. I thought, "thank you Lord, for sending me a friend." In reality, an angel. Jesus told us to "let your light shine before men, that they may see your good deeds and praise your Father in heaven."[13]

And we know where that light comes from.

"This is the message we have heard from him and declare to you: God is light; in him there is no darkness at all."[14]

---

12 Hebrews 4:12.

13 Matthew 5:16. Jesus said, "You are the light of the world. A city on a hill cannot be hidden. Neither do people light a lamp and put it under a bowl. Instead they put it on its stand, and it gives light to everyone in the house. In the same way, let your light shine before men, that they may see your good deeds and praise your Father in heaven."

14 1 John 1:5. See also verse 7. "But if we walk in the light, as he is in the light, we have fellowship with one another, and the blood of Jesus, his Son, purifies us from all sin."

Walk in the light.

Applied Christianity

I call the courthouses and rehab centers of life, the halls of applied Christianity. It was 8:35 a.m. I had just finished talking with my bailiff friend, Shifty Wallace. Dr. Ezekiel and I sat down at counsel's table. The judge took the bench. Shifty, the clerk, and court reporter were all in place.

But, there was no opposing counsel, no opposing party.

They were not there. *They were late.* The judge doesn't let the jury sit in the jury box until all the lawyers have arrived and he makes sure there is no business to attend to outside of their hearing. The judge will hold the jury in the jury room until the trial is ready to resume. No judge likes tardiness. That is why I was always at the little coffee shop outside the courthouse at 7:00 a.m. You can *never* be late. *Never.* And, today, Hatch was. He had been late a few times to pretrial hearings. Now he was late on a *trial day*. The judge stayed on the bench, and as the jurors came in, he told them, one by one, that "Mr. Hatch and his client, were late, please wait in the jury room." Usually, the judge would wait in chambers and the clerk would take care of this. But, in this case, the judge always took the bench at his pre-set time, and, you better be there. So, as each juror walked in to the courtroom, on time, and headed back to the jury room, the judge himself told them that Hatch and his client were late and to sit in the jury room until called. The juror would see me and Dr. Ezekiel sitting there, waiting. We were good to go. I think I heard the sound of crickets while we waited.

That's how the eleventh day of trial had started on a Monday morning. Hatch and his client banged and stumbled their way into court at about 9:03 a.m., apologizing about the traffic and their need to get some rebuttal evidence ready. There are no such real excuses; they were falling apart at the seams. As the jury proceeded in fill the jury box, their look of disgust toward Hatch and his client was obvious. Where was all of Hatch's bravado now? Where was all of Tarasov's confidence?

It took me a day and a half to put on my entire defense of the case, just Dr. Ezekiel, a few percipient witnesses, and an expert on damages. I rested by 4:00 p.m. on Tuesday, and shortly thereafter the case went to the jury. It was their turn to start the process of deciding who they believed, who was the most trustworthy, who should win. The jury could deliberate for an hour, or several days, or more. You just don't get to know.

Human skills plus divine intervention

I graduated from Pepperdine University in 1979 and was a member of the Law Review. I passed the California Bar the first time. By some earthly standards, I had done well. I had secured the necessary *human* skills to be a lawyer. But, within a few years, I realized that I needed human skills plus divine intervention to do anything of true or lasting value for my clients, and for me, as well. I try *so hard* to apply Christianity to my life, to where a stranger in the bathroom that might overhear me speaking victory over a case on behalf of my client, may consider me a little crazy. But, more often I've felt that the person who heard me *speaking* out, somewhat envied my dedication to my Savior. Perhaps down deep I had planted a seed. Perhaps the Holy Spirit whispered to them: "The tongue has the power of life and death."[15] I choose life. I simply trusted God that he was good to his word. And Jesus, my Senior Partner, was like a brother to me. I could always count on him, and the louder I cried out to him the better. I, myself, would go through that Eight-Step Program and ask Jesus to tell me specifically what he wanted me to know as it applied to the case and how to settle it. And, he would tell me. I don't remember ever getting a wrong answer, or no answer.

I often see the lessons of the *Parable of the Shrewd Manager*, Luke 16:8, in action. To this trial lawyer, the message is simple. The children of darkness are good, shrewd, and wise at setting down principles, acting in accordance with those principles, disciplining their selves, establishing goals, affirming victory, carrying out their plans, and succeeding at completing them. The children of darkness can become so good at it, so determined, so successful that they even command substantial respect from the world. They study, they set goals, they do affirmations, they find the "secret" behind these laws and they are "successful," in the world's eyes. They are children of this world. In this parable, Jesus warns us about the people of this world. Indeed, he admonishes us.

Dr. Ezekiel, a godly man, was no match for Georgy Tarasov and Chris Hatch. He simply never saw it coming. He saw it after a one-hour meeting with me in January 2006, when I told him that Tarasov's management contract was illegal and should be thrown out of court. Later on, it was. Long before I met with Dr. Ezekiel in 2006, I noticed something interesting about Luke 16:8. Verse 8 in my King James Bible says "the lord commended the unjust steward, because he had done wisely." The "l" in "lord" was not capitalized. The "lord" is *not* Jesus or God. In that same Bible, when Jesus referred to his father in Matthew 4:4 and 4:10, "Lord," is capitalized. Accordingly, the "lord" in Luke 16:8 is not God or Jesus. The lord is just the master of the house and business, the employer, and he was impressed. Indeed, the children of the world can be impressive. But, the children of this world are not, and shouldn't be, impressive to the children of light.

For the children of light, the children of this world can be overcome.

Dr. Ezekiel has lived a life as harmless as a dove. But he was often in the midst of wolves. At the end of the trial, as we walked down the hallway to go home, knowing that the case was now in the jury's hands, Dr. Ezekiel looked at me and quoted Jesus: "Behold, I send you forth as sheep in the midst of wolves: be ye

---

15 Proverbs 18:21.

therefore wise as serpents, and harmless as doves."[16] It was hard for Dr. Ezekiel to sit through a trial and stare into the face of his own folly. He had seen the signs early on of the risk he was taking with Tarasov and his partners. But he chose to ignore them. At times he just wasn't strong enough to take them on.

Until they wanted half of his practice, and several million dollars. Money, that Dr. Ezekiel didn't owe. Then he came to talk to me. Slowly but surely, Dr. Ezekiel was getting wiser. I doubt this, or anything like this, would ever happen to him again.

Never again underestimate the children of darkness

I recently asked a Jewish friend of mine, who doesn't read the Bible, "Where do you go when you want to read something in pursuit of wisdom?" He couldn't answer me. I felt sad for him that, although an heir to a rich biblical tradition, he ignored it. I asked a humanist friend "where do you go when you want to read something in pursuit of wisdom?" He couldn't answer me either. Both are highly educated, and had acquired lots of worldly knowledge. Indeed, they have accomplished a lot and the world sees them as very successful. They have the requisite "children of this world" wisdom. And with that wisdom they can put most Christians to shame.

Dr. Ezekiel underestimated Georgy Tarasov.

Never underestimate the children of darkness.

It is easy to acquire human knowledge. Applying that knowledge takes wisdom, and all wisdom begins with the fear of the Lord. As a trial lawyer, I have found one major advantage to "fear" the Lord: If you fear the Lord and keep his commandments, you don't have to fear anybody else. "The Lord is my light and my salvation—whom shall I fear?"[17]

Don't fear children of darkness. Don't fear man. Indeed, "Fear of man will prove to be a snare, but whoever trusts in the Lord is kept safe."[18]

And after three decades of litigation and trials, I have found that human skills plus divine intervention will always beat the children of darkness. But those human skills include serious application of God's teachings in your life, and certainly in the battles of your life.

On Wednesday morning of the trial, after the jury had deliberated for seventy-five minutes (to be exact), they said they had reached a verdict, and my friend, Shifty Wallace, went to find me where I told him I'd be:

. . . at the little coffee shop outside the courthouse.

T+

16 Matthew 10:16 (KJV).
17 Psalm 27:1.
18 Proverbs 29:25.

The Take Away 14
Children of light.

1. The **children of this world**, the **children of darkness** are often *wiser* than Christians, the children of light. "Wiser" in the ways of the world because they are of the world, they look for every opportunity to advance their own interests, to acquire more worldly goods and property, and more influence in the world. They are confident, self-assured, clever, cunning, and have worldly sophistication. Being "wiser" in the ways of the world, and pumped up with their own worldly confidence, they often won't think twice about taking advantage of you, or attacking you.

2. The Lord warned us about the children of this world, the children of darkness, in Luke 16:8 in the ***Parable of the Shrewd Manager***.

    "And the lord [the worldly master, *not* the Lord God] commended the unjust steward, because he had done wisely: for the children of this world are in their generation wiser than the children of light."
    We take the warning to heart.

3. Christians are **children of light**. Jesus said, "You are the light of the world . . . let your light shine before men, that they may see your good deeds and praise your Father in heaven." Ephesians 5:8-11 tells us: "For you were once darkness, but now you are light in the Lord. Live as children of light (for the fruit of the light consists in all goodness, righteousness and truth) and find out what pleases the Lord. Have nothing to do with the fruitless deeds of darkness, but rather expose them."

4. ***Never again underestimate the children of darkness***. The Bible is filled with the tools you need to do battle against the children of darkness, and the evil they inflict, or against a personal problem or challenge. Use those tools, and those weapons of warfare. Put on the armor of God, Ephesians 6:10-18; use Mark 11:22 and speak to your mountain (your adversary, your problem, your challenge); ask God for a customized set of tools, just for you, such as ***ddarssa***, and He will give them to you.

    Remember: "But be ye doers of the word, and not hearers only, deceiving your own selves."

Settle All the "Its" in Your Life, *part 2*

Even you have an "it"

By the time you finish this chapter, Part 2

Take out a simple standard issue, cafeteria-grade white paper napkin. Put a "T" at the top, and a "+" next to it. "T+". Take a moment, put out all the fires in your mind, and remove all the distractions. Let the one thing in your life come to mind that you would really like settled quickly. Write that on the napkin somewhere under the "T+". After you write down that one big thing, go ahead and add a few other things you'd like to settle, or a goal or dream you'd like to accomplish. That's "your list." Ask God to help you settle the matters on the list and receive in your heart the victory. If you don't believe in God, listen to your conscience (which was implanted in you by God) and commit to do everything within your power to settle the matters on the list, and keep an open heart to soulful leanings that you previously ignored. Date your list and sign your name on it. Fold the napkin and put it in your pocket. This is where journaling comes in. For the next forty days, get up early, while it is still dark,[1] and look at the list. Ask God to settle the matters on the list. Then ask him for guidance as to what *you* should do to settle the matters on the list, *your list*. You do your part, he will do his.

Don't worry, if you have come this far in the book, you have a certain amount of faith, certainly the size of at least, say, a mustard seed. You are so close. By the time you finish your forty days of looking at and praying over your list, you and God will have worked through settling the items or things on your list, and he will give you revelations.[2] Again, this is where journaling comes in. Write down the

---

1 Mark 1:35. See Chapter 6, fn 16, and Chapter 24, fn. 6.

2 Habakkuk 2:2. "Write down the revelation and make it plain on tablets so that a herald may run with it." Know this, in some cases, and with some problems, God will give you the starting place. But that is all you need. Remember, "he who began a good work in you will carry it on to completion . . . ." Philippians 1:6.

revelations! Write down everything God tells you. Forty days will go fast; eternity is forever.

"I tell you the truth, if you have faith as small as a mustard seed, you can say to this mountain, 'Move from here to there' and it will move. Nothing will be impossible for you."[3]

On Wednesday morning I was sitting at the coffee shop outside the courtroom with Dr. Ezekiel, waiting for the jury to render its verdict. We were sipping coffee. I was thinking of Arthur Blessitt. He's the man who spent forty years walking around the world with a cross. Arthur said: "The most important thing God will tell you to do is the next thing." I was waiting for the Lord to tell me the next thing to do. Dr. Ezekiel looked at me, paused, and said, "Tom, what is faith?"

I knew this was the culmination of my telling him over the past many weeks to "have faith, we'll win." I admit, I'm not the best at quoting Scripture, especially after a long trial, and my brain is worn out. But I did my best anyway to quote Hebrews: "Now faith is being sure of what we hope for and certain of what we do not see."[4] My eyes were tired when I looked back at my friend: "Ezra, I am sure of what I'm hoping for you in this case, and I'm certain you will win."

Ezra's tired eyes were peaceful, and he quietly said: "I think we have done all we can do. Now it's time to just stand, and stand firm."[5]

I wondered whether he knew he was quoting Scripture.

Just then, a lawyer friend, Joe Peary, walked up. He looked at me and Dr. Ezekiel. He nodded his head and said, "I know that look. You're 'between' aren't you?"

"Yeah," I said. Nodding to Ezra. "We are. How are you Joey?" I made the introduction to Dr. Ezekiel.

"I'm fine," Joey responded, slumping down and sitting next to us. He looked at Ezra. "We lawyers know that 'between' look. One trial finished, but you haven't quite gone home yet. And, soon another will start up." Joey looked at me, "I remember your poem, 'Between.' —I have one to share Friday night. Do you have any new material?"

"Yes, I have some new stuff. 'Between' was one of my first poems." I looked at Dr. Ezekiel. My bleary eyes were tired, I wanted to tape my eyelids up. "Some of us lawyers write poems, maybe just to deal with *it*. We get together once a month on a Friday night. We call it the 'Inklings,' after C. S. Lewis."

Dr. Ezekiel nodded and smiled softly. "Have you ever considered counseling?"

"The Inklings will have to suffice," I said.

That's when Shifty Wallace walked up. He looked at me with his big ol' smile and said, "I got good news and bad news for you."

"I'd like the 'between' news," I said.

Dr. Ezekiel wanted the good news.

---

3 Matthew 17:20.
4 Hebrews 11:1.
5 Ephesians 6:13-14.

Shifty helped us gather up our stuff: "The good news is, the jury's back."

"What's the bad news?" I squinted.

"The bad news is my judge has a case for you. She says, 'Only you can handle it.' They're Christians." Shifty smiled again. He knew his regular judge wanted me to try and settle a tough case she was handling. Shifty figured I was in for a complicated battle, and he knew I couldn't turn down a judge's request to try and settle a case.

I smirked at Shifty: "Okay, *but can I finish this case first*!?"

Shifty looked at me and Dr. Ezekiel and smiled, "Brother! Your case *is* finished." He nodded at us, and his smile gave us comfort. That's a smile I could read.

As we walked toward the courthouse entrance, Shifty threw his big arm around my shoulder and said: "Hey counselor?"

"Yes, Shifty?"

"Did you bring your toothbrush?" Shifty said with a laugh, and gave me such a slap on my back I almost fell over.

"Man, it just doesn't pay to hang around the courthouse," I blurted, while choking.

"Keeps you out of trouble, my man" said, *my man* Shifty.

As we went through the courthouse security line, Shifty couldn't help getting one more shot in at me. "Remember, Tom, you're an expert on marital sex."

Dr. Ezekiel was bemused. "What?!"

I looked back as he finished going through security. "I'm the last to know or understand marriage, and especially marital sex, or any other kind of—never mind!!" I looked at Shifty. "Obviously this is a marital dispute."

"Yep, and a big one. Judge needs you badly on this one," Shifty said.

Shifty had to keep firing away at me. "Hey! It's your fault."

"Why me?" I said

"Because you hang out at courthouses." And Shifty led us back to the courtroom where the jury was waiting on the Dr. Ezra Ezekiel case.

Everyone was in their place, the judge, the court reporter, the court secretary, the bailiff Shifty Wallace, Georgy Tarasov, and Chris Hatch. There were assorted witnesses, the public, and other interested parties in the gallery. And, a few people I recognized as federal investigators. They were looking at Georgy Tarasov. I hadn't seen them before.

After the normal formalities the judge reviewed the verdict and then announced the results. The jury voted 12-0 for Dr. Ezra Ezekiel.

With the Lord, *it's as easy as that.*

His life could go on. That's how a client feels at first. Later he'll be mad that Georgy Tarasov and his lawyer took the strike at him. I will help him with that. Everyone needs a "start day."

A jury verdict will also: settle a case. The judge finished, discharged the jury, and my staff and I and Dr. Ezekiel could now spend some time with the jury talking to them about the case, the details, and the obvious reasons they were on Dr. Ezekiel's side. The whole time, Shifty Wallace was pulling on my sleeve to get up the hall to his regular judge who had a case for me to try to settle. Dr. Ezekiel agreed that we'd all get together later in the week for dinner. To celebrate. It was 11:30 a.m.

It seems to me that throughout my entire legal career, I was always overextended. What I was wondering as Shifty Wallace led me down the hall to Judge Muriel McCullough's courtroom, was whether I was doing this to myself, or I was answering God's calling. That's a tough one. When I left Dr. Ezekiel's trial courtroom and started down that hall with Shifty, I had to stop. I realized just how tired I was. I felt my legs giving way. I realized I couldn't feel them. The last several months seemed to hit me hard, at that very moment. I looked at Shifty. "Shifty, I need coffee."

Shifty stopped. I could see he was about to insist I continue on. But he looked at me. He saw me. I'm sure in a heartbeat, he saw that I looked physically bedraggled. I had to blink to get my eyes to open. I ran my hands through my wavy unkempt hair. It took longer than usual. With no regimen for regular personal care, you eventually look tattered. Shifty had me sit down. He saw I was, well, crying. I had lost it. I suppose, too many 8-to-3s, too many trials, too little food. When I look okay, sometimes a person will say to me I look young for my age. My usual comeback: "My secret is no sleep, lots of coffee, and minimally invasive food." It's not funny. I know this feeling well.

It's a wall.

I sometimes hit it.

After a trial.

We all hit it on occasion after a trial. After whatever trial you have come through in your life.

Shifty puts his hand on my shoulder. "Tom, let me pray for you."

I was really crying. "Shifty, I'll be okay. I'm so sorry…This is just so embarrassing."

"Let me pray for you."

"Okay."

I wish I could remember the exact words of Shifty's prayer. But, I remember what it did for me. It fixed me. I felt the Lord said to me, "Tom, I'm with you, I will guide you, I will protect you, I love you." Or, something like that. I just felt the prayer healed my spirit, the core of my being, and that healed my soul, and that healed my body. And when the prayer was over—I was okay.

I stood up. Dusted myself off. "Shifty, I still need that cup of coffee."

"You got it, man." And we headed down a few flights of the escalator to the little store on the second floor so I could get a quick fix of coffee.

"Shifty?"

"Yes, Tom."

"Do you ever get lonely?"

He looked at me. "Do we need to sit down again?"

"Yeah."

So we sat down.

"Tom, stay here." Shifty left.

I waited. When I had that long trial in Shifty's courtroom a few years ago, I remember his wife, Ruby, would come on occasion and just sit in the audience close to Shifty. She had her Bible on her lap, and she didn't say a word as she read the Word. I could see the love they had for each other. Whatever that love is, I never had it. Shifty had a quick chance to introduce me to her once. But, in the middle of a trial, "quick" is really quick.

Shifty came back. He sat down next to me. "It's cool, I told the judge you needed a little time to compose yourself after the trial. Take your time; they'll wait for you."

"Shifty?"

"Yes, Tom, what's the matter, man?"

Drying your eyes on your coat sleeve is hard in a packed courtroom hallway when you know some of the people passing you by.

"Shifty, my wife told me our marriage was over."

"What?! Oh, man. I'm so sorry. I don't know what to say. Man, that hurts. I didn't even know you were married?"

"Just like that. She said it's over," I said, getting my composure together.

"Man, how long have you been married?"

I starting tearing up again.

I looked at Shifty through glazed-over eyes: "Three months."

I wasn't in the position, right then and there, midday, in the courthouse, to have a nervous breakdown. I had to rally. I had to recover. Quick. It was December 17 when my wife said our marriage was over. That was two months ago. I had held everything together to win Dr. Ezekiel's trial. My holding pattern was getting shaky. That's a skill you'd better have if you're going to be a trial lawyer.

Holding patterns.

I did that for three decades.

Finally, I just had to go to Department 64 and meet with the judge. Perhaps, I can help someone else.

Maybe I can't help when I'm this tired. But, maybe I can. I have no energy to put up with wasted energy—which most cases are. Maybe I should emphasize over and over again to those who go into battles like this that—it will wipe you out physically, mentally, emotionally, and financially. How many would actually go through this if they knew what they were going to go through?

And then I walk into Department 64.

It looks like a warzone. I can see counsel at their tables, the clients next to them. Both sides are hunkered down, talking in whispers. Boxes of evidence and pleadings everywhere, blow-ups of evidence standing here and there, overhead projector equipment idling just in case the battle resumes, and witnesses and onlookers in the audience. A few photographers glancing around. The energy in the courtroom is thick. Everyone turns around and looks at me. I'm now in the present. I suddenly forget what I had been doing. Everyone looks wasted, tired, worn out. Shifty takes his usual place at the bailiff's desk and I hear his co-workers, the court reporter and judge's clerk, and a few law clerks get happy because they have their old friend Shifty back, miffed that their judge loaned him to my trial. Shifty was really needed back here. They missed him, badly. The judge was standing by her clerk's desk. She signals me to join her alone in chambers. I walk into her back office.

We exchange greetings. She looks exhausted also. She lays her weary head in her hands.

"Tom, here's the lay of the land: Two doctors, ophthalmologists now married to each other, met in medical school. Famous in their field of medicine. Built five offices in five cities. Fly around in a helicopter and a plane between offices. Very successful, wealthy, have two kids, eleven and thirteen years of age. Husband has an affair with Genevieve ("Jenny"), a nurse that accompanies him on his surgeries. The two were married fifteen years, officially divorced two years ago and have been fighting over the assets ever since. Each has spent hundreds of thousands of dollars on attorneys fees. Husband's affair is no longer relevant, but it keeps coming up. She never stops crying. He is stoic and resolute. Wife had a meltdown earlier today and all counsel decided to take one more shot to settle, even though we are two days into the trial to determine how the assets are to be divided. Custody of the kids will be joint. They'll end up drug addicts with parents like these."

"Judge, I'll take it from here," I said.

A simple standard issue, cafeteria-grade white paper napkin

I walked out the judge's chambers; I wasn't tired anymore. I asked Shifty to go to the cafeteria and get me a standard issue, cafeteria-grade white paper napkin. He did, in record time.

"Hello counsel, and parties. Judge McCullough has asked me to sit in as a mediator on your case. She has given me the lay of the land. I'd like all present who are not parties, or their lawyers to leave the courtroom. It's lunch time anyway."

Everyone leaves, including the court personnel. Everyone is introduced. I take a seat in front of counsel's table, facing the lawyers and the parties: Husband and Wife, *past tense.*

I have the parties sign a standard confidentiality agreement, and then explain the mediation process to them. Everything said during the mediation would remain confidential and inadmissible in the trial. I would start off hearing from both sides in a joint session, and then caucus with both sides separately as I tried to hone a way to resolve the case for them. Except, in this case, as it turned out— there was no need to caucus. Only God can do that.

The joint session lasted forty-five minutes. Both sides gave their side of the story. When they were done, I looked at them and said:

"Jill and Bryan, I can see how hurt both of you are. Jill, you feel that Bryan cheated on you, ruined the marriage, and then ruined a wonderful, very successful medical practice. Bryan feels that you left the marriage a long time ago when you stopped having sex with him, which is a very important part of marriage. Because your father is an alcoholic, you have some unresolved issues with your father, and with men in general. Bryan, you feel abandoned by Jill and therefore justified in starting a relationship with your nurse, a relationship you didn't want, but has now developed into something you value, and with long- term potential. Still, what you did is an act of adultery, disruptive to the medical practice, and the final element that destroyed the marriage. In reality, this trial is about a division of the assets of your marital estate and therefore the personal side of this is not considered relevant. And yet these issues are prominent. I've often said that, with but few exceptions, most cases can settle over lunch on the back of a napkin. So, I'm going to suggest how this case should settle, and then we can meet separately all you want, and we will try hard to settle this case. I have all the energy in the world, we will stay until midnight if you'd like, and Judge McCullough sometimes orders that, if she decides that's what it will take."

I reach over and grab the napkin.

"This is a standard issue, cafeteria-grade white paper napkin." I write as I talk. "I put a little "T" at the top and a little + next to it. 'Trust God.' Under that, I'll write 'Jill and Bryan's Settlement.' So, here's your list:"

I continue writing and talking. What I write is a short version of what I say:

"First, I'm putting two columns, A and B. You have five offices that operate pretty much independently. So, I'm putting three in column A, and two in column B. Because I've heard all the financial numbers and figures, I believe this division is fair, or as fair as we can get;

"Second, the revenue at each practice will stay at each practice and goes to the party that gets the column A or B practices;

"Third, strict joint custody of the children, with time with them and expenses divided 50-50;

"Fourth, you will sell the house in the Palisades, and divide the proceeds 50-50. Same with the retreat in Palm Springs.

"Fifth, finish dividing up the assets in the bank accounts and brokerage accounts 50-50;

"Sixth, finish dividing up the furniture, art, and everything else;

"Seventh, Bryan, agree to counseling twice a month with Genevieve. Otherwise, you will ruin that relationship, because you have communication problems. Ask her to consider writing an apology to Jill. And, in counseling, focus on communicating with Jill. Communicating with love and respect.

"Eighth, Jill, agree to counseling to finally deal with your alcoholic father, who I believe abused you. You never worked through all that. It's time. Counseling, twice a month. When you get in a new relationship, have sex, lots of sex, a minimum of two or three times a week. No exceptions, except normal exceptions. Have it whenever, wherever, however—just, have *it*.

"Now, I'm putting two signature lines for Jill . . . and Bryan.

"I'm optimistic.

"On a personal note: Jill, whether you get column A or B, you should sell the practices in two years. You never wanted to be a doctor. You did what your father wanted you to do. In two or three years, sell your practices, travel and take up photography. You love it, and . . . it's time to live your life.

"On a personal note: Bryan, you should buy the practices from Jill, and pay her a good price. You may be a better doctor technically than Jill, but the patients love Jill, and she has the healing touch. Pay her to stay on as a consultant and let her continue to be the face of the practices. You'll never regret it.

"Last personal note: Jill and Bryan, forgive each other. Both of you have incredible futures in store for you. God will rebuild your lives and continue to bless you.

Now go, meet separately with your lawyers. I will sit here and wait as long as you want. No hurry. Who wants the napkin?"

"I do," said Jill. Holding back tears.

Later that night, after the mediation, I went downtown to The Dream Center. Mike Conner, the director of The Dream Center Rehab Center asked me to speak at the Tuesday night service, which is mostly attended by all the people in the program. My topic: *Settle It! . . . and do it quickly.* It is such a blessing to look out at three hundred or so faces, of people determined to get their life together. In the front row, was Stanley, a twenty-four-year-old heroin addict who had been in the program and off the streets for three days. Next to him was Ben, who'd been in the program for a year. Stan was shivering uncontrollably and Ben was helping him with a blanket and support. Stanley was determined to stay and hear me speak.

Me?

How absurd?

I hadn't even started and I was humbled. I had just finished a trial, I had fought like hell. Was the fight even close to what Stan was fighting?

No.

Stanley was white, tats everywhere, scars everywhere, tracks, even on his neck. Ben was black, forty years old. Divorced, two kids. Sober one year. Lord, how can I possibly help, even in the slightest?

I can't. I toss the mental outline I was going to speak about.

"Guys, my friends Danny and Patty have passed out to all of you a simple standard issue, cafeteria-grade white paper napkin. Just kind of hold that between your hands for a moment, while I pray for you, while I pray for all of us, and me, your brother in Christ."

I pray, letting the Holy Spirit lead me.

When I finish, I ask everyone to pray out loud, right now, for the one thing they would like the Lord to settle in their life right now. They pray.

"Guys, I'm in my fifties now. I have been in more battles, fights, wars, and brawls than you can imagine. And then I look at all of you. And, I realize: *you can imagine.* What kind of sinful pride do I possess that allows me to think I've had greater fights than you? . . . My whole life has come down to just one message: God wants you to settle the matters in your life, and do it quickly. He has told me that he wants to pour out his blessings on his sons and daughters and that to do so they must do all they can to settle all the burdens and trials that have come their way and will come their way. He wants nothing separating us from a close relationship with Him.

"On the napkin in your hand, at the top put a "T" and a little cross "+" next to it. "T+" Trust the Lord.

"Now, under that, write down the one thing in your life you would really like settled quickly. After that, go ahead and add a few other things you'd like to settle. That's your list.

"Sign and date it."

Everyone takes a moment and does it. And, so do I. I've had a few lists in my life. And now I need another one. The little church is quiet as the Holy Spirit moves.

"Most of you, perhaps all of you have made the list. If I gave this speech, sermon, whatever it is, to a less hurting group than you, few would make the list, and fewer would keep it.

"My friend here is Ben. I've known Ben for about a year. Ben has a little faith. Maybe a puny little amount of faith. Maybe the size of a mustard seed. But Jesus said: "I tell you the truth, if you have faith as small as a mustard seed, you can say to this mountain, 'move from here to there' and it will move. Nothing will be impossible for you."

"The size of my friend Ben's faith is enough."

Earlier in the afternoon, Jill and Bryan and their lawyers came back about one hour after the joint session had ended. They all sat in front of me. Jill's lawyer went first:

"We want to settle."

Bryan's lawyer went second:

"We want to settle."
"Who wants column A, and who wants B?" I asked.
Jill's lawyer went first:
"Either one is fine with us."
Bryan's lawyer went second.
"Either one is fine with us."

In my estimation, both Jill and Bryan had good hearts. They were children of light. Georgy Tarasov had a bad heart. It didn't improve. Children of darkness eventually are struck down. He would eventually be arrested for a whole host of illegal things. He is still in jail.

At the end of the day, Jill and Bryan chose column "C". They each took two practices, and combined their efforts and talents in the fifth and most successful practice. They are booming. Jenny even assists Jill in her surgeries. Jill found a new love and is engaged. God repairs our lives, over and over again. Just keep going back to Him. Both Jill and Bryan did.

Only God can settle that

When I was finished speaking to the Dream Center rehab group later that night, I looked over at Stanley. He was sobbing, so a few more of us went over to just be with him.

Then, well, I thought it was a little rude of me, but I looked at Stanley and asked him: "What did you write on your napkin?"

He clutched the napkin and lowered his forehead into his hands. Through his sobs he said:

"That the only thing I ever, ever, again inject into my life . . . is God."

Then he dropped his arms in his lap and I saw the track marks, bruises, and scars running up both his arms.

Only God can settle that.

And on that day, He did.

T+

The Take Away 15
How to settle the problems in your life.

1. Some people will make the conscious effort to settle the problems in their life, especially those people that really need to settle a major problem in their life. With God's help, it is actually quite easy:

    Take out a simple standard issue, cafeteria-grade white paper napkin. Put a "T" at the top, and a "+" next to it. "T+" ("Trust the Lord"). Take a moment, put out all the fires in your mind, and remove all the distractions. Let the one thing in your life come to mind that you would really like settled quickly. Write that on the napkin somewhere under the "T+". After you write down that one big thing, go ahead and add a few other things you'd like to settle, or a goal or dream you'd like to accomplish. That's "your list." Ask God to help you settle the matters on the list and receive in your heart the victory. Date your list and sign your name. Fold the napkin and put it in your pocket.

2. This is where journaling comes in. For the next *forty days*, get up early, *while it is still dark*, and look at and pray over your list. Ask God to settle the matters on the list. And ask Him for guidance as to what *you* should do to settle the matters on the list, *your list*. Write down the revelations! Write down everything God tells you. Write down everything that is on your heart. Turn it all over to the Lord. "Write down the revelation and make it plain on tablets so that a herald may run with it." Habakkuk 2:2.

3. In some cases, and with some problems, God will give you the starting place. But that is all you need. Remember, "he who began a good work in you will carry it on to completion . . . ." Philippians 1:6.

4. It would be impossible for me to say how many people I have helped to settle their problems or conflicts in this way with just a simple standard issue, cafeteria-grade white paper napkin. *I don't understand it.* But, then again, I don't lean on my own understanding. "Trust in the Lord with all your heart and lean not on your own understanding; in all your ways acknowledge him, and he will make your paths straight." Proverbs 3:5-6.

    Spend the next forty days working on your list. Start getting up early, while it is still dark. Turn your list over to the Lord. And, have faith.

    "I tell you the truth, if you have faith as small as a mustard seed, you can say to this mountain, 'Move from here to there' and it will move. Nothing will be impossible for you." Matthew 17:20.

Journal Entry, June 18, 1999

Friday morning, 4:30 a.m.
Spirit, Soul and Body

Another birthday

Mercy. This is painful. Depressing. Intense. I've spent twenty years in courthouses and courtrooms. And if you count law school, college, and most everything I did since I decided to be a lawyer when I was twelve, it is even longer than that. I was clerking in the Santa Barbara Law Library when I was in high school and college. I spent a lot of time watching my various bosses over the years try cases, and that was *before* I even went to law school.

Lord, I guess you *did*, have a plan for me. It took me a while to know where it came from, but I know now. I wanted to be a lawyer, and some of my earliest memories were of sitting outside the courthouse in the nearest coffee shop talking to my boss, a lawyer, and listening in while he spoke to his client. It was usually about 7:00 a.m. The trial would start in a few hours. Jury selection, then opening statements. I felt I was in the right place. It was summer in Santa Barbara, the surf was up, my friends were at the beach. I was wearing an old herringbone sport coat, white button-down shirt, and stained tie. Maybe the surf was up, but I was at the courthouse. I was the son of a rocket scientist and my afterburners were already fired up.

That was twenty-five years ago.

On that morning, a long time ago in Santa Barbara, sitting in the little coffee shop outside the Santa Barbara courthouse, I took a sip, my first sip, of coffee. The taste was kind of bitter, so I added some cream. No sugar. And tried it again. I liked the smell, the aroma. I took another sip. It tasted perfect. Strong, smooth, warm, lots of aroma. It had attitude. I felt I had found a friend. My father and his

Jewish friends smoked. I tried it, but didn't like it. Instead, I'd drink coffee. My dad's affectation was smoking, mine would be coffee. Around 8:15 a.m., my boss finished his discussion with his client, looked at me and said: "Are you ready?" I said, "Yes." He said, "Let's go." I remember saying in response, *"For such a time as this."* Back then, it was just a phrase I picked up from a Jewish friend of my father's. I didn't know what it meant, but it was kind of catchy, so I would use it. I was exactly where I was supposed to be. I believe I was where you wanted me to be.

Thank you for that.

A question for God

I'm sipping coffee now, and thinking. It's 4:30 a.m. It's my birthday. I'm alone as usual and I have to be in court in a few hours. My khaki suit is waiting, my white button-down shirt, and a striped tie, no stains (it's early still). *Lord, I have a question for you.* And I'd really like you to answer it truthfully. I need an honest assessment. My bosses over the years gave me assessments, so I figured you could give me one. Anyway, here's my question: Is the path I'm on such that at the end of it, you will say "well done, good and faithful servant?"[1] Look, I want to know that. Nobody's listening, I can ask a question. Can't I?

I don't understand why when I'm so beaten down and broken, so tired, so lost, that you don't criticize me. You always build me up. I've made some brutal personal mistakes and yet you never condemn me, just like your word says. Why would anyone *not* want you as a friend? I criticize myself horribly. I'm getting older, I'm alone, no family of my own, no personal life, not close to my parents and brothers, don't know my neighbors. Don't have much to show for myself. I'm a talented lawyer, but not much else. Plenty of clients, plenty of work. And, sadly, more comfortable in a courthouse than on a date. More comfortable in cross-examination than in a hug. Better able to read a jury than read a menu, better able to draft a brief than write a letter, more comfortable in suits than in jeans.

I'm at least half way done with life. My life seems much longer than a mist. But I still want to know: am I doing a good job? I feel like I'm putting absolutely everything I have in to this thing, my life, my path, my career, my everything. I win my trials, but everything else seems shaky.

I was wondering if at the end of the day, if you could answer my question. Please?

Amen.

Another little coffee shop outside the courthouse

It's now 7:00 a.m. and I'm at the little coffee shop outside the courthouse. The little coffee shop has gone through various permutations over the years, but, it's

---

[1] Matthew 25:21-23 (NKJV). The Parable of the Talents. "His lord said to him, 'Well done, good and faithful servant; you were faithful over a few things, I will make you ruler over many things. Enter into the joy of your lord.'"

still there. I will be there, no matter what they call the place. It's right outside the courthouse, literally on the same property. In the "*court*yard." I can't get used to its new name. To me, it's still: *the little coffee shop outside the courthouse.* That's what I can relate to. It's Friday, it's my birthday, I have big plans for the day: Be in court all day, or until this case settles (I'm being positive), then go home and go to sleep after a little more journaling. Lord, please help me settle this case today. I'm tired, and I've done everything possible to settle it. This case is six months old, I've worked very hard on it, so have my clients.

I remember the day I met them, my clients, David and Shirley Miller.

It was six months ago, sitting at this same coffee shop, 7:00 a.m., waiting to spend a full day in court, sipping a cup of coffee, with cream, no sugar, and waiting to meet with a potential new client, David Miller, who wanted to catch me before I carried on with another day in trial, which would resume in a few hours. I wondered at the time if David was Jewish or Gentile, knowing that "Miller" is the third most common surname among Jews, but also one of the most common names among Gentiles.

I think of these things when I pick a jury.

Then David saw me as he walked up. And I saw him: older, about seventy, white and gray hair, hastening at whatever he did. I already sussed it up: he was walking at four miles per hour. Too fast. If his case ever went to trial I would tell him to keep his walking to 2.5 miles per hour. That's normal. I wouldn't want jurors in the hallways thinking he was nervous.

And he did start right in: "Tom, so good to meet you, thank you so much for meeting me, ugh!, *for such a time as this*, I really need you."

"Jewish," I thought.

Then, trailing behind him, rushing to catch up was *Yenta*, no, actually, "Shirley." He brought his wife, *how cute*. They *hastened* together. She was doing 4.5 miles per hour. And that was just her walking. They were still rushing to get out of Egypt. David and Shirley Miller offered to buy me another cup of coffee. I tried to decline, but Shirley would not hear of it. It took me a while to convince her I didn't want sugar in it, any type of sugar, any type of sweetener. No additives. Coffee is blessed as it is. That being settled, Shirley/Yenta allowed David to lead the conversation, for about one sentence, while echoing everything he said; they both wore the pants in the family, belt and suspenders, but he wore the garments of praise.[2] All I knew was that a jury would side with them on whatever they wanted. Trustworthiness defined these people; they measured exactitude with deeds over words. They had spent a lifetime measuring things, and the measurements were perfect. They were in the clothing business. Clothes were not clothes to them, they were instruments of worship.

David asked: "Tom, did you read the complaint I sent over to you last night?"

---

2 Isaiah 61:1-3. "He has sent me to bind up the brokenhearted . . . to bestow on them a crown of beauty instead of ashes . . . and a garment of praise instead of a spirit of despair."

"Yes I did, and I have the lay of the land," I responded.

Yenta took over, "Tom, I heard you win all your trials. We really need you. Our company has been sued and we must win or we will lose everything. We will spare no expense," she said in a low hushed voice designed for extra drama. Or, maybe she was actually concerned. "Thomas, we believe God sent us directly to you, no other lawyer will do."

"Have you tried to settle the case?" I asked.

"No, we want to destroy them, for doing this to us. We don't want to settle. Why would we settle?" Shirley emphasized. Whew, what an accent; Brooklyn Jewish. I love my friends from Brooklyn.

I looked at David and Shirley and said, "Look, in a few hours I will carry on with my current jury trial. I *expect* to win. But, that's because my client has done everything he can to settle it. *Everything*. You don't qualify to win the case, until you've done everything you can to settle it."

"Why should we settle with these—these children? These—Jezebels!" screeched Shirley.

"Don't you believe in blessings, Yen (*Yenta; I almost said*)—I mean Shirley," I asked, pausing, sipping my coffee, pausing, like my father used to, before and after taking a drag from his cigarette. I had studied that gesture; I had it down.

"Oh, Thomas, Thomas, Thomas, everything Rabbi said about you is true. I can see that. He also said I would have to read the Beatitudes," she said, casting her head back, adding every Jewish Yiddish accent possible. "What is that about?"

Ouch. That was accusatory.

"Well, if you want to win, you need to be a peacemaker," I said. "You okay with that?"

"I am!" David rushed to add, looking at his wife.

"Hmmm. Okay, but will you help us?" She pleaded.

I shook my head with feigned concern. "Mercy, David and Yenta, doing the Eight-Step Program. This could be fun. I'll call you tonight," I said.

I had one more question for them: "Did your Rabbi tell you who my Counselor is?"

Yenta/Shirley rushed to her answer: "No! But Harry Goldberg did."

They started to walk away.

"Please call us tonight!" Shirley called back.

"Harry Goldberg!?" I swear, I teared up.

I was glad they walked away.

Lord, send me to serve, not to win

I remember that day well, when I met the Millers for the first time. After that encounter early in the morning, I asked you: Lord, am I getting a bad reputation? I don't want to be known for winning my trials. I want to be known for helping people settle their conflicts, their problems. Your son, Jesus, wasn't known for "winning." That's ridiculous. And yet he won everything. I see the arc of his battle from beginning to the end. From Genesis to Revelation. In the end he wins. I think of Jesus as my Savior, but on a daily basis, as a servant. When he was here, he was the ultimate servant. And at the end of his earthly walk, he died on the cross for my sins, and everyone's. He was our servant Savior. How trite to look at him as a "winner," which is some modern-day concept taught by the accumulators, those that accumulate treasures on earth, not in heaven. Those graduates of our modern day "feel good" seminars. Jesus would not have gone to those seminars and would not have approved of them. Jesus focused on being about his father's business, and serving in that regard. Help me to learn this. Lord teach me to be about my father in heaven's business, teach me to serve. Lord, *send me* to serve, not to win. "But seek first his kingdom and his righteousness, and all these things will be given to you as well."[3]

Clothed in majesty

It's now 8:00 a.m. Here come the Millers. Six months have gone by in a flash. We will be in mediation all day. I have to admit, I've really come to love them. Here are these orthodox Jews that have studied the Beatitudes, did Jesus' Eight-Step Program, even did the 8-to-3 rule, and are now lecturing me as to why they should settle this case. They have threatened to adopt me. Hey, maybe I'd get a birthday party tossed in. It took them about two months to drop their demands on me to just pummel the other side, then take them to trial, then beat them to death, win the case, and go home. The third month in, after David went through Jesus' Eight-Step Program, after I convinced him it was mostly based on the Old Testament (although I wasn't sure it was; Lord forgive me for that), he decided two things, he wanted to teach Jewish history at the local college, and he wanted to settle this case. He knew why he wanted to settle the case, he didn't care how. That was up to God, he said. And Yenta, she's planning to teach fashion design at the same college. "Thomas," she barked, "the primary reason to be a teacher is to be a student." So, now—they want to settle the case. But, they didn't want to lose Jericho, or City of Palm Trees ("Jericho," was described in the Hebrew Bible as the "City of Palm Trees") their beloved clothing companies. Teaching and fashion were to be their hobbies.

The Millers have been in the schmatta (clothing) business for thirty years.[4] It is religion to them. The problem is, their partner, really David's partner, Joseph Schwartz, died three years ago, his adult children took over his interest, and now the company, Jericho, and its main subsidiary, City of Palm Trees, is in trouble. There is no agreement as to how to position the eleven brand names for the future, there's distrust, money arguments, power struggles, jealousy, and other problems. David misses the days when it was just he and Joseph running

---

3 Matthew 6:33.
4 Genesis 35:2.

the business, which is worldwide, eleven well-known brands, selling in all the major stores, and worth a lot of money. Now, it's David (and Yenta/Shirley) that own 50 percent, and Joseph's three adult children, three girls, that own the other 50 percent. Out of the blue six months ago, Joseph's kids sued David to split up the company, Jericho, and of course, City of Palm Trees. David was heartbroken. He misses his friend, but he believes Joseph's kids will kill the business. In one outburst, David cried:

"This younger generation. They simply don't understand the great importance God places on clothing. Clothes should serve as reminders and symbols of God's truths and commandments! These kids, they have never read Genesis 35:2 and Psalm 104:2." He raises his pitch to a scream, "Don't they know —our God clothes himself with splendor and majesty, he wraps himself in light as with a garment. This is what our clothes SHOULD DO! These kids, they only know the book of Saks, the book of Neiman Marcus. They think "Leviticus" is a line of clothing! I will spew them OUT OF MY MOUTH!!"

Shirley would then calm David. "Now, now, David. Please. This will get us nowhere. We will give them the younger lines. They will be out of fashion by yesterday. And they don't even know it." The three Schwartz girls were between twenty-three and twenty-seven. The case was between the old and the young. The case was between Jericho, the oldest city in the world, and Beverly Hills, one of the newest. David, Shirley and Joseph were born in Israel. Joseph's three girls were born in Beverly Hills. They had hired a young lawyer, Leonard Klein ("Lenny"). He'd been a lawyer for five years. He was "cool." Our mediator was retired judge Lawrence Hornbaker. He was as old as me. He wasn't cool.

It was going to be a long day.

12:00 noon. The case is messy. Discovery and investigation to date has unveiled the fact that the Schwartz' children have diverted corporate opportunities to another clothing business they have started, one that would eventually compete with some of Jericho's eleven brands. The girls are vying for their own reality show. They're up against another group of sisters that are the daughters of a famous athlete and an actress, the Simonians. They are pulling out all the stops. David is devastated because it was David who started the business, and he had brought Joseph over from Israel thirty years ago to help him run it and grow it. Unfortunately, in David's mind, Joseph's kids were Beverly Hills secular Jews that were only in it for fame, money, and did he say, "fame." The girls looked at David and saw an old, and doddering man. (I'm not that far behind David in age.)

After a long discussion at lunch, Shirley and David, were resigned to the possibility that after thirty years the company would be split up, which meant splitting up the brands. David felt he was breaking a promise to Joseph to keep the company together, guide his daughters, and teach them the business. But, the daughters were "teaching" David the business—that was clear. After all, they had been in the business three years, *they knew everything*.

And they *knew* they wanted to be television stars.

The handwriting is on the wall

The mediator struggled back and forth with the offers as the girls, and their young turk of a lawyer vied for all six of the younger, trendier brands. Three of those brands were collectively referred to as the "Fig Leaves" brands. The girls had developed the styles, but liked the trade name chosen by David, "Fig Leaves." Apparently, the girls never knew why David had cynically suggested that they name the styles "Fig Leaves." He told me that in Genesis 3:7 after their fall, "they" ("they" being Adam and Eve) sewed fig leaves together and made themselves garments—the first unisex clothes. David said that was disgusting to God, who forbids such conduct. Indeed, he said, "it is clear in Genesis 3:21 that God made separate coats of skin for "Adam and his wife." In another outburst, David yelled at the girls: "You girls. You don't know God. You don't know that God specifically said: 'A woman must not wear men's clothing, nor a man wear women's clothing, for the LORD your God detests anyone who does this.' Deuteronomy 22:5!!"

The youngest girl tittered at this with a smirk, and rolled her eyes. David then looked her in the eye, and then the other two girls in the eye and said: "You don't know, the handwriting is on the wall." . . . Then he looked at the mediator and said: "Give the girls what they want: the six brands, including 'Fig Leaves,' I will drop my claims against them for stealing and diverting corporate opportunities. My wife and I get the remaining five brands. They take their six, we take our five and go our separate ways."

He looked up to the heavens: "Joseph, I tried. But, it was your daughters that sued me."

The youngest again chirped out one final comment, proud of her new negotiation skills: "You're going to have to augment the offer."

"Haven't all of you girls had enough—*augmentation*!!" Shirley screamed.

The settlement was written up, signed and put on the record before the judge. The girls got their wish, succeeded with their demands, felt justified that they had sued David and Shirley. They were celebrating by 4:00 p.m. They had won their first court battle. Mr. "cool," Lenny Klein was ecstatic. His future was secure. They were all happy. They were convinced they would now, "for sure," get their reality television show. They would beat out the Simonians. "Those girls were ugly anyway," I heard one say as they strutted down the hall. "The Schwartz sisters couldn't be stopped," another said, and they danced and twirled.

I walked David and Shirley to their old Buick. David and Shirley were sanguine about keeping their older more established brands. But, secretively, they knew that by keeping the main brand names, "Jericho" and "City of Palm Trees," they could rebuild the company. The trade names and styles that the girls readily walked away from, meant everything to David and Shirley.

David called me at 10:15 p.m. One of the entertainment channels just announced a new reality show. One centered around "the Simonians." David referred again to the Book of Daniel 5:5, and said: "I tried to stop them, but the handwriting was on the wall."

He thanked me, and hung up.

The Dream Center

The Miller case settled at 4:30 p.m. Then, I decided, because I'm already downtown, I think I'll go to the Dream Center.

At first I thought the Dream Center in downtown Los Angeles was only a rehab center. I'd been to a lot of other rehab centers, mostly to volunteer, or work with my lawyer friends as they tried to get off drugs or alcohol. Other programs are good, I suppose, but I see the prescription drugs that the doctors give my friends, just seem to blanket over the problem, and they are right back in trouble. My friend Walt, has been back to the rehab center in Malibu three times. And, thirty days in rehab is just not enough. Forty days is the minimum, don't they know that? When I first went to the Dream Center I realized they don't do "rehab." They change lives. And their prescription is simple: water, Tylenol, and the Bible. Nothing else. That simple. Amazing. And, a person, male or female can stay there a year. A year! And, amazingly, it's free. Free? The rehab centers I know and have taken friends to are $10,000 to $20,000 a month. Or more. How does the Dream Center do it for free? The director said they usually have about 150 adult men and women in the program. For free!

So, I was first brought to the little Dream Center church on a Thursday night in January 1998, and it changed my life. Who are these guys, Tommy and Matthew Barnett? Are they crazy? They raised money to buy the old deserted, rundown Queen of Angels Hospital by Echo Park, in Rampart, the worst area in town, drug dealers, gangs, crime, destitution, prostitution, homeless, everything else. They turn the old hospital into a church. My actress friend, Dyan, took me to one of their church services on a Thursday night. The service was in an old gym, in the old hospital. Old, rundown, beat up. But, Lord . . . you were there. Clearly, You were there. And, your *angels* had returned to the old Queen of Angels. After I went to that service on that first Thursday night, I was hooked. I started going there every week. If I was in court, it was easy, I was already downtown. If I was in my offices in Beverly Hills it was also not too hard to get down there by 7:00 p.m. when the service began. There were no lukewarms there. I felt at home. I didn't care how far I had to drive, I drove to my newfound ghetto church.

Spirit, soul, and body

Lord, it is so helpful that I have come to learn that "I" am not my "mind." Perhaps it was the book of Daniel that first gave me the clue. God sent a messenger to Daniel and when the messenger appeared he said: "Do not be afraid Daniel. Since the first day that you set your mind to gain understanding and to humble yourself before your God, your words were heard, and I have come in response to them."[5] There is so much in this verse that helps me Lord. I have come to learn that we are spirit, we have a soul, and we live in a body.[6] I am spirit, and I have a soul (which is my mind, will, and emotions), and I live in this body.

It was Daniel's *spirit* that set his *mind* to gain understanding and to humble himself before you, God. I know that those who live in accordance with the Spirit have their minds *set* on what the Spirit desires, and I know the mind controlled by the Spirit is life and peace.[7]

Lord, when I was born again, it was my spirit that was born again, certainly not this slowly wasting away body. My body wasn't born again, my spirit was. When I was born again, it is my spirit that received eternal life. This is truly a marvelous and wonderful experience when this sinks in. I have begun to see that we are all spirit, even my adversaries in court, my adversaries in life. It is so much easier to understand them when I see them as spirit beings struggling with life just as I am, but also so lost if their spirit hasn't been born again. If they are not born again, their souls are not being renewed, they don't have a new life, they can't discern the evil forces trying to rule their life, they are cut off from the true source of life, and strength, and guidance and counseling that brings true peace and joy in this life. I know, as Daniel knew, that his prayers, his "words" were heard by you, and you responded to him.

Lord, I know you are sovereign, but thank you for the times, so numerous to list, that you have responded to my words, and my prayers.

Lord, thank you for my soul. Lord, I realize that it was my spirit that was born again, not my soul. But, because my spirit is born again, my soul (my mind, will and emotions) is being saved also and is going through a process. Lord, I can see that you are renewing and restoring my soul, you are renewing and restoring my mind, will and emotions. Lord, I accept your "word" planted in me,[8] and I no longer wish to conform to the pattern of this world, but wish to be transformed by a renewing of my mind.[9]

And I thank you for restoring my soul.[10]

Lord, I get it.

I've *settled it* in my spirit.

---

5 Daniel 10:12.

6 1 Thessalonians 5:23. "May God himself, the God of peace, sanctify you through and through. May your whole spirit, soul and body be kept blameless at the coming of our Lord Jesus Christ."

7 Romans 8:5-7. "Those who live according to the sinful nature have their minds set on what that nature desires; but those who live in accordance with the Spirit have their minds set on what the Spirit desires. The mind of sinful man is death, but the mind controlled by the Spirit is life and peace; the sinful mind is hostile to God."

8 James 1:21.

9 Romans 12:2. "Do not conform any longer to the pattern of this world, but be transformed by the renewing of your mind. Then you will be able to test and approve what God's will is—his good, pleasing and perfect will."

10 Psalm 23:3.

At the end of the day

Lord, it's late. It's the end of the day. This is one of my longer journal entries. My fingers are sore. I wish I would type softer.

Lord, at the end of this day, and at the end of all my days, at the end of my life, and when it's all been said and done, I pray that you can say to me: "Well done, good and faithful servant!"[11]

Down deep, deep in my heart, I hear your still *small* quiet voice:

For today, well done good and faithful servant. I'll have your list for you in the morning. Carry on.

So, I do. Amen.

T+

---

11 Matthew 25:23.

The Take Away 16
The godly examined life is well worth living.

1. The godly examined life is well worth living. Psalm 139:23 says: "Search me, O God, and know my heart; test me and know my anxious thoughts. See if there is any offensive way in me, and lead me in the way everlasting." The godly examined life is everlasting.

2. Socrates said "The unexamined life is not worth living." We live in a world where the examined life means *self* examined. This chapter explored a mediation between self examined lives and godly examined lives. Between the young and the old, the temporal and the everlasting, the worldly and the godly.

3. From the ancient aphorism of Plato to "Know Thyself," to the poet Samuel T. Coleridge's cry, "Ignore thyself, and strive to know thy God!"—man fluxes with a desire to justify his life and find a deep and true purpose.

4. Sometimes I see the Gospels, including the book of Acts, as journals. There's history, there's story, there's teaching, and there's honesty, integrity and finally truth. Where would we be today if the Gospels had not been written? Is your life worth writing about? Start your life journal, and ask God to bless the entries. God may have something very important for you to write down. Ultimately, God wants a relationship with you. What are you doing to foster that?

Matthew 25:21-23 (NKJV). The Parable of the Talents. "His lord said to him, 'Well *done*, good and faithful servant; you were faithful over a few things, I will make you ruler over many things. Enter into the joy of your lord."

Settle It!

Watch and Pray

Watch and Pray

The spirit is willing

The speed of construction can't compete with the speed of destruction

On a flight to New York, Mike Harrison met a very pretty woman who sat next to him. They spoke for a while during the flight, just about life, and business. Then they went to work on their own projects as the flight progressed. Then they landed. As they walked up the jetway together she asked if she could have a drink with him later that night, just to talk business. She was interested in "his company."

He said "yes."

What's the big deal?

It's just business.

Later that night they had the drink together.

The conversation up the gangplank took less than five minutes.

An executive is crossing town in Chicago in her company limousine. She gets a call on her cellphone from her broker. The broker tells her to sell a certain biopharmaceutical stock she has a large position in. The broker goes on to tell the executive nonpublic information that the owner of the biopharmaceutical company and his family were selling all of their shares because the FDA was going to refuse the company's application for a new cancer treatment drug.

She sells her shares based on this illegal, insider information from her broker. They ask about each other's health and life in general.

The conversation on her cellphone while being driven across town took less than five minutes.

Martin Reader called me up in the summer of 2004. I was at my desk, swamped, coffee in hand, trying to get a document together. Reader was the CEO of a hospital in Los Angeles, a hospital that needed patients. He said he just finished a short meeting with a marketing guy who, for a rather large fee, could guarantee an additional forty patients a month if Reader would just sign a simple marketing agreement under which the services of the hospital would be marketed to the nearby communities.

Reader asked the guy, "Is it all legal?"

The marketing guy said, "Yes, of course it is. You can count on me! Will you sign?"

Reader was ready to say, "yes," and sign the marketing agreement. Then he remembered the Five Minute Rule that says most major mistakes happen in less than five minutes. Reader told the guy he would think about it. So the guy left with his unsigned marketing agreement. And Reader thought about it. He decided it didn't smell right.

Reader called to tell me he really wanted to sign the contract. If the guaranteed patients came in, the hospital could easily afford the high monthly marketing fee. The marketing guy could easily give the contract to hospitals in the area, Reader's competitors.

Reader told me: "Tom, I was all ready to sign and give him a check and then I remembered your Five Minute Rule. He just left. He wasn't here very long. Did I do the right thing?"

"Yes," I told him. "Don't sign those marketing agreements. What the guy does is go down to skid row, pick up homeless people, pay them a few bucks, get them to hop in his van, bring them to the hospital and get them admitted. Because they are homeless, they all have at least some problems. Then you can bill the Medicaid and Medicare system. Problem is, you're basically paying for patients, which is illegal. Don't do it. I have to get back to work now."

"Okay, I won't sign it. Thanks." Reader hung up.

It took almost six years for the CEOs from two other hospitals in the area to be indicted, along with the marketing person, for Medicaid and Medicare fraud related to the marketing agreements. They all spent time in prison, were hit with major fines they could never pay, and ruined their careers.

Before signing, Reader decided to take five minutes, wait, and listen to his conscience. Then he called me.

His conscience said there was something wrong with the proposal.

His conscience was right.

The five minutes of deliberation saved his hospital, and his career.

Reader and I were having coffee about a week later at the Pantry in downtown Los Angeles. We were discussing his decision not to sign the marketing agreement, and he was thanking me. We didn't know that he would be even more thankful six years later. Then, he was talking about how long it took him to painstakingly build a career, buy his first hospital, then buy his second hospital and his projections for future growth. He was old enough to know just how fast someone could destroy his or her career with just one wrong move.

"The speed of construction can never compete with the speed of destruction," I said.

"And the ugliness of destruction can never compete with the beauty of construction," Martin shot right back at me.

I knew my friend Martin pretty well, I knew his wife, and his kids. He was slowly but surely building a great business and a great home life.

Whether it is a building, or a life, if it is slowly and methodically constructed, it is a thing of beauty, or a life of beauty. And the beauty of it, or the beauty of a life, will always magnificently surpass the ugliness of its or a person's destruction.

I nodded in agreement to Martin, and added, "'Slow,' is not a popular word anymore, but if applied correctly, it will always beat out 'fast.'"

Martin and I finished our breakfast. Martin's hobby is photography. As we were leaving he was still musing:

"You know in photography, 'slow' means a longer exposure. I personally like my photos after a longer exposure. I also like my decisions that way."

I still don't know if that analogy applies. But for Martin it does. And it helps him make a lot of great decisions.

The Five Minute Rule, part 2

The Five Minute Rule is simple: *most disasters are caused in under five minutes.* That's because the first reaction of your body (your flesh) cannot be trusted. The second reaction of your mind could be wrong. But the reaction of your spirit will be right.

When the woman made the proposal to Mike, if he had remembered the Five Minute Rule, the worst he would have done is say "I'll think about it." Then, he would have deliberated for five minutes, and he would have known what to do.

When the broker made the call to the executive, if she had remembered the Five Minute Rule, the worst she would have done is say, "No rash decisions here; I'll call you back in five." She would have listened to her own spirit, and just said "No."

Martin Reader knew to take five minutes. His first reaction was to take the deal. Instead, he took five minutes. Martin is spirit-filled. He could count on getting the answer right.[1]

He did.

The power of life and death

The tongue has the power of life and death,[2] therefore—use it wisely. Watch every word you speak. Every word. "For by your words you will be acquitted,

1 "Feeling is the voice of the body. Reason is the voice of the soul, or the mind. Conscience is the voice of the spirit." Kenneth E. Hagin, *How You Can Be Led by the Spirit of God* (Faith Library Publications, 2nd edition 2001), p. 63.
2 Proverbs 18:21. "The tongue has the power of life and death, and those who love it will eat its fruit."

and by your words you will be condemned."[3] Words, and deeds, must never be rushed.[4] That's when mistakes happen, and sometimes disasters. "Even a fool is thought wise if he keeps silent, and discerning if he holds his tongue."[5]

And on the other side of the coin is *listening*. Teaching a client the fine art of listening is a challenge in this world. And it takes some time. But, at a minimum, they have to learn the power of their tongue, and the power of their listening. In business dealings, and in life, and in every conversation they must come to understand that: *Every word spoken is a word not heard.* When you're speaking, you're not listening. And, so often, that's not good. Was what you said in the conversation more important than what you didn't hear the other person say? So often it's clear: You're not learning when you're talking.

The spirit is willing

Your spirit is willing to guide you, if you give it the chance. Your conscience is the voice of your spirit. We are spirit, we have a soul (our mind, will and emotions), and we live in a body. When Mike was asked by the pretty girl to have a drink that night, his body, his flesh reacted fast; the answer was "yes!" Even his mind would have just analyzed it: "Well, it's just business, she's interested in my company, the work we do, we're professionals, there's nothing wrong with having a drink together, besides, I've been working hard, I deserve it."

But, his spirit, if he had given it a chance would have said: "No!" And, Mike should have listened.

He didn't give it a chance.

It's actually quite simple. The Holy Spirit, speaks to your spirit, your conscience is the voice of your spirit, you listen to your conscience, and you know what to do.

Trust your spirit.

Your spirit will guide you. Give it a chance.

Lying, it's easy . . . until the end

Lying as an offense is codified in both state and federal law. In California where I try most of my cases, it's codified in Civil Code Sections 1709 and 1710. Lying is fraudulent deceit.[6] It has existed from the beginning of time as noted below.

I used to tell my law students at Pepperdine University that it is easy to deceive. It's amazingly easy. And, you will be dealing with it for the rest of your life, personally, in your business life, and in your professional life. People lie. And it is easy for someone to lie, especially if they put their mind to it, if they *set their mind* to it. And it will bring you much strife and pain. That, I can assure you. We

---

3 Matthew 12:37.

4 See Proverbs 21:5. "The plans of the diligent lead to profit as surely as haste leads to poverty."

5 Proverbs 17:28.

6 California Civil Code Section 1709. Fraudulent deceit. One who willfully deceives another with intent to induce him to alter his position to his injury or risk, is liable for any damage which he thereby suffers.

lawyers have to deal with it extensively in our professional life. There are laws everywhere dealing with it, directly and indirectly. When you see a case, like I did with my client Dr. Ezekiel, you think, "okay, the other guy lied, he lied extensively and over a long period of time, I get it, it's not hard to understand, he's a liar, and if he gets away with his lie, he thinks he will profit from it." And then I pause and think further, "he is one 'who loves and practices falsehood.'"[7] I know what happens to him in the end.

So, it doesn't faze me. Deception, lying, was here from the very beginning. We have been fighting it from day one. How do we fight all this deception, all this lying?

Watch and pray.

You barely get the story of man started in Genesis, chapters one and two, before deception kicks in by chapter three. It kicks in with amazing ease. The key is in the dialogue.

Now the serpent was more crafty than any of the wild animals the Lord God had made. He said to the woman, "Did God really say, 'You must not eat from any tree in the garden?'"

The woman said to the serpent, "We may eat fruit from the trees in the garden, but God did say, 'You must not eat fruit from the tree that is in the middle of the garden, and you must not touch it, or you will die.'"

"You will not surely die," the serpent said to the woman. "For God knows that when you eat of it your eyes will be opened, and you will be like God, knowing good and evil."

When the woman saw that the fruit of the tree was good for food and pleasing to the eye, and also desirable for gaining wisdom, she took some and ate it. She also gave some to her husband, who was with her, and he ate it."[8]

Done.

The first deception was complete, and the consequences are still continuing.

Welcome to my life as a lawyer. How do you fight this deception, the day-to-day deceptions, lies, half-truths, and attacks?

Watch and pray.

Get used to it.

But, there is so much to hope for. In the end, the liars, *indeed,* "everyone who loves and practices falsehood," are cast "outside." Jesus, himself, wraps up this problem with those that lie as follows:

> "*Blessed are those who wash their robes, that they may have the right to the tree of life and may go through the gates into the city. Outside are the dogs, those who practice magic arts, the sexually immoral, the murderers, the idolaters and everyone who loves and practices falsehood.*"[9]

---

7 Revelation 22:15.
8 Genesis 3:1-6.
9 Revelation 22:14-15.

In the end, the liars, and everyone who loves and practices falsehood will be *outside* and their evil will no longer be able to touch, corrupt or hurt God's people. They are done. They are with the dogs.

Watching and listening are highly underrated. All wisdom begins with the fear of the Lord,[10] and ends with watching and praying. When it comes to the best of the best, the truly professional, you see their quiet demeanor, the pleasant look on their face when someone speaks to them, the quiet calm as they take it all in, the quiet reserve as they weigh the words, the soft smile as though a simple prayer is their background music, and you know that it will be hard, indeed, impossible to deceive him.

Jesus said, "Watch out that no one deceives you."[11]

He also said: "Watch and pray so that you will not fall into temptation. The spirit is willing, but the body is weak."[12]

And Paul said, be joyful always and "pray continually."[13]

Watching and praying will fend off 98 percent of the deception thrown at you, the attacks, the garbage, the deliberate attempts to bring you down. But, you will still get hit on occasion. The Lord will still be there for you. He will never leave you nor forsake you.[14] He will help you.

"Blessed *is* he that watcheth."[15]

Gift of understanding

Why oh why would Jesus himself, over and over again toward the end of his ministry tell all that would listen to him, to watch, and to watch and pray? Why would he do that? What was his point?

"What I say to you, I say to everyone: 'Watch!'" Jesus said.[16]

It's nice to have thirty years of hard-core lawyering behind me. Because I certainly know. Perhaps a certain *donum intellectus* sets in.[17] If you don't slow down, learn God's way of watching and praying, you are going to make a lot of mistakes, a lot of mistakes that are disasters, and a lot of mistakes that could destroy your life. On the other hand, if you do watch and pray, the few mistakes you still might make will turn out to be a blessing, and your way back to newer and stronger blessings.

---

10 Proverbs 9:10. "The fear of the Lord is the beginning of wisdom, and knowledge of the Holy One is understanding." Also, Proverbs 1:7. "The fear of the Lord is the beginning of knowledge, but fools despise wisdom and discipline."
11 Mark 13:5. Matthew 24:4.
12 Mark 14:38.
13 1 Thessalonians 5:16-17.
14 Hebrews 13:5; Deuteronomy 31:6.
15 Revelation 16:15 (KJV).
16 Mark 13:37.
17 *Gift of understanding.* "Accordingly, then, the intellectual light of grace is called the gift of understanding in so far as man's understanding is easily moved by the Holy Spirit, the consideration of which movement depends on a true apprehension of the end. Wherefore unless the human intellect be moved by the Holy Spirit so far as to have a right estimate of the end, it has not yet obtained the gift of understanding however much the Holy Spirit may have enlightened it in regard to other truths that are preambles to faith." Thomas Aquinas.

By the time Mike Harrison's case, Blackdog vs. Harrison Interactive was scheduled for its first mediation, six months had passed, we had done a ton of investigation, research, and discovery, and we were now aware of how deep and extensive was the fraud that Blackdog, and its owner, Julius Rotello, had committed on Mike and his company. Mike was despondent, knew his company was on the line, he could lose everything. Blackdog had stolen Harrison Interactive's software and done a pretty good job of covering it up. There was just one problem: Mike had technically given the software and technology to Blackdog pursuant to a deal that allowed them to test the software to see if it would work for their movie streaming system. Mike had given away the family jewels. But, the reason he did it was because the principal of the company, Julius Rotello, misled him into thinking Blackdog would license the software from Harrison Interactive for a hefty sum. But, the other reason he did it was because he didn't watch and pray on a certain weekend at a trade conference in New York, when a woman asked him if he'd like to have a drink, later in the evening.

And Mike said, "yes."

One wrong "yes" is all it takes.

Two hours before the mediation was to begin at JAMS[18] in downtown Los Angeles, Mike and I met at the Pantry. We sipped coffee and discussed our settlement position. Thanks to the work of our forensic experts, we were prepared to tell the mediator, retired Judge Judith T. Rosenthal, that we believed we could prove fraud against Blackdog, and its owner, Julius Rotello. Mike was sure that Rotello would never own up to the fraud. Rotello thought he was too dang smart and he would get away with it. Rotello was prideful of his skullduggery. A person's 'pride' can be pretty handy if you're the guy fighting him. Pride is a weakness. Always look for the guy's undoing when they engage in fraud, and other skullduggeries.

Then Mike looked at me and said, "Tom, I really messed up."

I looked back, and said, "No you didn't, Rotello's a *professional* liar, he could have taken anyone. Indeed, our research indicates that he has defrauded other people, other companies, but no one's challenged him yet. We will, we can win this case, we got 'em."

"Tom, I really messed up," Mike breathed out. It was a long breath.

"Mike, okay, you messed up, if you insist, but we can win this case. We will save your company. I promise!" But my confidence was suddenly checked.

"Tom . . ."

I stopped. Okay, *three* "Toms," I thought. That's not a good sign.

How is it possible for the countenance of a man to change so abruptly? I was with Mike Harrison, but it wasn't the old Mike Harrison. He suddenly looked

18 Judicial Arbitration and Mediation Services, Los Angeles, California. The Honorable Judge H. Warren Knight, founded JAMS in 1979.

slumped over. My thoughts couldn't put words in my head to describe what I was seeing in my friend. But it was there. In a long second I saw it.

So, I waited.

Mike's words started very slowly. "When this whole thing started with Blackdog, I—had an affair. It's that simple. All I did was let my guard down for the shortest period of time, and . . . bam, I had an affair. I can not even tell you specifically how it happened. But, I do remember the feeling of confidence I was under, the feeling of *competence* I was under, the feeling of being on top of the world. And, I let my guard down. And I know better. I met her on the plane to a trade show in New York, and I remember waking up with her in my hotel room the next morning. There I was Mr. Big Shot, flying to New York first class, of course, first time doing that, I would have never thought of paying for that in the past. I used to give my miles away to my best employees, but not this time. I was going to treat myself. I had earned it. Money was good, business was good, even my *marriage* was good. I remember Clare giving me the most amazing hug when I left that morning. *But,* I let my guard down. . . . It's that simple."

I was forced to look at my watch; Mike noticed. We had a half hour before we had to leave.

His head was heavy in his hands. "Tom, I feel I've let you down also. You and I talked about this before. *Watch and pray.* I know it inside and out. And just once, just once! I let my guard down." He shook his head. "This thing with Blackdog would have never happened if I hadn't let my guard down. I know how to watch and pray. I know how to 'be alert and always keep on praying.'[19] I know it, I know it. And, I didn't do it. It's that simple."

There is always something involved with a big mistake that isn't the big mistake. In this case it was Mike's affair. He let his guard down, and disaster swept in. And, a major business mistake swept in. And now, I had to get him out of it. A lot of things were going to get settled today.

"Tom, I invited Clare to meet me when the mediation is over. I plan to tell her."

"Okay."

And we got up, and headed off to the mediation.

My cellphone rang just before the mediation started. I saw who the caller was, my old friend Shifty Wallace. I took the call.

"Hey, amigo, I've been praying for you man."

"Hey Shifty, how are you?"

"Good, listen, I remember what we talked about before that last mediation, about your marriage being over and all. Listen, let me buy you some coffee. Let's talk man. I just want to be there for you."

"Thanks Shifty."

---

19 Ephesians 6:18.

"Same place. Tomorrow, 7:00 a.m."
"At the little coffee house outside the courthouse."
"You got it. See you there."
"See you there."

Speaking of *watch and pray*. I got out my napkin . . . and looked at my list.

T+

The Take Away 17
Watch and pray.

1. Why oh why would Jesus himself, over and over again toward the end of his ministry tell all that would listen to him, to watch and pray? Why would he do that? What was his point?

   "What I say to you, I say to everyone: 'Watch!'" Jesus said. He also said: "*Watch and pray* so that you will not fall into temptation. The spirit is willing, but the body is weak."

2. *Donum Intellectus. The gift of understanding.* If you don't slow down, and learn God's way of *watching and praying*, you are going to make a lot of mistakes, a lot of mistakes that are disasters, and a lot of mistakes that could destroy your life. On the other hand, if you do watch and pray, the few mistakes you still might make will turn out to be a blessing, and your way back to newer and stronger blessings.

3. The Five Minute Rule: *Most major mistakes happen is less than five minutes.* Watch and Pray is a minute by minute exercise. *The speed of construction can't compete with the speed of destruction.* Disaster can strike quickly. We are called to watch and pray. Jesus warned us.

4. Whether it is a building, or a life, if it is slowly and methodically constructed, it is a thing of beauty, or a life of beauty. And the beauty of it, or the beauty of a life, will always magnificently surpass the ugliness of its or a person's destruction. *The ugliness of destruction can't compete with the beauty of construction.*

   Your spirit is willing to guide you, if you give it the chance. Your conscience is the voice of your spirit. We are spirit, we have a soul (our mind, will, and emotions), and we live in a body.

   The Holy Spirit, speaks to your spirit, your conscience is the voice of your spirit, you listen to your conscience, and you know what to do.

   Trust your spirit.

   Your spirit will guide you. Give it a chance.

   Watch and Pray. Be alert and always keep on praying.

Here Come the Assyrians
Rid yourselves of all the offenses

Just wait
   The Five Minute Rule, Part 1

Mike Harrison knew, somewhere deep down in his heart.
That he had made a big mistake: when he said "yes" to the nice woman that asked him out for a drink—just to talk business. No big deal, turned out they were at the same trade show. What a coincidence! Guys like me don't see those things as coincidences: *Be self-controlled and alert. Your enemy the devil prowls around like a roaring lion looking for someone to devour.*[1] Mike's "yes," turned into an affair. But that was just part of his problem. Because of his affair at the trade show, and letting his guard down, his business acumen was wasted—and he made very big mistakes in dealing with Blackdog and its owner, Julius Rotello.
   Julius knew what he was doing.
   He knew about the affair. He milked it for all it was worth.
   And he was going to do it again, that day, at the mediation.
   It was going to be a long day.

Over the years, I learned how so many huge mistakes were made in under five minutes. Just a short series of thoughts, or a short conversation, or a short intentional act, in just a few minutes could really destroy a person's life, or, hopefully, just *almost* destroy their life. Before making a decision, all you need to do is stop, ask God what to do, and wait for an answer. If an answer doesn't come right away, *no problem.* Just stand.[2] Do nothing. Whatever it is, if an answer doesn't come right away—you are called to *not* do it. Wait for the Holy Spirit to

---

1 1 Peter 5:8.
2 Psalm 4:4 (KJV). "Stand in awe, and sin not: commune with your own heart upon your bed, and be still. Selah." Psalm 37:9 (KJV). "For evildoers shall be cut off: but those that wait upon the LORD, they shall inherit the earth."

speak to your spirit. Just wait.[3] Indeed, be careful not to follow your own spirit. *Woe to the foolish prophets who follow their own spirit and have seen nothing!*[4]

There is a another side to the Five Minute Rule. In November 1984, in a little church in Westwood California, on a Wednesday night, I accepted the Lord. It took less than five minutes. Pastor Henry gave a short altar call after his sermon, and I went forward. I never looked back. That was the most permanent decision I ever made. In reality, the *only* permanent decision I ever made. In 2001, in the not-so-little Calvary Community Church in Thousand Oaks California, Mike Harrison made the same decision. The same permanent decision. And that's why his mistake was all the harder. But it is also why—he was going to make it back.

Back from the brink.[5]

A lesson learned early is a great blessing, a lesson learned too late a great punishment

The Assyrians were a tough crowd. The Lord used them on occasion to punish. To punish even the good guys.[6] Believe in God, don't believe in God . . . doesn't matter. Someday, if you are doing something terribly bad, you're going to go down, you will suffer the consequences. You should expect that. But, so often in my life, in my life of standing at the crossroads of human conflict, I've seen that God, in particular, would discipline his chosen people, his children. And I saw, that the sooner he disciplined, the better.

"Woe to the Assyrian, the rod of My anger, the staff in whose
hand is My indignation *and* fury [against Israel's disobedience]!
I send [the Assyrian] against a hypocritical *and* godless nation
and against the people of My wrath; I command him to take the spoil
and to seize the prey and to tread down like the mire in the streets.
However, this is not his intention [nor is the Assyrian aware that
he is doing this at My bidding], neither does his mind so think *and*
plan; but it is in his mind to destroy and cut off many nations.
For [the Assyrian] says, Are not my officers all
either [subjugated] kings *or* their equal?
Is not Calno [of Babylonia conquered] like Carchemish
[on the Euphrates]? Is not Hamath [in Upper Syria] like Arpad
[her neighbor]? Is not Samaria [in Israel] like Damascus [in Syria]?
[Have any of these cities been able to resist Assyria? Not one!]"[7]

---

3 Psalm 27:14. "Wait for the Lord; be strong and take heart and wait for the Lord."
4 Ezekiel 13:2-3. "Say to those who prophesy out of their own imagination: Here the word of the Lord! This is what the sovereign Lord says: Woe to the foolish prophets who follow their own spirit and have seen nothing!"
5 I know I spoke about the Five Minute Rule, part 2, first, in chapter 17. But, the Five Minute Rule, part 1, should always come first in your life. It gives you a chance to survive, to live through, to break through, the mistakes in your life.
6 2 Kings 17.
7 Isaiah 10:5-9 (AMP). See also Isaiah 5:26-29.

Your worst fate could be to not suffer until the very end, when it's the very worst, when it's way too late to turn your life around and leave a legacy, to be remembered for something good. So often, the punishment of the Assyrians was not immediate. But it would come, *eventually*. A lesson learned early is a great blessing, a lesson learned too late a great punishment. The Lord searches your heart. Will you be open to the lesson?

Just as Mike Harrison and I arrived at the mediation, I received a call from the FBI. I recognized the number; I thought I should take the call. I had received calls from them in the past several weeks regarding Georgy Tarasov, the defendant I beat in the Dr. Ezekiel case.

The FBI detective started quickly: "Tom, we wanted you to know we just arrested Tarasov. We wanted to put this courtesy call in to you. Will you tell your client, Dr. Ezekiel?"

"Yes, of course."

"Please remember, these guys run with some serious dirtbags. Call us—anytime. You know what I mean. You have my number."

"Yes, I have your number. Thank you for the heads up."

"You're welcome."

He hung up.

A thought passed through my mind: *The Assyrians took him down.*

A cynical thought passed through my mind: *it took them long enough.*

But then I thought, what's going to happen to my friend and client Mike Harrison? I could win his case, but now I know I'm fighting an additional battle. One I hadn't seen coming.

Georgy Tarasov was seventy-two years old when he was arrested. The FBI agent told me he was going to spend a long time in prison.

Mike Harrison was thirty-two when he had his affair. Would God bless him with the chance to rebuild his life?

I couldn't help but think about Solomon. *Why did he slowly over time disregard his wisdom?* As Solomon grew older, his wives turned his heart after other gods, "and his heart was not fully devoted to the Lord his God, as the heart of David his father had been."[8]

"So the Lord said to Solomon, 'Since this is your attitude and you have not kept my covenant and my decrees, which I commanded you, I will most certainly tear the kingdom away for you and give it to one of your subordinates. Nevertheless, for the sake of David your father, I will not do it during your lifetime. I will tear it out of the hand of your son.'"[9]

"Then the Lord raised up against Solomon an adversary, Hadad the Edomite, from the royal line of Edom."[10]

---

8 1 Kings 11:4.
9 1 Kings 11:11.
10 1 Kings 11:14.

Apparently, that wasn't enough to get Solomon's attention: "And God raised up against Solomon another adversary, Rezon son of Eliada. . . . Rezon was Israel's adversary as long as Solomon lived, adding to the trouble caused by Hadad."[11]

Still not enough. Then Jeroboam, one of Solomon's own officials, rebelled against Solomon.[12] God told Jeroboam through the prophet Ahijah that He was going to tear the kingdom out of Solomon's hand and give Jeroboam ten tribes, forming the Northern Kingdom of Israel. Solomon's son, Rehoboam, would end up with two tribes, Judah and Benjamin and form the Southern Kingdom of Judah. This would happen *eventually*, after Solomon's death. Punishment comes, eventually.

Why would God do this?

God said:

"I will do this because they [Solomon and the Israelites] have forsaken me and worshiped Ashtoreth the goddess of the Sidonians, Chemosh the god of the Moabites, and Molech the god of the Ammonites, and have not walked in my ways, nor done what is right in my eyes, nor kept my statutes and laws as David, Solomon's father, did."[13]

And as to Jeroboam, God said: "If you do whatever I command you and walk in my ways and do what is right in my eyes by keeping my statutes and commands, as David my servant did, I will be with you. I will build you a dynasty as enduring as the one I built for David and will give Israel to you."[14]

Solomon knew better. As we often do. This is one of his Psalms, a Song of Assents:

"Unless the LORD builds the house,
    its builders labor in vain.
Unless the LORD watches over the city
    the watchmen stand guard in vain."[15]

So, the Lord would use the Assyrians on occasion to chasten his people. But, the Assyrians should have taken no comfort from this.

"Therefore when the Lord has completed all His work [of
chastisement and purification to be executed] on Mount Zion and
on Jerusalem, it shall be that He will inflict punishment on the
fruit [the thoughts, words, and deeds] of the stout *and* arrogant
heart of the king of Assyria and the haughtiness of his pride."
    . . .

---

11 1 Kings 11:23 -25.
12 1 Kings 11:26-40.
13 I Kings 11:33.
14 I Kings 11:38.
15 Psalm 127:1. Attributed to Solomon. This is one of the Song of Assents. Psalms 120 to 134. Use these Psalms to praise, exult, and elevate God. (So, unlike Solomon, you don't forget God.)

"[The Lord] will consume the glory of the [Assyrian's] forest and of his fruitful field, both soul and body; and it shall be as when a sick man pines away *or* a standard-bearer faints.

"And the remnant of the trees of his forest shall be few, so that a child may make a list of them."[16]

Israel fell to Assyria in 722 B.C.

Assyria, was conquered and fell to the Babylonians in 612 B.C. Nineveh was the most important city in Assyria and became the capital of Assyria. The book of Jonah described Nineveh as a wicked city. God sent Jonah to warn the Assyrians that they would receive judgment if they didn't repent. They repented. For a while. Eventually God would judge the city of Nineveh for its arrogance, its idolatry and wickedness, and its oppression. Jonah's ministry was from approximately 785 B.C. to 753 B.C. But within several generations, evil and wickedness had returned to Nineveh and the prophet Nahum pronounced judgment on the wicked city of Nineveh and the nation of Assyria.

Read the book of Jonah to heed its warnings. Read the book of Nahum to see the results if you don't heed the warnings.

God used Assyria as his instrument of punishment against Israel. But Assyria itself would *eventually* be punished for its own wickedness.

The WHY-TOs are more important than the HOW-TOs

Why to settle it is more important than how to settle it. Why-to-do anything is almost always more important than the how-to-do it. You can always figure out how to do it, it's the why-to-do-it that is more complicated. Mike would learn his own personal *why-to* today. More specifically, why-to mediate was more important than how-to mediate.

The *how-to* would be easy today. We had retired Judge Rosenthal as our mediator. Both sides had already submitted mediation briefs about our positions on the case, the legal theories, the facts that support our case, and our settlement position, among a few other things. Judge Rosenthal would run a tight ship.

The mediation started in a JAMS conference room. Judge Rosenthal told us that she wanted each side to give an opening statement, and then she would meet separately with the Plaintiff and their lawyer. The Plaintiff was Blackdog and its owner, Julius Rotello, so, after the opening statements by both sides, she would meet with them first. Rotello's lawyer, Mac Fleister, gave his opening statement. He did his best to intimidate my client, and me, mostly with bombastic statements of Harrison Interactive's infringement on his clients' technology, massive damages they had suffered, and at least one powerful witness for their side—a witness that he brought to the mediation. His comments about Mike Harrison were designed to embarrass and belittle him. Every statement out of his mouth had a mocking

---

16 Isaiah 10:12, and 18-19 (AMP).

tone wrapped in supposed confidence for this case. He saw himself as the master strategist, putting together his case with the spit of wit and the art of connivance.

In the back of my mind I thought, "*Really*, are you mocking my client?"[17]

For my side, I kept it short and simple. I felt that all the action was in the sidebars when we met separately with the judge. So, for my opening statement, I just told the judge that about two years ago, Mike Harrison had several business meetings with Julius Rotello at a trade show in San Francisco. Rotello talked my guy into sharing a demo of his product with Rotello, Rotello kept the demo, reverse engineered it, stole the copyrighted software, and eventually launched Moviesonline. Then, Rotello had the audacity to sue my client who finished the development of the product and started selling it to major motion picture studios. Rotello sued Harrison, saying that Harrison stole Rotello's product, not the other way around. It happens all the time. The best defense is a good offense.

After the opening statements, the judge took Rotello and his lawyer, Mac Fleister, to another conference room for a caucus.

That gave Mike and me time to just sit in the main conference room alone, and wait for the judge to finish her sidebar meeting with the other side. We were just chatting when Mike looked at me and said: "Remember when we first met, before I became a Christian? I remember telling you I didn't believe in the devil."

"I remember."

"That's when we first discussed *watch and pray*. I came to a study group. You reminded the group: '*Be self-controlled and alert. Your enemy the devil prowls around like a roaring lion looking for someone to devour.*' I raised my hand. I told you I didn't believe in the devil. You said, 'so, what do you call your enemies?' I said, I didn't have enemies. And you said—"

"That's exactly what the devil wants you to think. It's much easier to prowl amongst the unwary," I finished the sentence.

"All I have to do is let my guard down, and an opportunity will present itself. I believe in the devil now," Mike said.

Mike sighed. "I asked the Lord, to forgive me for this one. This insane unfaithfulness to my wife, my business, my life."

"What did he say?" I asked.

"He said he would."

"Good."

"There's just one thing."

"What?"

"He said it wouldn't be easy. . . . I think he's a little mad at me for this one. Rightfully so."

I knew what he meant.

Just then the judge walked in. Quietly took a seat at the conference table. It was just the three of us in the room. It was very quiet. She looked at Mike.

---

17 Proverbs 14:6. "The mocker seeks wisdom and finds none, but knowledge comes easily to the discerning."

The judge quietly said, "they brought a certain witness with them. Her name is Betti. Do you know her?"

Mike looked at me, then looked at the judge.

He said: "Yes, I know her."

The judge looked at Mike: "This makes things difficult for you. You know that, don't you?"

"Yes, I do."

I knew what she meant.

Five minutes later I ran into opposing counsel, Mac Fleister, in the men's room. He didn't say a word. He just chuckled. Kind of a deep, slow chuckle. He was happy with himself. I had heard that chuckle before. Then he strutted out of the bathroom and down the hall. I had seen that strut before.[18] It reminded me of an incident years ago in the Harry Goldberg case.

For some reason that made me feel at peace.

I thought of my friend Mike Harrison: "*If a wicked man turns away from all the sins he has committed and keeps all my decrees and does what is just and right, he will surely live; he will not die. None of the offenses he has committed will be remembered against him.*"[19]

Mike was going to be alright.

Right then and there I knew. Let Mac gloat.

The Lord was there.[20]

Rid yourselves of all the offenses

At lunch I sat there with Mike.

Finally he looked at me and said, "Tom, I feel that at the very moment I said yes to that girl, the Lord started preparing a lesson for me. The affair happened on a Thursday night. The very next day, in the morning, I first met with Julius Rotello. I can completely remember the feeling. The heaviness of the night before weighed on me. I felt liberated at the same time. I felt energized. I had a swagger to my walk. I had a swagger to my talk. I felt powerful. I was in command. I knew what I was doing. I felt good. I know that feeling now. . . . I never want that feeling again. —Never."

Mike and I, and some of our friends had talked about the Assyrians in the past. How God had used them, Israel's mortal enemies, to punish the Israelites for their sinful ways. Indeed, when Israeli king after king "did evil in the eyes of the Lord,"[21] eventually, God allowed the kings of Assyria, Tiglath-Pileser, Shalmaneser, and Sargon II to conquer Israel, and deport all the Israelites to Assyria. Then the king of Assyria brought people from Babylon, Cuthah, Avva, Hamath and other lands and settled them in the lands the Assyrian kings had taken from the Israelites.

18 Psalm 12:8. *The wicked freely strut about* . . . .
19 Ezekiel 18:21.
20 Ezekiel 35:10.
21 2 Kings 15:18; 17:2.

"All this took place because the Israelites had sinned against the Lord their God... The Israelites secretly did things against the Lord their God that were not right.... They followed worthless idols and themselves became worthless.... "[22]

We agreed with some well known scholars: "In the end Assyria destroyed God's people only after God's people had destroyed themselves."[23]

Mike and I, and some of our prayer partners would sit around and discuss the Assyrians and ask ourselves: *does the Lord still work like this, even today?* After story upon story from our own lives, and lots of additional experience, we would conclude, *yes.*

But we also knew: *Rid yourselves of all the offenses you have committed, and get a new heart and a new spirit.*[24]

We were just a bunch of haggard Christians. Doing our own fieldwork. Not a theologian amongst us. *In* the world, but not *of* it. Who would understand us if we, actually looked at these principles of God as working in our own lives on such a macro and micro level? Nobody, we figured. But that's okay, we just kept up our fieldwork. We trusted God' promises. They are everywhere in the Bible:

> *"I will cleanse you from all your impurities and from all your idols. I will give you a new heart and put a new spirit in you; I will remove from you your heart of stone and give you a heart of flesh. And I will put my Spirit in you and move you to follow my decrees and be careful to keep my laws."*[25]

Indeed, we knew: *Woe to the foolish prophets who follow their own spirit and have seen nothing!*[26] We counted on the *Holy Spirit* guiding our spirit so that we would know what to do. Those who are led by the Spirit of God are sons of God.[27] Our *spirit* is really who we are. We are spirit, we have a soul (which is our mind, will and emotions), and we live in a body.

Mike and I finished our lunch. We had a long afternoon ahead of us.

As we got up, I said: "Mike, the case won't settle today. I believe that God has a different plan for you. It will take some time to play out. We'll work hard this afternoon with Judge Rosenthal, we'll still try the best we can to settle. But, I don't think it will settle."

"That's okay. I've learned enough for a lifetime today.... I will never forget this lesson."

"Mike, don't worry. You will rise again."[28]

---

22 2 Kings Chapters 15-17. And, see verses 17:7; 17:9; 17:15.
23 R. Laird Harris, Gleason L. Archer, Jr., Bruce K. Waltke, *Theological Wordbook of the Old Testament* (Chicago, IL: Moody Publishers, 1980), p.78.
24 Ezekiel 18:31.
25 Ezekiel 36:25-27.
26 Ezekiel 13:3.
27 Romans 8:14. See also, Romans 8:16. "The Spirit himself testifies with our spirit that we are God's children."
28 Proverbs 24:16. "For though a righteous man falls seven times, he rises again, but the wicked are brought down by calamity."

God has gone out in front of you, Part 1

The case didn't settle that day. That's okay, some other things did. Mike Harrison's wife met him after the mediation and they headed off for dinner. Mike called me that night. Mike told Clare everything. She said she knew something was wrong the moment he came home from the conference, and she had been praying ever since. She watched how their relationship, the family, and his business deteriorated since the weekend of the affair.

There would have to be more discussions and a lot more prayer.

Clare didn't walk out.

Mike said he never saw the girl again.

He asked Clare to forgive him. He told her he would never, never, ever again be unfaithful to Clare or his family. He had learned how destructive sin could be in his life.

He felt he had a new start day.[29]

I told Mike I had been praying for him and Clare. I told him I felt in my spirit that God had laid a verse on my heart. *God has gone out in front of you.*[30]

I told him I didn't know exactly what the word I'd received meant.

But we'd find out in good time.

From past experiences, I had learned to be thankful when God laid that verse on my heart. Because, I knew:

The goal is to settle matters quickly, not hastily.

Give God the chance, to go out in front of you.

He will. Expect him to.

T+

---

29 Ezekiel 36:26-27. "I will give you a new heart and put a new spirit in you. . . . And I will put my Spirit in you and move you to follow my decrees and be careful to keep my laws."

30 1 Chronicles 14:15. See also, Acts 2:25, the words of David: "I saw the Lord always before me. Because he is at my right hand, I will not be shaken."

The Take Away 18
Here come the Assyrians.

1. The Assyrians were a tough crowd. The Lord used them on occasion to punish. To punish even the good guys. Believe in God, don't believe in God, doesn't matter. Someday, if you are doing something terribly bad, you're going to go down, you will suffer the consequences. You should expect that. So often in my life of standing at the crossroads of human conflict, I've seen that God will discipline his chosen people, his children. And I saw, that the sooner he disciplined, the better. I learned: *A lesson learned early is a great blessing, a lesson learned too late a great punishment.* Your worst fate could be to *not* suffer until the very end, when it's the very worst, when it's way too late to turn your life around and leave a legacy, to be remembered for something good. A lesson learned too late is a great punishment. The Lord searches your heart. Will you be open to the lesson? *When* will you be open to the lesson?

2. God used the Assyrians, Israel's mortal enemies, to punish the Israelites for their sinful ways. Indeed, when Israeli king after king "did evil in the eyes of the Lord," eventually, God allowed the kings of Assyria, Tiglath-Pileser, Shalmaneser, and Sargon II to conquer Israel, and deport all the Israelites to Assyria. All this took place because the Israelites had sinned against God. The Israelites secretly did things against God that were not right. They followed worthless idols and themselves became worthless. In the end, the Assyrians destroyed God's people only after God's people had destroyed themselves.

3. Does the Lord still work like this, even today? Answer: *Yes.* All our secret sins and bad choices play out eventually. The *watch and pray* generation knows: *Be self-controlled and alert. Your enemy the devil prowls around like a roaring lion looking for someone to devour.*

4. Therefore: *Rid yourselves of all the offenses you have committed, and get a new heart and a new spirit.* Ezekiel 18:21-22 says: "*If a wicked man turns away from all the sins he has committed and keeps all my decrees and does what is just and right, he will surely live; he will not die. None of the offenses he has committed will be remembered against him.*"

    Speak in agreement, the words of David: "I saw the Lord always before me. Because he is at my right hand, I will not be shaken."

19

The Cost of The Settlement

Measuring the costs comes down to one word:
sacrifice

Sacrifice

All trials come down to one word: trustworthiness. All settlements come down to one word: *sacrifice*. How much are you willing to sacrifice to settle the case? To settle the personal problem? To settle problems with your spouse? With your partners, neighbors, friends, and foes? How much are you willing to sacrifice to settle the problem with yourself?

I'd give anything to convince you that after watching and taking part in more than thirty years of court battles and life battles: those that sacrificed to settle were always better off for it. That's the way it is. That's the way it should be. And, those that sacrificed to settle their personal problems or problems in their relationships were always better off. They were always blessed. The price, and the effort, was well worth it.

I haven't learned much about God and his ways from academic study, classes, and teaching. I've learned about God at the crossroads of human suffering and despair: courthouses and rehab centers, in mediations, arbitrations, and trials, and in the one-on-one counseling dramas that occur in a typical day of lawyering. These are places where people go before they take the law into their own hands. Resolution requires sacrifice. *The one that sacrifices nothing learns and discerns nothing.*

The right to survive it

This week looked like any given week in my life. On Monday, the Mike Harrison case didn't settle. But I knew it would at the right time. When I get that feeling, I'm always right. I know where those "feelings" come from. We were not going to be able to go "straight up" and settle this case, or straight up and win this case. We would have to "circle around," first, while God went before us.[1] Yes, that's His way on occasion, or maybe quite often. Be patient.

And then, of course, today was the Sarah Bleu mediation.

Then on Wednesday, I would start the Janie Blythe medical malpractice jury trial, unless that case settled.

It was 7:00 a.m. on Tuesday morning. It would be an hour before Sarah Bleu met me. Then at 9:00 a.m. the mediation would start.

I was again sitting at the little coffee shop telling Shifty that after three and a half months of marriage, my wife told me it was over. The bottom line was simple, she had come from a foreign country, she felt she had her U.S. citizenship locked up, she had stacked up complaints about me, she was done. It was over.

I had no idea how I would survive this. On so many levels, my life seemed over.

No matter how skilled and qualified I was as a professional, those skills and qualifications didn't seem to carry over to a personal life.

My best friend that morning was Shifty Wallace, a court bailiff. The only one that knew I had this problem. I hadn't turned to anyone else yet. At the end of the Dr. Ezekiel trial I had basically collapsed, and God had put Shifty there to catch me.

Thank God. Because I had imploded, more than Shifty knew, more than even I knew.

But, apparently, not more than God knew.

I'm sure the world knows that even professional people that are trying to help people professionally, can also have their own problems. I needed someone to pray for me. But no one knew I had problems.

Shifty looked at me, took a long sip of his coffee, like I'd seen him do before and said: "I've been praying for you, man."

"I was hoping so. Thanks." I heard right then in my heart: *The prayer of a righteous man is powerful and effective.*[2]

"You'll survive this, you know that don't you?"

"It doesn't feel like it right now."

"But, you will, I promise you. But, even better, God promises you. The Lord gave me this word for you: 'The Lord himself goes before you and will be with you; he will never leave you nor forsake you. Do not be afraid; do not be discouraged.'"[3]

---

1 1 Chronicles 14:14-15.
2 James 5:16.
3 Deuteronomy 31:8.

I knew that was from the Lord. "I hear that man. I can't thank you enough for your help," I said. That's about all I had the energy to say. I hung over my coffee like a drunk.

"Now, here's what you do. Stand up. Come on, throw your shoulders back! Stand up straight!"

I stood up.

"Now, repeat after me: I can do all things through Christ who strengthens me. . . . Louder! *I can do all things through Christ who strengthens me!* The Lord will make me the head, not the tail. The Lord will restore to me double for my trouble. And, if God is for us, who can be against us?"[4]

I repeated the words that Shifty spoke over me.

"That's a Word from the Counselor.[5] Now get to work, counselor."

As Shifty gave me a big hug, up walked Sarah Bleu.

Sarah joked: "Can I get in on some of that?"

Shifty gave a big smile: "*That*, is from up above."

I saw that Shifty's wife, Ruby, was waiting in the wings. I smiled over to her. She smiled back. So much said in just the simple exchange of smiles. I saw Shifty give his wife another big hug. His big frame seemed to smother her.

Angels come in all forms.

The cool resolve of a taker

It was 8:00 a.m. Sarah was on time.

"Tom, that wasn't fair."

I didn't know what she meant.

"I was prepared to come this morning and fight like hell . . . ."

She was telling me her reasons to fight. *Her* reasons. I looked at her. She seemed dejected. But, she did look pretty. She had put a little makeup on, minimally. I could see that she had lost her hair from chemotherapy. I couldn't help remembering her long brown hair wonderfully chaotic most of the time. She wore a stylish skier's cap.

It had been eight months since her husband of eleven years served her with divorce papers. I remember when she called me.

"Tom, how are you?"

"Sarah, I'm fine. How are you?"

"Well, I had a good day. I visited three of my clinics, taught a course in nutrition at the one in Thousand Oaks, exercised Chelsea in my favorite dog park, picked flowers from my garden, arranged them on the kitchen table overlooking the ocean, planned a scrumptious dinner for my husband and my daughter Emily . . .

---

4 Philippians 4:13; Deuteronomy 28:13; Job 42:10; Romans 8:31.
5 John 14:16. "And I will ask the Father, and he will give you another Counselor to be with you forever—the Spirit of truth." See also John 15:26.

and then the doorbell rang. Which is weird, because my friends just walk in, or, at best, knock briefly and barge in. But . . . the doorbell rang, and no one just walked in. So, I opened the door, and was served with divorce papers. Todd is divorcing me. Just thought I'd tell you. Oh, and did I tell you I was diagnosed with breast cancer last week?"

That was eight months ago.

Sarah was finishing with *her* reasons to fight.

"I don't know, I was all geared up to fight like hell. Todd wants half my clinics, joint custody of Emily, spousal and child support. He's already taken what he wants from the house, he has his cars, golf clubs, sail boat, and coin collection. He won't talk to me. Since the day he left, he hasn't spoken to me except pro forma, regarding Emily, and needing money. That's it."

She looked up at me. "I've lost my hair now." And then she started crying.

And therein lies the complete incompetence of someone like me to help her.

She talked as she cried: "I did what you said Tom. I studied the Beatitudes. You called it Jesus' Eight-Step Program."

Mercy, sometimes my ideas seem so trite when they come back to me. So many thoughts rippled through my head. It's just that I've seen divorces as the great windfall for lawyers. Insanely expensive for such small results. And then you see the victims. I see those engaged in the relentless pursuit of answers as to *why someone would do such a thing to me?* The very act itself, of leaving abruptly, with no explanations, is designed to make you pursue the "why"—and waste your time. You, the friend and lawyer, try to tell someone you care about to not pursue it.

Rarely does it help to engage in the relentless pursuit of answers, or the relentless pursuit of compensation. It is best to proceed. Proceed on with your life.

Sarah's husband Todd, has the cool resolve of a taker. I didn't see him as too complicated. He was just a taker. An extreme tunic collector, but, *taking* is sometimes just not good enough. Some takers also want to hurt you.

In eight months of family law lawyers fighting over the divorce, and the division of property, Sarah still had no clue as to why Todd left her. Not a trace of a clue. As her old business lawyer, she had asked me to help her with the mediation. She trusted me. She was spending tens of thousands for her divorce lawyer, and her husband's divorce lawyer, because, in this case, the community property laws favored Todd, the husband. Sarah was the breadwinner in the family.

Sarah's divorce lawyer had given us our marching orders: *we don't compromise, we want full custody of Emily, we want all the clinics, all forty-five of her weight loss clinics. Todd gets nothing. He defrauded her. He waited savagely for the ten years of marriage to pass, lulled her into putting all her clinics in both of their names, and then dumped her. He was a dog, a scumbag. Give as little as possible. We will win at trial.*

Perhaps. We might win. But at what cost?

On the other hand, what would be the cost of settlement?

I had gotten to know Todd through the divorce proceedings. And like all divorce work, you end up learning a lot about the marriage. Throughout the marriage, Todd made sure his needs were met in a mechanical self-centered way. He could send out a smile that most people believed, but it was vacuous. There was an impenetrable nothingness about him. I told Sarah that a search for answers from Todd would be worthless. With Todd, you will never get to know. There may be nothing to know.

In the back of my mind, I couldn't help thinking, *you don't want to know.*

You don't want to be on a cruise ship, with a nice outside deck, with a person like Todd.

Our mediator was Judge Teresa Swenson. She herself had gone through a divorce several years before that. It was long, messy, expensive, and a somewhat public affair. Even family law judges have no inside track on an easy approach to a divorce. This was a mandatory settlement conference. Judge Swenson would spend the whole day juggling at least five cases to settle, a nearly impossible task. But like most good judges, she was up to it. She would methodically try to settle a few easy ones quickly, if such things existed and then concentrate on the hard ones.

She viewed our case as a hard one.

It wouldn't be that hard.

The peaceful resolve of a giver

At lunch, Sarah and I had a chance to assess the morning. The judge juggled her five cases. She met with me and opposing counsel at about 10:15 a.m., without our clients present. We summed up our positions. Todd and his lawyer wanted everything. That was the bottom line. Every last little thing they could ever even possibly get—they wanted. Then the judge met separately with Todd and his lawyer. Because Todd was the Petitioner in the divorce case because he filed it and started the process, he and his counsel were the first to meet separately with the judge. They met for twenty-five minutes. The Judge hadn't called us in yet. She had to juggle the other cases. We weren't sure where she was in the process.

Sarah told me that she had originally wanted to fight like hell against Todd. She realized what he had done to her. He was ready to cash in. But, she had lost her hair, and was concerned that she would lose one or both breasts. Todd was the cancer in her life. She was ready to sacrifice whatever it took for resolution, and, to get him out of her life. She just wanted to be with her daughter and move on.

Sarah looked at me. "Me of all people. I run health and exercise clinics. And, I got cancer. I know that Todd is the real cancer in my life. He has been feeding off me for eleven years. He basically doesn't work anymore. He started working for me in administration and PR about seven years ago. Now, he thinks he owns the place. He wants half. Half of my life. I don't care. I will die if he stays in my life any longer. Tom, let's settle today. Get me out of this case, so I can heal. And . . . (she lifted off her skier's cap) heal, I will."

"Okay."

"Tom, when I started to read the Beatitudes, nothing penetrated my cold heart. So, I decided to read through them forty times. I read them thinking the reason was that I would get influenced into settling with Todd. I'd compromise. I'd compromise my principles. I remembered what your friend David told me: *you don't compromise your principles, you compromise for your principles.* Anyway, I studied away, read the eight beatitudes over and over again, forty times. I just felt the Lord healed me, starting with my spirit and all the way to my heart and soul. One night, I felt such a presence of the Lord, in my room. And he said to me: "Sarah, I'm going to heal you. Your daughter will be with you. Now, go and settle with Todd. I have a purpose and a plan for you. I will bless you and you will be a blessing. And, I was filled with the Holy Spirit. . . . That's it."

As her eyes filled with tears, I could see so much peace on her face.

And the verse I heard in my heart was similar to one Shifty had spoken over me earlier in the day: *O prisoners of hope, even now I announce that I will restore twice as much to you.*[6]

"Sarah, I promise you, we will settle today. Let me take a short walk now, if you don't mind. I have a little talking to do with the Counselor. We will settle today. Amen."

She looked at me. So peaceful now. She looked like she was healing right then and there.

"Amen," she said.

She slowly put her skier's cap back on, and then she softly patted her head to make sure it was in place.

Sarah had decided to rid her life of cancer.

In more ways than one.

And I went on my prayer walk.

T+

---

6 Zechariah 9:12; Cf. Job 42:10.

The Take Away 19
The one that sacrifices nothing learns and discerns nothing.

1. Resolution requires sacrifice. *The one that sacrifices nothing learns and discerns nothing.* Put another way: The one who is willing to give up something important and valuable (sacrifice), will gain and acquire knowledge (learn), and will perceive and recognize things about himself or herself, or others (discern), and thereby become a peacemaker, and therefore be blessed.

    Blessed are the peacemakers.

    If there isn't resolution in your life, measure your sacrifice. It is probably insufficient.

2. All settlements come down to one word: *sacrifice.* How much are you willing to sacrifice to settle the case, to settle problems with your spouse, with your partners, neighbors, friends and foes? How much are you willing to sacrifice to settle the problem with yourself? Those that sacrifice to settle are always better off for it. They are blessed.

3. The time spent away from settling the problems in your life is the time spent away from the purpose of your life.

4. Settle that problem in your life, the one that comes to your mind right now. Let the Lord restore you.

    O prisoners of hope, even now I announce that I will restore twice as much to you.

The Life-Light

But the darkness has not understood it

Set your heart and set your mind

Todd, the paradigm of self-centeredness, would never in a million years understand his own wife, Sarah. Julius Rotello, the master strategist, would never in a million years understand Mike Harrison. Richard Kahn, the patient that sued Dr. Blythe, the prowling opportunist hoping to make a killing, would never in a million years understand his former doctor, Janie Blythe. And, Billy Joe Hollister, the brilliant one, businessman *par excellence*, entrepreneur, bon vivant, would never understand what went wrong in his case against an old fuddy-duddy of a radio station owner, Harry Goldberg, and his cheap young lawyer with a stammering problem.

I had taken a leap of faith. I had told Sarah that her case would settle today. The odds seemed so stacked against her. Todd was prancing about[1] throughout the morning, emboldened by his legal position, a position he had methodically put in place over an eleven-year marriage. *Evil plots early and evil plots long.* He had waited the requisite ten years in California, such that his marriage was considered long-term. He would get a wonderful payout from Sarah, spousal support, half the clinics, joint custody, and bragging rights with his beer buddies. "Finally, a *woman* would take the hit; it's always the guys." Todd despised Sarah, she was soft, *weak* in Todd's mind, and now, she even had cancer. She, of all people, a person that runs forty-five health clinics. What a loser.

---

1 The strut of unjustified confidence is everywhere in the courthouses of life. See Chapter 22, fn 3.

Long ago, Sarah had made the decision to set her heart and mind on things above, not on earthly things.[2] And, one by one her clinics took off. No one could really figure out why.[3] Such simple approaches to life, health, mind, body and soul. Sarah had even written books. The books were pretty simple, but they sold, steadily, month after month. Sales slowly went up, not down. I suppose in my somewhat lowly and miserable state that day, I couldn't help but wonder how God had allowed a parasite like Todd in her life. On that day, I was particularly inspired by Sarah, but she didn't know. As the day went on she seemed to stand taller. Her head, with that ski cap on, was held high. When it was our turn to meet with the judge, we would have to walk down the hall, enter the courtroom and go back into the judge's chambers. Sarah would walk with pride, she knew her Lord was right there with her. She would always stop just before we would enter the judge's chambers, check herself over, pat her head to make sure her ski cap covered her hairless head, then she would smile softly, nod to me, and I knew she was ready to walk in.

I felt ashamed at myself. Down deep I was mad at God for my wrecked marriage. *Why didn't God warn me not to marry that girl? Did I not inquire of the Lord?*[4] I wanted so badly to know what I did wrong. *What?* "Doubt" attacked me. A fiery dart flung from hell.[5] Faith's shield eluded me.

Sometimes the end of the day is impossible to see from the beginning.

I know that iron sharpens iron,[6] but with Sarah, I had never seen such soft iron.

We sat down in front of Judge Teresa.

She looked at Sarah. "How is your recovery coming?"

Sarah looked in the judge's eyes, "You noticed, I guess."

"I've seen a few skier's caps in my life. A few baseball caps, a few scarves."

She reached behind her desk. She held a baseball cap in her hand. A Dodgers' cap.

This cap was no souvenir. It had been worn out. It was tattered.

It was the judge's cap.

It was her version of a skier's cap.

The judge looked at it—and that was it. Tears flooded the judge's eyes. There was no holding them back. She bit down on her lower lip.

Then Sarah started crying. So loud, I don't think I could have heard anything else.

Then I started in.

Protocol broke down. Sarah left her seat and went behind the judge's desk to give her a hug. They were hugging, and they were crying. Finally, my own deluge

2 Colossians 3:1-2. "Since, then, you have been raised with Christ, set your hearts on things above, where Christ is seated at the right hand of God. Set your minds on things above, not on earthly things."
3 Matthew 6:33 (NKJV). "But seek first the kingdom of God and His righteousness, and all these things shall be added to you."
4 See Chapter 3, fn 2. There are consequences when one does not *inquire of the Lord*.
5 Ephesians 6:16 (KJV). "Above all, taking the shield of faith, wherewith ye shall be able to quench all the fiery darts of the wicked."
6 Proverbs 27:17.

poured out of me. What I was witnessing was hitting me; my wrecked marriage was hitting me; exhaustion was hitting me. I did what I could do to contain myself, and searched for something to dry my eyes, as the judge came to my rescue with her box of tissue.

We all grabbed a handful.

The judge was the first to speak, but it took a while.

"I was diagnosed with multiple myeloma three years ago. I was given six months to live. But, here I am. Still standing. Imagine that." She held up her Dodgers cap. "I came to love the Dodgers for all the wrong reasons."

Then they started crying again.

The judge slowed down her tears. She methodically dried her eyes. I noticed she didn't wear a stitch of makeup. But she shined. She looked at Sarah with such sympathy, "Todd told me you were a fraud. You run health clinics, he said, and you got cancer. You must be a fraud." She sadly looked down, "such coldness. Todd went on to say he doesn't understand you. You get cancer and yet . . . you're so upbeat. So pleasant. Like nothing happened. He doesn't understand why you haven't caved in. He wants you to cave in. Maybe he will have sympathy for you then."

But the darkness has not understood it

But Todd would never understand a person like Sarah, his wife that he lived with for eleven years, slept by her side, had a child with, watched her great unfailing faith, and yet, he wasn't persuaded to be a better person. His mind was set against Sarah. His mind was set on earthly things. And, in his case, he would get his earthly things. Todd was intent upon storing up his treasures on earth. He seemed to have no understanding that such a plan was not a good thing.[7]

The judge had composed herself and Sarah had gone back to her chair next to me and facing the judge.

"You know, Todd is baffled by you," she said to Sarah. "But, I totally understand you. You're just a good person. That's it. And there's no changing you. You're a keeper. . . . somebody is looking out for you."

As the judge spoke with Sarah, the Lord laid on my heart a verse: "The light shines in the darkness, but the darkness has not understood it."[8]

Todd would never understand Sarah. In the back of my mind, I figured Todd would have to deal with the Assyrians someday.

The judge looked at me. "I guess I've lost all neutrality in this case. I should recuse myself."

---

7 Matthew 6:19 . "Do not store up for yourselves treasures on earth, where moth and rust destroy, and where thieves break in and steal. But store up for yourselves treasures in heaven, where moth and rust do not destroy, and where thieves do not break in and steal. For where your treasure is, there your heart will be also."

8 John 1:4-5. "In him was life, and that life was the light of men. The light shines in the darkness, but the darkness has not understood it."

Sarah looked concerned. "What does that mean?"

"It means, I believe I may have lost my neutrality in this case and need to let another judge handle it."

"No, please stay on. You are such a gift to me today. We can't lose you."

"I may have no choice." Judge Teresa looked at me. "What do you think, Tom?"

But Sarah cut in—"Do you have to leave the case if we just give Todd whatever he wants?"

The judge looked at me. "What do you think, Tom?"

"Judge, stay on the case. It's going to settle today."

"Amen," Sarah said.

The Life-Light

I guess by worldly standards, Sarah got hammered that day. Todd made out like a bandit. He was so happy. He "scored." Sarah got to keep all her clinics, but Todd received a large equalization payment worth half the clinics Sarah kept, plus spousal support for five and a half years, plus joint custody of their daughter, and most of the other goodies and things he wanted. He was set. Sarah would carry on with her clinics, do all the work, and continue to pay Todd on a monthly basis for five and a half years. Todd sacrificed *nothing* to settle.

I understood a long time ago:
The one that sacrifices nothing learns and discerns nothing.

That was three years ago. I can't really tell you too much more about Sarah without giving her identity away, but she continued to shine. She had a full recovery from her cancer, her clinics are doing better than ever, and her daughter is with her full-time. The beautiful thing about a beautiful person is the source of that beauty. *The Life-Light blazed out of the darkness; the darkness couldn't put it out.*[9]

I also know what happened to Todd. It's not a pretty picture. Leave it at that. He has no idea why things haven't turned out well for him. He has no discernment.[10]

Once again, I am sure, more than anything, I want the Life-Light in me. In my world, every day, you see those that have it, and those that don't.

Children of light.

T+

---

9 John 1:5. Eugene H. Peterson, *The Message Bible* (NavPress, 2002), p. 1455.

10 1 Corinthians 2:14. "The man without the Spirit does not accept the things that come from the Spirit of God, for they are foolishness to him, and he cannot understand them, because they are spiritually discerned."

The Take Away 20
The Life-Light.

1. *The Life-Light.* "In him was life, and that life was the light of men. The light shines in the darkness, but the darkness has not understood it." This interpretation of John 1:4-5 from the *NIV Bible*, helps to explain why children of the world, children of darkness, can't understand those filled with *The Life-Light*. And, more importantly, it means that darkness can't, and never will overcome God's light. 1 Corinthians 2:14, says: "The man without the Spirit does not accept the things that come from the Spirit of God, for they are foolishness to him, and he cannot understand them, because they are spiritually discerned."

2. In Matthew 5:14-16 Jesus said, "You are the light of the world. A city on a hill cannot be hidden. Neither do people light a lamp and put it under a bowl. Instead they put it on its stand, and it gives light to everyone in the house. In the same way, let your light shine before men, that they may see your good deeds and praise your Father in heaven." God, and Jesus, are the source of that light. Those that accept Jesus into their life, reflect that light. Therefore, let your light shine before men. They *may* see your good deeds, but not always, and you have to accept that.

3. In this chapter, I discuss a person that sacrificed *nothing* to settle. *The one that sacrifices nothing to settle learns and discerns nothing.* He would be back for more later. He would suffer the consequences.

4. **"The Life-Light blazed out of the darkness; the darkness couldn't put it out."** This interpretation of John 1:5, by Eugene H. Peterson in *The Message Bible*, helps to explain the beauty of a person with unfailing faith in God and who is filled with the Holy Spirit. We can reflect that light, God's light. This Life-Light cannot be extinguished, and never will.

You Need an Advocate, Not a Lawyer

You want the ruling in your favor

The ruling is in the dirt

Perhaps you've heard the story of a woman who had a sudden need for an advocate. Not a lawyer, an advocate. Someone who could see the whole picture, and was selfless in doing so.

Hard to find, but sometimes you get blessed.

This woman was caught in the act of adultery and she was accused and taken before someone they thought would judge her harshly. A harsh judgment would give her accusers a certain sense of vindication, for they saw themselves as righteous and scholarly. Now this woman lived in a time when a woman and a man could be stoned to death for adultery. Still, only the woman was brought forth for judgment; the man wasn't included. The judge in this case was a well-known Teacher that the populace was growing to love and follow. The "righteous and scholarly ones" didn't like that, so they on occasion, like this one, tried to trap him into saying something incriminating so they could later bring charges against him.

The "righteous and scholarly ones" made the woman stand before the local citizens and then they said to the Teacher: "Teacher, this woman was caught in the act of adultery. In the Law, Moses commanded us to stone such women. Now, what do you say?"[1]

The Teacher stooped down and started to write on the ground with his finger.

A question from the "righteous and scholarly ones" was pending, and the Teacher was writing. In this case, the Teacher was the judge.

---

1 John 8:4-5.

I've been there many, many times. An argument is presented to the judge, and then both sides are waiting for the judge's ruling. Then, the judge starts writing. As an old trial lawyer, you know that the judge is writing his ruling, and you drastically want the ruling to be in your favor. In fact, in a heartbeat, you want to know that you know, that you know, that you have done everything possible to make sure the ruling is in your favor. Could I have done more, argued more, put forth a better case, cited better law? How could I have improved my case?

How could I have improved my life?

It is a very long moment as you wait for the ruling. And, if you are the one that could be ruled against, or ruled for, *it is a very, very long moment.*

The "righteous and scholarly ones" badgered the Teacher for a ruling.

In this particular case, the Teacher's ruling could wait. First, he wanted to do a little advocacy on behalf of the woman who had no one to speak up for her. That's when the Teacher made a simple statement to those that sought the ruling:

"If any one of you is without sin, let him be the first to throw a stone at her."[2]

I've been there many, many times. You are waiting for the ruling, but the judge makes a statement, or asks a question. I do *not* remember one time in thirty years of litigation when the statement or question did not give away which way the judge was leaning. Over two thousand years later after the Teacher made his statement, I, as a young lawyer, studied and studied that statement. And I studied the part about the Teacher bending down to write something in the sand, or the dirt, on the ground. To this young trial lawyer, the Lord, said: "I'm writing my ruling, on the ground."

I knew I always wanted that ruling to be on my side. On my client's side. So, I wanted to be the best advocate possible. Which was hard, because more than anyone else, I was well aware of all my flaws. And I had many.

I remember waiting for that ruling in the Harry Goldberg case.

I remember waiting for that ruling in the Ezra Ezekiel case.

I remember waiting for that ruling in the Janie Blythe case.

I remember waiting for that ruling so many times it makes me sick because my stomach remembers all the times it was so tied in knots that I couldn't breathe, I couldn't speak, I couldn't think.

I remember waiting for the ruling in the Harry Goldberg case. That case had burned like a brush fire after those first five days of trial. I seemed to gain momentum as the days went by. I fought hard, and I drove the case hard, putting everything I had into it. After the Plaintiff finally rested the case after twenty days of testimony, I brought a Motion For a Directed Verdict before Judge Roth. I paced back and forth making my arguments as to why the judge should right here and now—grant Harry Goldberg a directed verdict. Brendan Jones made his arguments. He wanted the jury to decide the case. He wanted the mob to decide.

---

2 John 8:7.

He saw the jury as nothing but a mob he could control. Why not? He always won didn't he? Frankly, somewhere along the way, he knew he was in trouble. Somewhere along the way, the plaintiff, Billy Joe Hollister knew he was in trouble. After the arguments were made, it was time for the judge to make his ruling. And the first thing he did was to start writing.

I remember that moment.

Everything is on the line.

I couldn't breathe.

Harry Goldberg couldn't breathe.

I wondered if the woman accused of adultery was able to breathe.

As she stood there and waited for the ruling, it was the Teacher's statement that hung in the air: *"If any one of you is without sin, let him be the first to throw a stone at her."*

Again, the Teacher stooped down and wrote something on the ground with his finger. What would be his ruling?

Those that heard the statement, including the righteous and scholarly ones, started to go away one at a time, the older ones first, until only the Teacher was left, with the woman still standing there.

The Teacher straightened up and asked, "Woman, where are they? Has no one condemned you?"

"No one, sir," she said.

Then the ruling came.

"Then neither do I condemn you,"[3] the Teacher declared. "Go now and leave your life of sin."[4]

You need an advocate

Sarah Bleu needed an advocate. If she chose her advocate well, she would also get a good lawyer. You can't be a good advocate unless you're also a good lawyer. But, you can be a good lawyer and yet, a poor advocate.

Sarah had a good lawyer already on board when she hired me. Her lawyer's advice was good. Indeed, maybe her lawyer would have won the case in trial, maybe Sarah would have been granted full custody of Emily, maybe Sarah could have kept all her clinics and Todd receive nothing, not even an equalization payment, maybe Todd would have been denied spousal support. But Sarah would have paid the lawyer hundreds of thousands of dollars to see if she was right, and Sarah would have suffered greatly through the process. And, Emily, well, she would have seen enough to be damaged for life. A lawyer is designed to sell one thing: the lawyer's services, the lawyer's time, and the more the better.

That's all the lawyer has to sell. Earthly time to reach earthly decisions.

An advocate wants godly resolution.

---

3 Cf. John 12:47. *"For I did not come to judge the world, but to save it."*

4 The story, Jesus Forgives an Adulterous Woman, is told in John 8:1-11.

Basically, my job when Sarah brought me on board was to be her advocate. My experience has shown that I did the right thing for her. I prayed that I would see the whole picture of what was right for her, and to use all my talents and gifts from God to get her out of a bad situation.

Be her advocate.

And be selfless about it.

Within that first three years after the settlement, Sarah was immensely blessed. And Todd went straight downhill. In the third year after the settlement, Todd hadn't even made an effort to see Emily. He had demanded joint custody during the settlement discussions, yet, he seemed to lose all interest in Emily.

Three years after the settlement agreement, Todd came back. For more. More money that is. Todd was not a man of resolution. And, Todd would never learn: *The problem with money is that it's a crude measurement for resolution.*

Money didn't, and wouldn't bring him any peace.

He no longer thought he received a good deal in the settlement. He had two years left on his spousal support, but he wanted more per month, he wanted child support for Emily, and he argued that the equalization payment had been inadequate. The value of the clinics had soared, Sarah was prospering, her business was growing. How could the equalization payment paid to Todd have been fair? He was slowly losing the fortune he had received in his settlement with Sarah, his business efforts were failing, he had no interest in seeing his daughter Emily, and when he did, he used the opportunity to criticize Sarah.

Todd was losing his mind.

You can lose your mind

At the crossroads of human conflict, every day you see people that are losing their minds, or have lost their minds. Years of negative thinking, self-serving thinking, years of sin, can destroy a mind. These are the people that did not think it was worthwhile to learn and retain the knowledge of God.

> "Furthermore, since they did not think it worthwhile to retain the knowledge of God, he gave them over to a depraved mind, to do what ought not to be done. They became filled with every kind of wickedness, evil, greed and depravity. They are full of envy, murder, strife, deceit and malice. They are gossips, slanderers, God-haters, insolent, arrogant and boastful; they invent ways of doing evil; they disobey their parents; they are senseless, faithless, heartless, ruthless. Although they know God's righteous decree that those who do such things deserve death, they not only continue to do these very things but also approve of those who practice them."[5]

5 Romans 1:28-32.

Wonderful authors, such as Joyce Meyer, have written great books on the mind, and how to have a good mind.[6] My job is twofold: first, to tell you that often when you are in the fight of your life you are dealing with people as Paul described them above; and, secondly, to tell you that when you are in the fight for your life, your mind will be attacked, will be tested, will be stressed, will be in torment—and you better have a plan. You need a plan, and you need to put it into practice, in a godly way.

"Finally, brothers, whatever is true, whatever is noble, whatever is right, whatever is pure, whatever is lovely, whatever is admirable— if anything is excellent or praiseworthy—think about such things. Whatever you have learned or received or heard from me, or seen in me —put it into practice. And the God of peace will be with you."[7]

Sarah was at peace. Todd wasn't.

Todd's lawyer sent threatening letters to Sarah, and she sent them to me.

Whatever you are about to do, do quickly

As I creep into my late fifties as a lawyer it all makes such sense to me now. And I now have over thirty years of practice to see how it plays out. Jesus said *settle matters quickly* with your adversary.[8] Such great counseling.

But there is also another approach that you sometimes have to take against your adversary, especially when they are so lost and the redemptive possibilities so remote.

Todd would call Sarah up and rail at her. And Todd's new lawyer, emboldened by a client with substantial, but dwindling resources, was incredibly aggressive. In one particular telephone call, after Todd's lawyer screamed at me his legal position and why they'd win, and how unjust the settlement was toward Todd, he demanded my response.

I quoted exactly what my Senior Partner told me to tell him:
Whatever you are about to do, do quickly.[9]

Just as Jesus said, settle matters quickly, there are those situations when the other side is so lost, so determined to do something so wrong, so evil, that it's okay to say: *whatever you are about to do, do quickly.* Because we live by faith, not by fear. Go ahead, take your best shot, and do it quickly, let's get this whole mess over with as quickly as possible. No more calls, no more threats.

And Todd and his lawyer did file a pretty massive motion against Sarah.

---

6 Joyce Meyer, *Battlefield of the Mind* (FaithWords, Revised edition, 2002).
7 Philippians 4:8-9.
8 Matthew 5:25.
9 John 13:27.

Sarah was to blame for everything that had gone wrong in Todd's life, Sarah had misrepresented the value of her clinics, Sarah this and Sarah that.

And after a mini trial over several days, the case was submitted, and Todd's lawyer was confident when he stood up and demanded the judge's ruling.

And the judge started writing.

And the knot in my stomach was twisting again, as usual.

What was the judge writing? I thought of Jesus writing on the ground. I said another short prayer, like Nehemiah.[10]

The judge tilted his glasses, and looked down at Todd.

"Mr. Bleu, do you think that maybe it's time you took responsibility for your own life?" The judge shook his head. He wrote some more.

Sarah's friends and parents in the audience gasped with happiness and delight. Her mother started crying.

The bottom line as to the judge's ruling on all of Todd's requests was: DENIED. He got nothing.

Then the judge suggested to me that I consider bringing a motion for full custody of Emily. If, by chance Todd showed supposed renewed interest in Emily, he felt it was too toxic of an environment for her to be in.

Then Sarah started crying.

I just held back.

Jesus the advocate

Jesus could have lawyered up the situation with the woman caught in adultery, but he went straight to the advocacy role. The ultimate advocate, would also be the judge. Jesus showed compassion and forgiveness to the woman while highlighting the hypocrisy of the supposedly righteous and scholarly ones. Jesus is the ultimate selfless advocate.[11]

I remember studying Jesus the Advocate, when I was a young lawyer. Exactly who was this person who, in one fell swoop, could end an accusatory attack, or fend off a question couched in trickery and subterfuge, or on the other hand, calm a storm, with just one statement?

"If any one of you is without sin, let him be the first to throw a stone at her."[12]

"Give to Caesar what is Caesar's, and to God what is God's."[13]

"Quiet! Be Still!"[14]

"Then the wind died down and it was completely calm."[15]

---

10 The spontaneous and quick prayers of Nehemiah. Nehemiah 2:4; 4:4-5,9; 5:19; 6:14; 13:14, 22, 29. "A short prayer pierces the heavens." *The Cloud of Unknowing* (Chapter 37, last sentence, and Chapter 38, "How and why a short prayer pierces the heavens."), referencing St. John of the Cross, *The Living Flame of Love.*

11 And, as discussed before, Jesus is the ultimate mediator between God and man. 1 Timothy 2:5. See Chapter 1.

12 John 8:7.

13 Matthew 22:21.

14 Mark 4:39.

15 Ibid.

In my life I've known so many of those moments, *when the wind died down and it was completely calm.*

And I know who to thank for those moments.

And who gets all the glory.

T+

The Take Away 21
You need an advocate, not a lawyer.

1. When you're in the fight of your life you need an advocate, not a lawyer. In the legal sense, a good advocate is also a good lawyer. But a good lawyer is not necessarily a good advocate.

2. The best advocates use Jesus as their model. Such an advocate wants a godly resolution. Such an advocate has a relationship with Jesus, is prayerful, and seeks godly wisdom to see the whole picture of what is right for the person they are called to help. Such an advocate will use all of their God-given talents and gifts to rescue the person, the client, the family member, or friend, from the problem or situation they are in.

3. When you're in the fight of your life, you want the ruling to be in your favor. You want to know that you have done everything possible to make sure the ruling is in your favor. Could I have done more, argued more, put forth a better case, been a better person? You need a godly advocate on your side. You need to be right with the Lord, and so does your earthly advocate.

4. Jesus could have lawyered up the situation with the woman caught in adultery, but he went straight to the advocacy role. Jesus showed compassion and forgiveness to the woman while highlighting the hypocrisy of her accusers, the supposedly righteous and scholarly ones. Jesus is the ultimate selfless advocate. Jesus is our role model for becoming, and being, an advocate.

22

God Has Gone Out in Front of You

When you're in the fight of your life

Settle it, or win it

In 1985, I did everything I could to settle the Knoll Radio Company vs. Harry Goldberg case. In those days it was mostly out of fear. I just figured that opposing counsel, Brendan Jones, and the rest of his team would kill me in trial. Together, they had about 120 years of experience, to my six. Yes, my boss, Murray Katz, had given me two associates to help, but one was strung out on cocaine (he was disbarred a few years later), and the other was scared to death. So, maybe I had six-and-a-half years of experience going for me.

But, one thing I did do was try my hardest to settle the case before the trial. Indeed, during the sixteen months of pretrial litigation, I had sent eight settlement letters. And, yes, my lead opposing counsel, Brendan Jones, never anticipated that I would put every one of those letters into evidence. Every single one. When I sent the letters, I did not make them confidential. The world could see them, for all I was concerned. Same with my client Harry Goldberg, he didn't care. Let the world see the settlement offers. Harry was an amazingly transparent guy. He had no secrets. One morning he told me that there is nothing concealed that will not be disclosed, or hidden that will not be made known.[1] I didn't know if Harry knew he was quoting Jesus. This was certainly an application of this statement by Jesus to a situation I hadn't considered before. But, it worked for me. And then I wondered if Harry was referring to the gun hidden in his briefcase.

In any event, both Harry and I were quite comfortable with putting all the cards on table for the judge and jury to see. Looking back, I feel like I begged Brendan

---

1 Matthew 10:26.

Jones and his cohorts to settle. But—they wouldn't. At least for nothing less than a giveaway by Harry of his beloved radio stations. So, I was forced to fight.

And I did.

If I could not settle it, I was going to win it. And over time I did learn: *You qualify to win it, if you've done everything you can to settle it.*

I had my Senior Partner to help me. He would make up for my 114-year deficit in experience.[2]

I was going to *march down* against them.

Be pleased, O Lord, to save me

In May 1985 after twenty days in trial, the Plaintiff Billy Joe Hollister and his lawyers rested their case. The next morning, I met Harry Goldberg at the little coffee shop outside the courthouse. It was 7:00 a.m. Harry and I had gotten our coffee and we were already talking about the day to come. It was a big day.

Harry looked at me and said, "Tom, this case has been the fight of my life."

I said something profound like, "I know what you mean."

And then I noticed the khaki suit I was wearing should have been at the cleaners. I needed a haircut, sleep, and a meal that someone somewhere would consider healthy. I looked like a wreck. I felt much worse. Deep down, I felt I'd be restored, so I didn't care. I knew who would restore me.

Harry slowly reached into his pocket. He pulled out the napkin from his back pocket. It was looking a little ragged. But there it was. Harry had kept the napkin I had pushed across the table to Brendan Jones with Harry's settlement offer. Brendan rejected the settlement offer, and with great aplomb, had pushed the napkin back at me, stood up, and strutted out. He had a TV interview to do regarding his latest victory. He didn't have time for us and our puny offer. He thought I was so desperate I would bargain against myself and come back with an even better offer for him. He was confident. He was the ruler of his world.

I was young; I marveled at his confidence.

Harry was remembering that moment from a few months before the trial began. He studied the napkin.

"The wicked freely strut about,"[3] Harry said.

Before the trial, Harry was a secular Jew. That had changed. A thought really jelled in my mind that morning that resonated with me for a long time. Harry had approached the trial almost like a drug addict knowing he's going to die approaches rehab as his last hope. He knew he was in the fight of his life. So, he made a decision to win, to conquer the problem that had beset him. Every day he was fighting for victory. Eventually, he also made the conscious decision to turn

---

2 "This is what the Lord says to you: 'Do not be afraid or discouraged because of this vast army. For the battle is not yours, but God's. Tomorrow march down against them....'" 2 Chronicles 20:15-16.
3 Psalm 12:8. "The wicked freely strut about when what is vile is honored among men."

the case over to God, and that meant getting out, dusting off and reading his old Hebrew Bible every day. I should say—*he studied it.* There was no *reading* it, he was studying it, looking for battle plans, ideas, and inspiration.

And protection.

I had told Harry I thought the trial could last thirty days. He saw the thirty days as going into rehab, or going into war.

It was springtime, and this king was going to war.

And he was going to emerge victoriously.

Of course he would.

God would go out in front of him.

I saw that Harry had written something on the bottom of the napkin. I had to read it upside down: "We are a mist, and we are here for a little while, and then we are gone," paraphrasing James.[4] And he had put the "T+" (Trust the Lord) next to it.

Harry looked up at me. "I put the gun away on the fifth day of the trial. And, held onto this napkin." He turned the napkin over:

"Be pleased, O Lord, to save me;
*   O Lord, come quickly to help me."*[5]

Harry had been speaking out that Psalm, loud and clear, daily, every chance he could, since the trial began. Not praying it out, *speaking* it out.

I looked at Harry and nodded my head, "When you're in the fight of your life, pull out all the stops. And for God's sake—*ask God for help!!"*

"Constantly," Harry said.

"Are you ready for battle?" I nodded at the courthouse entrance.

"Absolutely!"

"Be pleased, O Lord, to save me;
*   O Lord, come quickly to help me."*

Harry and I said that one . . . together.

As we walked to the courthouse entrance, Harry put his arm around my shoulders and said, "You know, that first week of trial, I noticed how you spoke with your *Counselor* every day. And I thought it was kind of strange. . . . I don't think so any more."

We kept walking. "This case has made me a better Jew. I like prayer again. And one thing I kept asking the Lord to do was go ahead of us, and help me win this battle."

Harry and I were definitely on the same track.

---

4 James 4:14. "Why, you do not even know what will happen tomorrow. What is your life? You are a mist that appears for a little while and then vanishes."
5 Psalm 40:13.

The ruling in the Harry Goldberg case, Part 1

By the twentieth day of trial in the Harry Goldberg case, Harry and I were on to something. After that first week, I felt, day after day, that God had gone out in front of us to strike down the other side.[6] As the pace of the trial sped up, things kept improving for Harry and me. Indeed, the Plaintiff, Billy Joe Hollister and his lead attorney, Brendan Jones, seemed to be less engaged. As our passion increased, theirs waned.

So I was ready that day to make my argument that Judge Roth should throw out the case against my client, Harry Goldberg—*before I even called my first witness.* By then our case was resonating. The series of deal memos did not amount to an agreement by Harry Goldberg to sell his beloved radio stations to William Joseph Hollister and his company, Knoll Radio Company. Within an hour of the start of the twenty-first day of the trial I was pacing back and forth before Judge Roth emphasizing that the case should be thrown out—now. There was no reason to carry on with this trial. The Plaintiff didn't have a case.

Then Brendan Jones argued. He stood mechanically at the podium. He made his points. Harry Goldberg should put on his defense and then, the case should go to the jury. Let the jury decide the case. He argued that the Plaintiff had made their case that Harry Goldberg had entered into a valid contract to sell his stations at a reasonable price, the market price. And the judge and jury should order the stations sold to Knoll Radio Company.

Period.

He sat down.

I was sitting. I really couldn't breathe. Harry was sitting next to me. He couldn't breathe. We both knew that the odds of winning a directed verdict were slim. Very slim. The Blue Angels and their client were smug in their blue suits. There they sat in a row: William Joseph Hollister, and his lawyers, Brendan Jones, Bruce Jenson, Philip Rawlings, and Ann Davis.

But, Judge Roth was writing.

And we were waiting.

God has gone out in front of you, Part 2

Twenty-six years later Mike Harrison and I were sitting at the Pantry, my favorite little back-up coffee shop in downtown Los Angeles. And I was thinking about that moment years ago sitting in the courtroom watching Judge Roth writing. What was taking him so long? He seemed so focused, but content. As the Harry Goldberg case wore on, I was certain that God had gone before us, and

---

6 1 Chronicles 14:13-15. "Once more the Philistines raided the valley, so David inquired of God again, and God answered him, 'Do not go straight up, but circle around them and attack them in front of the balsam trees. As soon as you hear the sound of marching in the tops of the balsam trees, move out to battle, because that will mean God has gone out in front of you to strike the Philistine army.'"

Harry Goldberg and his humble inexperienced lawyer would win. So, all I could do was watch the judge quietly writing.

It had been six months since Mike Harrison and I had engaged in the first mediation on his case. Everything had changed by then. I didn't know how the day would go, but I knew that the Plaintiff, Blackdog and its owner, Julius Rotello were in bad shape. Their online business, Moviesonline, was failing miserably. For some unknown reason, their business model simple didn't catch on with the public. Nobody was streaming or downloading the movies. Julius Rotello, desperate, and frantic, started offering pornographic movies to download for a dollar. And, there again, nobody wanted them. They didn't sell. Nobody downloaded them. Nobody streamed them. He was crazy with panic and fear. He had no answers.

It *had been* such a clever plot on Julius' part. He had conned Mike into giving him Harrison Interactive's technology, then they let some time go by and launched their own business, Moviesonline, then they sued Harrison Interactive for stealing Blackdog's supposed technology, that they stole from Harrison Interactive. The plot spread out over about three years. And because of Mike's mistakes, and his affair, it appeared as though Rotello could get away with it. After all, Rotello had some of the best computer and technology minds in the world working for him, and they were just as corrupt. Indeed, Julius considered himself a genius, one of the five smartest people on the face of the earth. That's what he told me in his deposition. He was quite happy with himself. He believed he had covered up the trail from stealing my client's trade secrets and using them in Blackdog's technology. But, of course, we had our own forensic experts and they had discovered and proven the trail, and we felt we were going to win at trial.

But, there wasn't going to be much of a fight.

Because Moviesonline was failing so dismally.

Blackdog had no resources to fight with. They were in no position to take us on in trial.

I felt the Lord had gone ahead of us and the battle was over. Over the years going all the way back to the Harry Goldberg trial, I saw how the Lord had gone ahead and fought the battle for us. Sometimes it was like when David had gone against the Philistines and won because God had gone before him. Other times it was a little more like when Jehoshaphat had to face off against the vast armies of Moab and Ammon, and others. They prayed, and put their faith in God. Then God spoke through Jahaziel and he said:

> "Listen, King Jehoshaphat and all who live in Judah and Jerusalem! This is what the Lord says to you: 'Do not be afraid or discouraged because of this vast army. For the battle is not yours, but God's. Tomorrow march down against them. They will be climbing up by the Pass of Ziz, and you will find them at the end of the gorge in the Desert of Jeruel. You will not have to fight this battle. Take up you positions;

stand firm and see the deliverance the Lord will give you, O Judah and Jerusalem. Do not be afraid; do not be discouraged. Go out to face them tomorrow, and the Lord will be with you.'"[7]

When it was time for King Jehoshaphat and his armies to fight with Moab and Ammon, and their allies, they looked toward the vast army, and "they saw only dead bodies lying on the ground; no one had escaped."[8]

Other times it was more like the time that Sennacherib threatened Jerusalem. The same God that would use the Assyrians to punish his unfaithful and sinful chosen people, would, on the other hand mercilessly annihilate when his people where faithful and cried out to him. "After all that Hezekiah had so faithfully done, Sennacherib king of Assyria came and invaded Judah." Hezekiah encouraged his military officers and his people with these words:

> "Be strong and courageous. Do not be afraid or discouraged because
> of the king of Assyria and the vast army with him; for there is a greater
> power with us than with him. With him is only the arm of flesh, but
> with us is the Lord our God to help us and to fight our battles."[9]

In the end, the Lord sent an angel, who annihilated all the fighting men and the leaders and officers in the camp of the Assyrian king. So the Assyrian King Sennacherib withdrew to his own land in disgrace and was later murdered by his own sons.[10]

Settle matters quickly, not hastily, Part 2

There is a big difference between settling a matter quickly, and settling something hastily. How can God go before you, if you don't give him the time?

"Watch and pray," Mike said. But I was getting a refill on my coffee at the Pantry. I love breakfast here. It tastes so good for some reason. Where you eat breakfast is at least fifty percent of what you eat for breakfast. Sitting at the Pantry, in downtown Los Angeles is a joy unto itself. I believe the place is anointed. Any person in this place would qualify to be on one of my juries. I think you have to be honest to dine at the Pantry.

"Hello, Tom?" Mike got my attention.

"Oh, sorry, just marveling over the beautiful cross-section of people that eat at this place."

"Clare and I are back together," Mike said.

"I had faith."

"A lesson learned early is a great blessing, a lesson learned too late is a great punishment. I think I heard that somewhere."

I nodded.

---

7   2 Chronicles 20:15-17.
8   2 Chronicles 20:24.
9   2 Chronicles 32:7-8.
10 2 Chronicles 32:20-21.

Pensive, Mike took a sip of his coffee. "In the past, I always prospered, I was protected, I was always happy, if I kept God's commands. So simple. When you walk they will guide you, when you sleep, they will watch over you, and when you awake, they will speak to you."[11]

"Mike, we will settle today."

"It's back in God's hands. Finally." We started to get up. Both of us asked for more coffee to go. The Pantry's coffee is anointed. Did I say that?

Mike looked at me and sighed deeply, "I'm glad I'm going through this. It has been the hardest thing in my life, both the business and with Clare, but I'm glad I went through this."

We were walking next door to where the mediation would take place. We were quiet. It had been somewhat of a long haul until today.

Mike looked at me again and said, "The haste that got me into this problem would not be what gets me out of this problem."

"I know. God's timing is everything. It is important to settle a case quickly, not hastily.[12] Haste got you into the problem, but will not get you out of the problem."

"This case has been going for seven months. In my case, 'quickly' may turn out to be seven months. But, I'm settling a lot more than this case."

Lead me in the Way everlasting[13]

Julius Rotello and his lawyer Mac Fleister had lost their luster. They made every effort all day long to strut, to gloat, to intimidate, to prevaricate. But, their company, Blackdog was dead, it had failed, they couldn't prove damages, they couldn't prove infringement, and all they had left were bullying tactics. At the end of the day, they gave it up, agreed to pay my client a significant sum of money for attorneys' fees and costs, and agreed to not use Harrison Interactive's technology.

The case was over.

Our mediator, Judge Rosenthal helped us draft a Settlement Agreement, and as it was being signed, I got a phone call. Normally, I wouldn't pick it up. You shouldn't do that. But, by this time of the day everything was more relaxed, and I had already signed the Settlement Agreement.

The phone number was unusual. And, I just felt I was supposed to answer. So, I did.

It was Harry Goldberg's daughter.

Harry had died earlier in the day. Would I come over?

T+

---

11 See Proverbs 6:22.

12 See Proverbs 19:2. "It is not good to have zeal without knowledge, nor to be hasty and miss the way." Proverbs 25:8. "What you have seen with your eyes do not bring hastily to court, for what will you do in the end if your neighbor puts you to shame?"

13 Psalm 139:23-24. "Search me, O God, and know my heart; test me and know my anxious thoughts. See if there is any offensive way in me, and lead me in the way everlasting."

The Take Away 22
God has gone out in front of you.

1. "This is what the Lord says to you: '*Do not be afraid or discouraged because of this vast army. For the battle is not yours, but God's. Tomorrow march down against them. . . .*'" 2 Chronicles 20:15-16.

    For children of light, the saints of the Lord, his children, the battle belongs to the Lord. This is what the Lord says to you: Do not be afraid or discouraged because of your enemy, the vast army against you, the problem you are facing, the challenge before you. *For the battle is not yours, but God's.*

2. 1 Chronicles 14:13-15. "Once more the Philistines raided the valley, so David inquired of God again, and God answered him, 'Do not go straight up, but circle around them and attack them in front of the balsam trees. As soon as you hear the sound of marching in the tops of the balsam trees, move out to battle, because that will mean *God has gone out in front of you* to strike the Philistine army.'"

    Over the years going all the way back to some of my first trials, both professionally and personally, I saw how the Lord had gone ahead and fought the battle for me. Sometimes it was like when David had gone against the Philistines and won because God had gone before him. Other times it was a little more like when Jehoshaphat had to face off against the vast armies of Moab and Ammon, and others. They prayed, and put their faith in God. Similarly, the children of God can pray, put their faith in Him, and He will go out in front of you and fight the battle for you. I ask Him to, I've counted on the Lord. He has never let me down.

3. Proverbs 19:2. "It is not good to have zeal without knowledge, nor to be hasty and miss the way." Proverbs 25:8. "What you have seen with your eyes do not bring hastily to court, for what will you do in the end if your neighbor puts you to shame?"

    There is a big difference between settling a matter quickly, and settling a matter hastily. How can God go before you, if you don't give him the time?

4. Ask the Lord to save you, to protect you, to preserve you, to go before you, quickly, and help you.

    "Be pleased, O Lord, to save me;
       O Lord, come quickly to help me."

The Settlement Club

The contemplatives

I sat toward the back when I went to the Harry Goldberg funeral. That was the only place I could find a seat. It was packed. I recognized some of my friends from the Settlement Club. We nodded. I thought of my old boss and senior partner, Murray Katz. He had died probably ten years ago. He had retired at least fifteen years ago. I sometimes hate how fast time goes by. We are a mist.

But, I had been so blessed to have had lunch with Harry about six months before he died.

My last lunch with Harry

We sat at a restaurant called the Buffalo Club on Olympic in Santa Monica, California. Harry was in his mid-eighties. We tried to do the math on how old both of us were in the spring of 1985. I was about thirty-one, and Harry was about sixty-one. Or so we figured. It didn't matter anymore. Right next to him on the floor by his chair was his trusty old tan leather briefcase that must have been about fifty years old by then. Harry saw me looking at it.

"Looks like you've had it refurbished a little," I said.

"Yeah, it's on its last run with me. We've been together a long time. A man and his briefcase." Harry mused. What was left unsaid by two guys that had grown older together was: *wish we could refurbish ourselves like we can our old briefcases.* It's okay I thought: our hearts had been refurbished many times.

"I'm still concerned you have that old handgun hidden in there somewhere," I smirked.

"I discovered something more powerful, a long time ago." he said.

The ruling in the Harry Goldberg case, Part 2
Today, if you hear his voice

We both ordered Cobb salad, sipped iced teas and remembered.

"Tom, that old Judge Roth must have spent ten minutes writing before he looked up at us."

"I remember."

Harry looked up to the sky above. "You know, ever since he finally looked down at us and granted our motion for a directed verdict, and we realized we had won . . . I never looked back again. Never questioned, never underestimated God. Never." Harry looked at me. "I've been at peace ever since. I got to keep my radio stations and live my life out. I thank God."

"And looking back, I now know: *with God, it's as easy as that*," I said. With a stroke of his pen, Judge Roth had ruled in our favor. I thought of those last two battles in Revelation.

Harry looked at me: "And, is this a good time to thank you?"

I was thinking about how much God had taught me through all those battles, starting with Harry Goldberg's case.

"Harry, that trial ended twenty-five years ago! You're thanking me now?" and I smiled.

He smiled back at me. "Well, I've been meaning to get to it."

"Well, you're welcome. Did you ever figure out I didn't know what I was doing?"

"Hell yeah! That wasn't hard," Harry snarled, and then coughed a little.

"I was making it up as I went."

"You, with the help of your Counselor, gave me the second half of my life. I never doubted anything ever again. I put all my faith in God. I realized he was on my side. I realized he'd go out in front of me. He'd protect me. He'd preserve me. And he has! You know, I'm still an old Jewish guy. But it was that trial that it first happened. I remember it well."

"What was that Harry?"

"It was on the second day of the trial on a Tuesday morning. I started praying, and I heard God speak to me in a still small voice. It was a simple statement, but in the context of the moment I knew exactly what I was being told. God said, 'Harry, do not harden your heart.' On that particular morning I had lost all faith. I thought I would lose the case, lose everything. I was done. So, I knelt down and I prayed, and that's what God said to me and he led me to Psalm 95:8.[1] And I never looked back. You know what happened that day, Tom?"

"No."

"I was at peace. I felt rested. You know? I have to tell you, I've been at rest ever since that day. I did hear his voice. And I've been hearing it ever since. And I never

---

1 Psalm 95:7-11. "Today, if you hear his voice, do not harden your hearts as you did at Meribah, as you did that day at Massah in the desert, where your fathers tested and tried me, though they had seen what I did. For forty hears I was angry with that generation; I said, 'They are a people whose hearts go astray, and they have not known my ways.' So I declared on oath in my anger, 'They shall never enter my rest.'"

wanted to lose that. Because I knew what it was to hear his voice, to be at peace, and to be at rest, in the Lord. You know something, Tom?"

"What Harry?" I said.

"Rest doesn't have much to do with sleep."[2]

"I know, Harry. Indeed, I never got much sleep."

"Tom, you know those losers that sued me. They never got a radio station. Not mine, not anyone's. They lost out big time. Just greedy. They made me a rich man by overreaching, because with your help, I never did the deal with them." And Harry looked up. "You know, I feel like I'm close to the end. But this has been the best rest ever. It's 'today,' if you hear his voice. '*Today*.' And, every day. Never lose that Tom. Never."

Harry coughed again. He waived off my concern.

To be at rest. I knew what Harry was talking about. It was code to us. Harry was a simple Jew, I was a simple Christian. We would spend most of our lives in some type of battle. So, basically, we counted on hearing God's voice, receiving it into our heart, and then every day making every effort to enter God's rest.[3] There comes the time when you know that the only rest that counts is God's rest. We could never really put this in preacher's words. We had a yeoman's knowledge of spiritual matters. We just felt we knew how to do it, and did it.

We were just two guys sitting there reflecting on decades of battles and victories. But in the end only one victory counted. Where you spend eternity. And, every day, if you hear his voice, and take it to heart, you can even live *now*, in that eternity. There is great rest in that.

And, peace.

"Is this a bad time?" Janie Blythe walked up to our table. She was full of smiles and sass as she arrived.

"What are two of my favorite boys up to?" There were hugs all around.

Harry studied us both, his eyes showed their age, but they sparkled.

"Whatever happened to that malpractice action filed against our good friend here Dr. Blythe?"

Janie leaned in. "It went all the way through trial. The jury came back in forty-five minutes, 12-0 in my favor."

Harry groused at both of us. "Why'd they take forty-five minutes?"

We laughed.

Janie offered: "We tried to settle. Did everything we could."

"They only wanted a million dollars," I said.

Harry groused again, "These cases are just lottery tickets to some."

"We tried everything we could to settle, and our last offer was just under the amount that would have forced us to report the settlement to the Medical Board of California."

---

2 Proverbs 20:13. "Do not love sleep or you will grow poor; stay awake and you will have food to spare."

3 Hebrews 4:11. "Let us, therefore, make every effort to enter that rest, so that no one will fall by following their example of disobedience."

"Well, that just wouldn't have been right," Harry said. "There are just some battles you have to fight."

Then Mike Harrison walked up.

I was totally surprised. "Okay, this is a conspiracy. Can't a man have lunch in peace with an old friend?" I mused.

Mike Harrison gave me a hug. "Hey, don't blame me, Harry called this meeting."

And Harry must have, because just like that more people showed up, old clients, old friends, and old comrades I had fought with or sometimes fought against. It was good to see them all.

And sure enough, the waiters seemed to know this was happening, because tables and chairs fell into place, iced teas were poured all around, and someone brought me a cup of coffee, and promised that it had been blessed by Pope Clement VIII.

The Settlement Club

Once everyone was seated, and after greetings all around, Harry slowly stood up. It was a little hard for me to watch Harry struggle to stand. It really was sinking in how, oh how!, so many years had gone by.

"I called this meeting, and I wanted to thank you all for coming. The best I can tell we have had good lives, and are having good lives. I'm eighty-six years old now. And, at my station of life you can't help but want to sum things up a little bit, or at least be part of the process. Which is why I called this meeting. All of us, at one time or another were in the middle of a pretty serious battle in our lives and we ended up working with Tom to help us, and we also worked together to build each other up and support each other. And we all resolved, or settled, or prevailed one way or the other, or got through the battles we were faced with. So, I decided to call each of you and ask you for the one thing that stood out as the most important thing you learned from going through that battle. I asked you all to think about it, and come today prepared to speak briefly about it. So, without further delay, and so that I can sit down as soon as possible, I'd like to turn this meeting over to my co-host, Dr. Janie Blythe."

Janie managed to spring up while I helped Harry sit back down. She lit up the room with her energy.

"Welcome to the first of its kind Settlement Club! Harry and I have been talking about this for a long time. We wanted to get everyone together and just share their thoughts and victories and experiences from going through the fight of their lives. I called around, and, looking out among all of you, I'm just so excited that so many showed up. We know that we learned a lot by going through the fight of our lives, and we also think we can share what we learned with others. Somewhere along the line, some of you started asking me when we were going to have the first "Settlement Club" meeting, so that's what Harry and I eventually called it. To be honest, we have no idea what will come from today, but we are so glad you came, that you are willing to participate, and . . . we love you!!"

Janie sat down.

Settle it! . . . and be blessed

Sarah Bleu stood up.

Nicely placed on her head was the ski cap I recognized from the last day in court I spent with her. I remembered she felt more comfortable covering the effects she was suffering from chemotherapy. It had been a while since I had seen her. On this day, Sarah was radiant. She had a pretty summer dress on to match her ski cap.

"Well, first, I want to tell you something." Mercy, we were all tearing up right then. Why, oh why, I don't know. But it hit us all. We all know Sarah.

"I have been cancer-free for a year."

Then with a relish, she removed her ski cap, and her hair flowed out like a fresh forest of red and auburn.

She choked a little and said, "I am so thankful for all your prayers, and I praise God for healing me." There was applause all around, and we all stood up to hug her.

"I got cancer one day. And then, within a week, my husband served me with divorce papers. I decided my life was over. But then, through early morning prayer, getting up at 3:00 a.m., spending maximum amounts of time with the Lord, I felt he said to me, 'Sarah, just settle it, and I will bless you, and restore you for all the trouble you have gone through.' So after that, I pretty much did everything exactly opposite of what my family law lawyer suggested, that I fight for every little thing I deserve. Instead I settled, moved on, and I was blessed. And, I did the same with my cancer. I just decided in my heart to not worry about it, and turn it over to the Lord. I still did what my doctors said to do, but mostly I just stopped all the fretting and worrying. I just turned it over to God. And, here I am. It is such a simple concept. But, in the midst of my hurt, pain, my suffering, I felt God told me to just settle it, he would bless me, and would restore me for all the trouble I went through.[4] And, I'm here to tell you: he did. Except for one thing. He restored much more. I have been blessed more than I could ever have imagined." And just then her daughter Emily came running up and gave her Mom an amazingly long and warm hug.

As the applause and hugs subsided, they sat down.

---

4 Isaiah 61:7. "Instead of their shame my people will receive a double portion, and instead of disgrace they will rejoice in their inheritance; and so they will inherit a double portion in their land, and everlasting joy will be theirs." Zechariah 9:12. "Return to your fortress, O prisoners of hope; even now I announce that I will restore twice as much to you." Job 42:10. "After Job had prayed for his friends, the Lord made him prosperous again and gave him twice as much as he had before."

Settle matters quickly, not hastily

Mike Harrison stood up.

"I cheated on my wife, which led to some horrible business decisions and the general decline of everything I valued in my life. I did an "excellent" job of keeping it a secret for close to a year. I never got caught, I was never found out. But, then I got sued and was in the battle of my life. Everything was on the line. I tried my best to try to settle the lawsuit quickly, but basically, my whole life kept getting worse. So, I went back to prayer, and I got up really early every morning for a week. That was the goal, but the "week" lasted even longer than that. But, I tried my best to compartmentalize my sin, and not deal with it. I figured that no one would find out. The bottom line was that *I* couldn't settle the case quickly, and certainly not without God's help. I did everything *I* could do, but it got me nowhere. I even did prayer fasts, battle plans, and read the Bible, but until I came clean with my sin, my life kept going downward.

"I learned so much from my experience, but if I have to emphasize just one thing, it would be to *settle matters quickly, not hastily*. Once I told my wife what I had done, my life started to get better. Eventually, I got right with God, I got right with my wife and family, and the case settled. At least in my case, you can't settle matters quickly without God on your side. And, God's timing is never "hasty." While I put things right with my life, God went out in front of me and, well, helped me eventually obtain victory in my life. No matter what it is in your life that has to be worked out, in my case it was sin, it could be anything, give God a chance to work it out ahead of you. Settle matters quickly, but not hastily.

"If you don't know the difference, you haven't prayed enough yet."

"I was thirty-two years old when this all happened to me. I found out: 'A lesson learned early is a great blessing, a lesson learned too late is a great punishment.'" He nodded to me.

And I nodded back.

You Be the Peacemaker; The Eight-Step Program

Doug Cooke stood up.

"Twenty-seven years ago, in the fall of 1984, one night I did enough heroin and cocaine to land me in the hospital and then rehab for about the fifth time. I would have to read the hospital report to remember any details of that night, because I blacked out. So within a few days of that night I was in rehab for the fifth time. And, this time, within a few days I was suicidal. I was done, I couldn't recover, I knew I couldn't, and I made the decision to be done with my life. Anyway, *Tommy* said he was ready to bail on me, but then in a last ditch effort to save my pathetic soul suggested we do Jesus' Eight-Step Program. Tommy was clearly making it up as he went, but he said that Jesus had this Eight-Step Program, and I should do it. He even said he'd do it with me. So, I thought, 'suicide, or the Eight-Step Program?' and I decided 'what the heck' I'd do the Eight-Step Program because I'm used to programs, but I'd never heard of this one.' I had heard of Jesus, and if he really had a Step Program, why not give it a try. I know now that Tommy didn't know what he was doing either, but, week by week we did it together. Little did I know he was heading to his first really big trial defending some old dog Jewish guy who was obsessed with his radio stations." Harry and the rest of us smiled joyously on that comment. Doug nodded and smiled at Harry. "Anyway, Tommy and I worked through the Program:

Blessed *are* the poor in spirit: for theirs is the kingdom of heaven.
Blessed *are* they who mourn: for they shall be comforted.
Blessed *are* the meek: for they shall inherit the earth.
Blessed *are* they which do hunger and thirst after righteousness: for they shall be filled.
Blessed *are* the merciful: for they shall obtain mercy.
Blessed *are* the pure in heart: for they shall see God.
Blessed *are* the peacemakers: for they shall be called the children of God.
Blessed *are* they which are persecuted for righteousness' sake: for theirs is the kingdom of heaven."

"It was the seventh Step that got me. I realized one cold night in LA, that I was not a peacemaker, I was a moneymaker, and that I would never be called a child of God. I *knew* it. And I was scared. And that was it. At that moment, hanging with Tommy in a little coffee shop I decided to get my life right with God, make amends to everyone I needed to, and there were lots of them, and turn my life around. I started by paying back a vendor that I had ripped off for a small fortune. I had been a thief of his money. I slowly, but surely paid him back, with interest, fees and costs. I saw 'him' as nothing more than a vendor, until God made me see him as a 'person' that I had really hurt. His name is Sandy Collins. He's been a close friend ever since.

"I never wavered after that. The eighth Step: Blessed *are* they which are persecuted for righteousness' sake: for theirs is the kingdom of heaven. The eighth Step is the anti-waver step. As Aquinas said: if you are confirmed in poverty of spirit, meekness, and all the rest, it follows that no persecution will induce you to renounce the first seven Steps.

"I have now spent twenty-seven years confirming that the Eight-Step Program is a battle plan. It's a plan to turn the battle over to the Lord."

Speak to your problem

Stanley stood up.

"In my best of days, I suffered from manic depression. They now call it bi-polar disorder. And my biggest problem they said was 'rapid cycling.' Which means that I cycle from elation to desperation throughout the day so fast that I don't know which feeling to follow, or what is real. Those were my better days.

"I was homeless down on skid row in downtown Los Angeles when one day I got on a big white bus with the words 'Dream Center' on the side. I was high, and I figured this was my ticket to get higher." More smiles went around. "I don't remember much that day, but they did feed me, and they offered to help. As I sobered up, I decided to give them a chance. I checked into their rehab center, that Tom says we shouldn't call a rehab center." He nods at me: "Tom says we only treat with Tylenol, water, and the Bible. I was disappointed at first to find that out, and indeed, by the third day at the Dream Center, I was going through some heavy withdrawal. The third day was a Tuesday night. And I hit a wall, my body was convulsing, I spent a lot of time in the bathroom throwing up, I was freezing, I couldn't seem to get warm, but I went to the Tuesday night Chapel service and sat in the front row, except for the bathroom visits. I was amazed they let me stay there, especially in the front row. Both Mike and Tom spoke. I was a forty-six-year-old heroin addict, homeless man, dealer, and a criminal. I had lost my mind. My mind was my enemy. The vortex of thoughts and insanity was killing me. As I got sober I got desperate to kill myself. But Mike spoke about Romans 10, the whole chapter.

"On the day I hopped on the white bus, I had already seen it pass about a 100 times. Looking back, I realized how bad of shape I was in that day, and in my own little way, I had asked God for help. And his answer to me was: 'Time and time again I have held out my hand to you, and you have ignored me, refused me, and disobeyed me.' So I thought he told me to, this time, 'Get on the bus.'

"So, I did.

"And Mike spoke that Tuesday night from Romans 10, he ended up reading the whole chapter by the time his sermon was done, and he ended his sermon with these words: which my cold, freezing, shaking, convulsing, pounding body heard: 'All day long I have held out my hands to a disobedient and obstinate people.'

"So, I knew God had called me, so when Mike gave an altar call, I managed to stand up and give my life to Christ. Mike said: 'That if you confess with your mouth, 'Jesus is Lord,' and believe in your heart that God raised him from the dead, you will be saved.' Mike said: 'Everyone who calls on the name of the Lord will be saved.' And, I *had to be saved.*

"That was a year and a half ago. So, I have been sober for eighteen months. For the last eighteen months I've become an expert on Romans, Chapter 10. The whole chapter. I know that faith comes from hearing and hearing from the word of the Lord. So, if I'm not hearing the word from someone else, I'm speaking it out to myself. Speaking it out. I speak it out. And I speak to my problems when they arise and cast them into the sea in Jesus' name, cast them into the sea in Jesus' name, cast them into the sea in Jesus' name. I never let my mind wander. I have learned not to listen to myself, but to speak to myself. And I speak the word of the Lord. For eighteen months now, and counting. Praise God."

T+ Trust the Lord

Lydia Ann Winslow stood up.

"My first three novels, I would like to think, were good, and they met with some success. Indeed, I was getting well known, and—it went to my head. But, there was a lie trickling through my books, and the lie was, that they were co-written with my best friend Zoe Jin Zhao. I call her "Jinny." But the success went to my head, and I caused a dispute with Jinny, my publisher, and just about everyone in my life. Tom was our mediator one day in court, and *we*, I mean *I*, didn't take his advice and settle the case. He said something at the end of the day that really stuck with me, day after day, after that first mediation day: "I've never seen a longer fight land less wounds." Oh, that stung. I couldn't sleep for a few nights, but I kept right on hurting people.

"As we walked out of the mediation, I heard Tom level another jab at me. He told me I should study the Prayer of Saint Francis. I told him, proudly, *I don't pray*. Well, there was such a hole in my heart after that day, I wasn't doing any writing, it was as if my fountain had run completely dry. Well, I decided to study *that stupid prayer*. Reading it the first time was hard. *I* felt like the one that was injured and hurt. *Me, me, me*. But, I read the prayer anyway, with *an attitude*. And, slowly but surely, it changed my heart. One day, as the litigation struggled on, and I wasn't writing even one word, and I really missed my friend Jinny, I read the prayer one more time. We were scheduled to go to trial that day. That was the lowest day of my life. I was suicidal. So, me, an atheist, looked up and said: 'Okay, if you God are really there, please let me run into Tom in court today. That's the only hope I have of settling this matter, and ending this pain.' Well, I didn't believe in miracles, so I figured I'd be able to wallow in my self-pity on that particular day. But, after a really nasty morning in court, I left the lawyers to battle it out over the lunch break and I went up to the cafeteria to get a salad—and walked straight into Tom, who was sitting with Harry.

"I was stunned. Totally stunned. To this day I have never told that story to Tom, but it was amazing. So, he told me to get a napkin and write down exactly the terms to settle, I put a 'T+' at the top. And, the case settled within two hours. Done. On the exact terms on the napkin." She reached into her purse. She held up the napkin. "This napkin."

"Jinny and my fourth book was on the bestseller lists for eighteen months. We've gone on to write seven more books.

"Tom, I've been meaning to tell you, I do believe in miracles.

"And, I do: *Trust the Lord*.

"I put that sign on everything. *Everything* that matters to me."

Do you talk to God? Part 2

Giovanni Jr. stood up. His thick Italian accent took center stage.

"I once spent nine years fighting with my brothers, nine long years. My father had died. He was the anchor in our lives, and so, we fought. But then, in one day, only one day, we settled nine years of warfare. I know Tommaso has said, 'God has a plan for you, but he doesn't plan for you.'[5] Well, God had told me his plan for me. One that would always bring around my family, my friends, *and* a few enemies that would become friends. And I sat on it for twenty-five years until I started talking to God, and finally I asked God to make it happen for me. And he did. *The day I asked, was the day I received.* I know it's not always that fast for some people, but it was for me. I believe you receive it the day you ask for it. The timing of the delivery is God's timing, not mine, not yours.

"I have learned that praying is simply talking to God. Hey, I'm Italian, I know how to talk. And, better still, I, *now*, know how to ask. My God has given me everything I've ever asked for. I am a thankful man.

"You know my friends, this 'asking' thing,[6] it really works.

"And in all your talking . . . *talk to God*."

There was applause all around. Giovanni's brothers were there, Francesco and Paolo, and they applauded the hardest. Italians! They always cry. I could relate.

Transformative mediation; Philemon

Giovanni's brother, Francesco stood up.

"I am a lawyer, like Tommaso, but much smarter." He received the laughs he was looking for.

"What actually happened one day in mediation with Tommaso was, *transformation*. You see, I'm a lawyer, and sometimes we lawyers talk about 'transformative mediation.' 'Oh, please! I say'. What a joke! Paul, in A.D. 60 was the first transformative mediator. Paul's letter to Philemon is in reality, Paul's letter to *me*. When I think I'm in the 'right,' and sometimes, when I'm *definitely* in the 'right,' my Italian tendency is to mow down the other person with my self-righteousness. But, I remember Paul's personal letter to Philemon. Philemon had a slave named Onesimus that ran away. Somehow Onesimus ended up in Rome where he came to work with Paul. Onesimus became a Christian. So Paul sent Onesimus back to Philemon, not as a slave, but as a brother in the Lord. Paul put it this way to Philemon:

'Perhaps the reason he was separated from you for a little while was that you might have him back forever—no longer as a slave, but better than a slave, as a dear brother. He is very dear to me but even dearer to you, both as a fellow man and as a brother in the Lord.'[7]

---

5 I was quoting Dr. Myles Munroe.

6 Matthew 21:22. "If you believe, you will receive whatever you ask for in prayer."

7 Philemon 1:15-16.

"Paul told Philemon that he could have been 'bold' and 'ordered' Philemon to do the right thing, but instead, he appealed to him on the basis of love, and Philemon's commitment to God. And if Onesimus owed anything to Philemon, Paul said: "Charge it to me." This parallels exactly what Christ has done for each of us.

"So, my point is, among many others, is that what happened that day in mediation with Tommaso, was that my relationship with my brothers was reconciled, reestablished . . . *transformed.*

"And also, now, when I approach people on any topic, especially if, as usual, I feel I'm in the right, I think of Paul and his use of tact, grace, and peace. Paul, the great transformative mediator.

"And I think of Christ, the great mediator between God and man."

The problem of evil is a problem for the other side

Dr. Ezra Ezekiel stood up.

"It is so wonderful to see you all, *for such a time as this.* Thank you for inviting me to your *Settlement Club.* I trust that the Club will meet often in the years to come.

"I learned so much from the battle I was in several years ago. My case was a blueprint for naiveté. I had done so well most of my life, medical school, and building my dream of practicing medicine that, I basically had no watchtower in my life, no protection, no discernment. I was a master at acquiring knowledge, and a fool at acquiring wisdom. In my case, evil plotted early and evil plotted long. And I never saw it coming. I, too, tried everything I could to settle the case. I agree, that even though I was struck by men with evil intentions, I didn't deserve to win it, unless I did everything I could to settle it. Because you don't get to know and understand all the workings of the Lord in the process. Since I had that fight of my life I have taken Luke16:8 (KJV) to heart:

'And the lord commended the unjust steward, because he had done wisely: for the children of this world are in their generation wiser than the children of light.'

"For the children of light, the children of darkness can be overcome.

"Indeed, the problem of evil is ultimately a problem for the other side. Because evil loses in the end.

'No weapon formed against you shall prosper.'[8]

"And against me, they definitely didn't prosper."

---

8 Isaiah 54:17 (NKJV).

The watch and pray generation
Hold onto your wings

Shifty Wallace stood up. Mercy, it was good to see him. And his wife was sitting next to him. She patted his arm as he slowly stood up.

"Like my friend Thomas, I have spent thirty years in court. Not as a lawyer, but as a bailiff. I knew early on that God had placed me there to pray over the disputes and battles that I would witness for thirty years. And, although I have been a witness to thousands of battles over the thirty years, indeed, tens of thousands, he blessed me with a simple life, and a simple wife." Shifty lovingly put his hand on his wife's shoulder. "I thank the Lord, for giving me a Strong Tower in Him, and also in a Proverbs 31 woman, like my wife Ruby. She is truly a wife of *Noble Character*.

'A wife of noble character who can find?
She is worth far more than rubies.'

"Saints, I look out at you and I see the *watch and pray* generation, those that are extraordinary, those that have wings. 'The net is spread in vain before the eyes of them that have wings.'[9] Minute by minute, hour by hour, day by day, you may assume that the world will try to entice you, the world will call to you to 'Come along with us,' that you will get all sorts of valuable things. Be in the world, but not of it.[10]

"Hold onto your wings. And when the world entices you, *fly away*.

"I can assure you, as a witness to thousands of battles, that in the end, always, *always*, the Lord's will be done. So, endlessly, I say to you, seek out His will. Indeed, please remember:

'Every good and perfect gift is from above, coming down from the Father of the heavenly lights, who does not change like shifting shadows.'"[11]

There was applause as Shifty sat down.

The contemplatives

I stood up.

"The 8-to-3 rule started out as something so simple, that over time it just became simpler. Warfare is lonely business, and it affects people differently. But for those that get up early and spend those first hours with the Lord, the first fruits, there are great blessings. By now, so much time has gone by, and I've seen the benefits and victories that have come from short or long periods of time with

---

9 See Proverbs 1:17. And I was blessed to find it phrased this way in *Story of a Soul*, The Autobiography of St. Thérèse of Lisieux, Manuscript C. (Washington D.C.: ICS Publications, 1996), p. 224. "All the nets of the hunters would not be able to frighten me, for '*the net is spread in vain before the eyes of them that have wings.*'" (Italics in original)

10 Romans 12:2. "Do not conform any longer to the pattern of this world, but be transformed by the renewing of your mind. Then you will be able to test and approve what God's will is—his good, pleasing and perfect will." See also, John 15:19. ". . . you do not belong to the world, but I have chosen you out of the world."

11 James 1:17.

the Lord, early, early in the day, that I know this is a great gift from God. Who would have known that those in the heat of the fight of their life would find peace in the contemplative life? What I've discovered of value in life has come from hearing the still quiet voice of the Lord. Which I discovered can be heard in noisy courtrooms, busy sidewalks, bustling airports, and fast freeways. But, I hear the Voice the best and clearest as a contemplative at 3:00 a.m. Thomas Merton, in discussing *contemplata tradere* said this:

> 'There is only one vocation. Whether you teach or live in the cloister or nurse the sick, whether you are in religion or out of it, married or single, no matter who you are or what you are, you are called to the summit of perfection: you are called to a deep interior life perhaps even to mystical prayer, and to pass the fruits on your contemplation on to others. And if you cannot do so by word, then by example.'[12]

"After all these years it was a little daunting to learn that Merton started his days at 2:00 a.m. Perhaps like me, he enjoyed the surprises that the Lord had in store for him, and the work that the Lord was doing in his life. Merton eventually came to realize and said about himself, that while speaking to God, 'without knowing how or why, I had actually done the right thing, and even an astounding thing. But what was astounding to me was not my work, but the work You worked in me.'"

"Indeed, for all of us, what is astounding, is not the work we have done, but the work the Lord has done in us.

"Amen."

And everyone said: "Amen."

  T+

12 Thomas Merton, *The Seven Storey Mountain* (New York: Harcourt Brace Jovanovich, Inc., 1948), p. 419.

The Take Away 23
The Settlement Club List.
Ten blessings.

1. Settle it, and be blessed.

2. Settle it, and do it quickly.

3. Settle it, and *you* be the peacemaker.

4. Settle it, and *you* turn the battle over to the Lord.

5. Settle it, and use the tools God has given you.

6. Settle it, and *Trust the Lord.* T+

7. Settle it, and transform yourself, and all those involved.

8. Settle it, and *watch and pray*, just like Jesus told you to.

9. Settle it, and know that the Lord will make even your enemies be at peace with you.

10. Settle it, and you will become, and be, and stay, a child of God.

The Fight of Your Life, Is the Fight for Your Life

Thursday morning 4:30 a.m.
Journal Entry, June 18, 2009

Thirty years is a long time. Actually, thirty-three years since I started law school in 1976. As I write my last thoughts I think of Thérèse of Lisieux who, when making a reference to the completing of her written "memories," said: *"I am not breaking my head over the writing of my 'little life.' It is like fishing with a line; I write whatever comes to the end of my pen."* Ultimately, we want to hear from you Lord and know that what comes to the end of our pen, is what *you* inspire. I know that feeling of being an open vessel. I first learned it a long time ago when I was in the fight of my life, helping someone with the fight of their life.

I am thinking this morning of just one simple concept you taught me so long ago: *All settlements come down to one word: sacrifice.* How much are you willing to sacrifice to settle the case? To settle the personal problem? To settle problems with your wife or husband? With your partners, neighbors, friends and foes? How much are you willing to sacrifice to settle that problem, challenge, or addiction with yourself? When in a dispute with another person, are you willing to think in terms of blessing the other person first before thinking of yourself? . . . Well, now the years have gone by and I've witnessed over and over again what you showed me from Genesis 13: There had been quarreling between Abram's and Lot's herdsmen. So Abram said: "Let's not have quarreling between you and me, or between your herdsmen and mine, for we are brothers. Is not the whole land before you? Let's part company. If you go to the left, I'll go to the right; if you go to the right, I'll go to the left."[1] Abram placed full confidence in the Lord and gave the first choice to his nephew Lot, and for his faithfulness God promised Abram that it would be Abram and his offspring that would be blessed *forever* and would receive all the land, even what Lot had chosen.

---

1 Genesis 13:8-9.

Lord, I've been blessed to witness your faithfulness in hundreds of battles where just this one simple concept has played out. Ultimately, you bless the person who sacrifices the most, or gives the most. I am a witness.

The fight of your life, is the fight for your life. Is that true? Well, I have been so blessed to help clients, friends and family that have been given great gifts and talents from you Lord, but people have attacked them, the devil tried his best to steal those gifts and talents from them, and those blessings. I would tell them "God's gifts and his call are irrevocable."[2] In each case, the fight of their lives was the fight for their lives, so that they could continue to give their life away. To be a blessing to others. The joy I have had to help people get through the fight of their life, so that they could carry on and be a blessing to others, their family, friends, and the world, is immeasurable. That was basically why I was here. No other reason that I can discern.

I asked you to send me.

And, you did.

"Better *is* the end of a thing than the beginning thereof."[3] Lord, is it okay to say that I have really tried to be a good person, to do your will. I was figuring that since November 1984, when I got to know you, I have kneeled down by my bed *very early in the morning* approximately 9,125 times to get your to do list for me for the day. I called it "God's To Do List." "GTDL." I still call it that. I remember that the list was based on your Word: "Therefore do not worry about tomorrow, for tomorrow will worry about itself. Each day has enough trouble of its own."[4] So often, the only way I could push forward for what I knew would be such a stressful day, was to focus *only* on what you wanted me to do that day, just that day *only*. If I did that, I felt I was automatically doing what you said to do in the previous verse, which I prefer from the King James: "But seek ye first the kingdom of God, and his righteousness; and all these things shall be added unto you."[5]

Lord, I sense the sacredness of what you want us to write down in those early hours, *while it is still dark.*[6] And more and more I sense what you mean by us being the *watch and pray* generation. As many times as I have knelt down to pray, to talk with you, you have now had me *stand up*. The watch and pray generation is the stand-up prayer generation. We are inspired by Ezekiel's call and commission.[7] You speak to us. You are sending us. And you tell us: *do not be afraid, do not be*

---

2 Romans 11:29. And see *The Message Bible*, Eugene H. Peterson, Romans 11:29, 30-32: "God's gifts and God's call are under full warranty—never canceled, never rescinded. . . . In one way or another, God makes sure that we all experience what it means to be outside so that he can personally open the door and welcome us back in."
3 Ecclesiastes 7:8 (KJV).
4 Matthew 6:34.
5 Matthew 6:33 (KJV).
6 Mark 1:35. "Very early in the morning, while it was still dark, Jesus got up, left the house and went off to a solitary place, where he prayed." As noted before, some secrets must be caught, not taught. See Chapter 6, fn 17. Have you learned yet, the power of secret prayer early in the morning, *while it is still dark*?
7 Ezekiel 2:1-7. "He said to me, 'Son of man, stand up on your feet and I will speak to you.' As he spoke, the Spirit came into me and raised me to my feet, and I heard him speaking to me. . . ." We are advised three times: "Do not be afraid."

afraid, do not be afraid. And what could be more powerful than to stand up and pray Psalm 35?

> "Contend, O Lord, with those who contend with me:
>   fight against those who fight against me.
> Take up shield and buckler;
>   arise and come to my aid.
> Brandish spear and javelin
>   against those who pursue me,
> Say to my soul,
>   'I am your salvation.'"

Lord, I'm sorry for all those times I botched some of the items on your list, *GTDL*. Mercy, the failures loom in my heart on occasion. Still, especially in my professional life, I have seen so many victories. More victories than I can enumerate. And, all glory to you Lord for those victories. But the battles have taken a toll on me. As you know, I have fought depression on occasion along the way. Maybe too many occasions. I am definitely one of those that "groan inwardly."[8] But, I'm a pretty good fighter. I'm good at stepping up to the plate and speaking out against depression, and bringing myself around. *"I speak to my mountain, my mountain is depression, and I say to my depression 'be gone in Jesus' name. Cast into the sea in Jesus' name. Cast into the sea in Jesus' name."*[9] I only have you, Lord, to work with. Nobody else. No one else knows. There is no one else to tell. And why would I tell them? It's not even a question. I know how to beat it. And, I'm beating it now. This was the first tool you gave me, a long time ago. But still, I wonder who is happy? Who has clearly beaten it? I'm doing pretty good. With your help Lord.

And so, it's my birthday again. Here I am. I'm still standing. And I'm still "standing up," on my feet. I'm getting old doing my fieldwork. But that's a good feeling. I feel like my old friend Harry Goldberg, I'm amazed that you preserve me. I felt like David on so many occasions, shouting out to you Lord: "Preserve me."[10] Time and time again, I felt I could easily lose a battle, I was outmatched, over my head, no hope, but you came through. I, again, acknowledge what Spurgeon said: "We are constantly opposed, and yet perpetually preserved!" In my case, I was perpetually preserved, and perpetually blessed. But, Lord, I do admit, I really look forward to the "new heaven" and "new earth" you reference in Revelation 21. Mercy, that's a whole other topic. I basically agree with Randy Alcorn on this topic. He said:

---

8 Romans 8:22-23. "We know that the whole creation has been groaning as in the pains of childbirth right up to the present time. Not only so, but we ourselves, who have the firstfruits of the Spirit, groan inwardly as we wait eagerly for our adoption as sons, the redemption of our bodies." Also see, 2 Corinthians 5:2. "Meanwhile we groan, longing to be clothed with our heavenly dwelling . . . ."

9 Mark 11:22-25.

10 Psalm 143:11. "For your name's sake, O LORD, preserve my life; in your righteousness, bring me out of trouble." Psalm 119:88. "Preserve my life according to your love, and I will obey the statutes of your mouth."

"God never gave up on his original plan for human beings to dwell on Earth. In fact, the climax of history will be the creation of new heavens and a   New Earth, a resurrected universe inhabited by resurrected people living with the resurrected Jesus (Revelation 21:1-4)."[11]

"New heavens and a New Earth": I'm at the point of my life where I don't need a whole lot of details on this topic Lord. I have so much faith in you now, that I can truly live in the *now*. Just be right here, right *now* with you. Everything's in good hands, your hands Lord.

Your hands.

Settle It! . . . *and be Blessed.* In the end, I suppose I'm like the sparrow: All I did was dip my beak into the ocean of your ideas on this topic. But my humble beak is full. I am so blessed. Amen.

Is this a good time to thank some of the Mighty Men?[12] Those fellow warriors that have fought with me, blessed me, and tried their best to hold me accountable, despite my many flaws. I'm thinking of Greg Jesson, Jed Nibbelink, Danny Ovando and Dan Cislo, and some of my new warrior friends, Ron Brown, and Don Coley. Thank you so much for sending them, and many others, my way. Certainly, I know, where two or more are gathered in your name, there you are in our midst.[13]

Lord, David had four stones left after he finished off Goliath.[14] I feel like I have some stones left in my shepherd's bag. What did David do with his remaining stones? Lord, I'm ready if you have a few more assignments for me.

And so, as I come to the end of my little book, of my *little life*, I think of Thomas Merton's last words of his book, *The Seven Storey Mountain*: "SIT FINIS LIBRI, NON FINIS QUAERENDI."

"This may be the end of the book, but not the end of the search."

Well, I'm a little older than Merton when he finished his book, so I shall quote Jesus:

"Surely I am coming quickly."

To which I repeat: "Amen. Even so, come, Lord Jesus!"[15]

T+

---

11 Randy Alcorn, *Heaven* (Carol Stream, Illinois: Tyndale House Publishers, Inc., 2004), p. xviii.
12 2 Samuel 24 (KJV).
13 Matthew 18:20 (KJV). *"For where two or more are gathered together in my name, there am I in the midst of them."*
14 1 Samuel 17:40. "Then he took his staff in his hand, chose five smooth stones from the stream, put them in the pouch of his shepherd's bag and, with his sling in his hand, approached the Philistine."
15 Revelation 22:20-21 (NKJV).

The Take Away 24
God's gifts and His call are irrevocable.

1. ***The fight of your life is the fight for your life.*** You have been given great gifts and talents from the Lord. You will, on occasion, be attacked, and the devil will try his best to steal those gifts and talents from you, and all the blessings that go with those gifts and talents. But, "God's gifts and God's call are under full warranty—never canceled, never rescinded."

2. ***The fight of your life is the fight for your life***—so that you can continue to give your life away—to be a blessing to others.

3. ***Better is the end of a thing than the beginning thereof.*** God has given you life, and gifts and talents that go with it. To stay on track to fulfill His purpose in your life, get up early every morning, and make a list, God's To Do List, and He will make sure you accomplish all that He has planned for you.

4. We are inspired by Ezekiel's call and commission, "Son of man, stand up on your feet and I will speak to you." Lord, you speak to us. You are sending us. And you tell us: *do not be afraid, do not be afraid, do not be afraid.* And what could be more powerful than to stand up and pray Psalm 35?

"Contend, O Lord, with those who contend with me:
    fight against those who fight against me.
Take up shield and buckler;
    arise and come to my aid.
Brandish spear and javelin
    against those who pursue me,
Say to my soul,
    'I am your salvation.'"

And in this way, *His Way*, you will be perpetually preserved.

"Amen. Even so, come, Lord Jesus!"

Acknowledgements

I'd like to thank Pastor Henry, who gave an altar call on a Wednesday night at a little church in Westwood, California way back in November 1984. I answered that altar call and in less than five minutes changed my life for an eternity. I'm so thankful to him and all the pastors that will never know just how much their simple short altar calls change millions of peoples lives just like me —forever.

I'd like to thank the 8th Row Prayer Team at my church, Angelus Temple/ Dream Center. Everyone needs a good prayer team and I have one.

I'd like to thank my accountability brothers, Greg Jesson, Jed Nibbelink, Danny Ovando and Dan Cislo. Accountability brothers are in the habit of saving your life on occasion, as they have mine.

I'd like to thank my Senior Partner and Co-Laborer, as I do every day. This day is no different.

Amen.

Start Day

I always wanted a
    start day . . . that lasted.
The day I would always remember
    as the day . . . I started.
The day when everything that
    was before ~~ was
    definitely ~~ before.
The day when everything after
    was
    definitely . . . after.
And one moment, one
    crossover moment
    was definitely
    the line between.
No day after, would ever
    again look like
    a day before.

Because I finally said
    that's it,
    no going back,
    no looking back,
    no thinking back.
Because this is it ~~~
    start day.

A day in my life
    that God blessed
    in a powerful way.
A day when God said
    "follow me."
    And . . . I did.
A day when God so
    renewed my mind that
    I got it,
    I heard,
    I listened.

And then one day
    it happened.
What really changed
    was that this time
    I listened . . .
And I left myself
    behind.

And I had my
    Start Day.

Between

It is the morning between,
    between a battle waged
    on a field where law
    settles all and some
    are changed forever.
And . . . the going home ~ ~ ~
    shield and sword
    folded up in a briefcase
    and frayed nerves
    evening out to warmer
    thoughts.
Between . . . is always
    so much shorter than
    the battle before and
    the being home thereafter.
Between is when good
    decisions can be made
    because its so hard
    when in battle . . . and,
    strangely even harder
    when at home.
I want to become a
    specialist at "between."
    To listen at this moment,
    To really understand
    what happened . . .
    and what is to come.
And know that I do
    have choices and that
    The Greater Plan is so
    real . . . so alive
    in my life
    . . . that I can
       feel it.

Finish Day

Finish day
 is still to come,
 for me and you
 if you're reading this.
Still part of all,
 the arc of life,
 here on earth
 but we're fading mist.

I found a battle
 plan that works
 and chose a warrior
 who can lead.
Ultimately what
 serves as right
 is that which surely
 gets us freed.

Tossed and turned
 at times I felt,
 forced again
 to check my ways.
But then I'm back
 on track again,
 whence I learned
 -- number my days.

Sanctity
 is our telos,
 God's chosen endpoint
 for me and you.[1]
Holiness is
 not a luxury,
 meant for only
 just a few.[2]

So help me finish
 all that You planned,
 and pull me back
 when I go astray.
Because all I want
 is to be ready,
 when I have,
 -- my finish day.

---

1 James Martin, S.J., *Becoming Who You Are* (Mahwah, New Jersey: HiddenSpring 2006), p. 82,
2 Mother Teresa.

About the Author

Tom Gehring is a lawyer with offices in Santa Monica, California.
For more details, feedback, prayer requests, help, or comments, he can be reached at Tom@tomgehring.com.

_____

_____

_____

_____

_____

_____

_____

_____

_____

_____

_____

Date:

_____

_____

"Write down the revelation and make it plain on tablets so that a herald may run with it." Habakkuk 2:2.

_____

_____

_____

_____

_____

_____

_____

_____

_____

_____

_____

Date:

_____

_____

"He who began a good work in you will carry it on to completion . . . ."
Philippians 1:6.

_____

_____

_____

_____

_____

_____

_____

_____

_____

_____

Date:

_____

_____

"I tell you the truth, if you have faith as small as a mustard seed, you can say to this mountain, 'Move from here to there' and it will move. Nothing will be impossible for you." Matthew 17:20.

Telos.